98-95

IN~YOUR~POCKET

by
D. Roger Maves

Sequoia Publishing, Inc.
Littleton, Colorado, USA

This book belongs to:

_____

_____

_____

_____

_____

_____

To my mother and father,

*Thank you for teaching me how to read and write,
work hard and persevere.*

*Most of all, thank you for sharing your love of books—
it's added a dimension to my life
I couldn't have lived without.*

*Thanks to my wife, Rachel,
and my children, Nathan and Randi,
for being so patient with me,
supporting me and cheering me on.*

*Thanks to Tom Glover, Mary Glover, and Mary Miller
at Sequoia Publishing for all their help
in making this book possible.*

*In remembrance of my grandparents:
Ernest and Rose Maves
William and Beatrice Knospe*

Biography

D. Roger Maves is an author, instructional designer, trainer and photographer. He has a degree in Illustrative Photography from Brooks Institute of Photography and worked for many years in advertising and design. He has worked with computers for the last 20 years and has extensive experience in both hardware and software. Roger has trained users in corporations across the United States, both publicly and privately. He has developed and taught courses in database programming, network installation and administration, and custom business applications.

Roger continues to write, develop courses and train. Founder and principal of The Knowledge Group, Inc., he specializes in thinking, creativity, innovation and communication training.

Publisher's Note

Sequoia Publishing has made a serious effort to provide accurate information in this book. However, the probability exists that there are errors and misprints, and that variations in data values may also occur depending on field conditions. Information included in this book should only be considered as a general guide and Sequoia Publishing, Inc. does not represent the information as being exact.

The publishers would appreciate being notified of any errors, omissions, or misprints which may occur in this book. Your suggestions for future editions would also be greatly appreciated. See Sequoia address and phone numbers on the copyright page.

The information in this manual was collected from numerous sources and if not properly acknowledged, Sequoia would like to express its appreciation for those contributions.

Errors and omissions which have been identified in any Sequoia publications have been compiled into an errata sheet. Errata sheets are available on Sequoia's web site at www.sequoiapublishing.com. (Once on the web site, click "site map" on the main menu bar and then look for "Errata sheets.")

More Sequoia Products

Bell's Guide ···$14.95
    A comprehensive, pocket-sized real estate handbook for everyone

DeskRef ···$29.95
    The desktop version of PocketRef

Highpoint Adventures ·····································$9.95
    A pocket guide to the highest elevation in each of the 50 states

How To Ski the Blues and Blacks *(Without Getting Black and Blue)*
···$9.95
    Expert ski instruction + nationwide ski area data

Measure for Measure ···$14.95
    THE conversion factor handbook!

MegaRef, Version 2 ··$39.95
    IBM/PC and compatibles software version of PocketRef.

Pocket Partner ··$9.95
    Comprehensive law enforcement pocket reference

Pocket PCDIRectory ···$14.95
    Contact information for the PC computer industry

Pocket PCRef ··$14.95
    Comprehensive PC computer reference

PocketRef ··$9.95
    BEST SELLER! Everything you ever wanted to know - and then
    some! Shirt-pocket size.

Seldovia, Alaska ···$24.95
    An historical portrait of Seldovia, Alaska

TechRef ···$29.95
    Pocket PCREf + PCDIRectory, and MORE!

**Troubleshooting Your Contracting Business to Cause
Success** ···$39.95
    Secrets for running a successful contracting business

Resources and Trademarks

The following are Registered Trademarks or Trade names:

ANSI - American National Standards Institute

ASCII - American Standard Code for Information Interchange

IBM - International Business Machines

Microsoft, Windows, MS-DOS - Microsoft Corporation

NetWare - Novell, Inc.

OS/2 - International Business Machines Corporation

Table of Contents

Introduction

About This Book

WinRef 98-95 In Your Pocket is designed as a reference for all users, whether beginning, intermediate or advanced. Its purpose is to provide a convenient quick reference to the commands, functions and operations of Microsoft's Windows 98 and Windows 95 operating systems. WinRef is unique in its comprehensive analysis of the differences between the two operating systems, thereby making it an ideal reference for users who are upgrading from 95 to 98.

It is not written as a step-by-step tutorial; rather, the information is concise and to the point. The format used allows us to provide a wealth of information which anxiously awaits your review.

How to Use This Book

WinRef 98 - 95 is organized in several sections which are listed in the table of contents.

Section 2, "Subject List," is a listing of topics by subject. If you want to learn everything about a particular subject such as Communications, File Management or Maintenance you can look here for all the related topics and feel confident you're covering all the areas thoroughly.

The main section, "Commands & Features," comprises the bulk of the book. It alphabetically lists commands, tasks, modules and features so that you can quickly and easily get to the information you need.

This is where you want to look first for your topic. The topics are listed alphabetically by name. Most topics will be listed there; however, if your topic is listed in another part of the book you will be directed to the appropriate location by the notation See: *Topic*.

When you find a listing for the topic you are looking for, always take a look at the end of the listing where you may find additional references to related subjects, listed under *See Also:*.

Some topics within **Commands and Features** include *"QuicKeys"* that list brief, concise methods of access you can use to perform common commands and tasks. These methods may include mouse, menu and hot key combinations. In many cases there may be several ways to accomplish the same task.

Many different types of files are used for Windows 98, Windows 95 and the applications that run on these operating systems. The **"File Types"** section contains a list of the most common file name extensions and the files that they normally represent. Also included is a reference to whether the particular file type can be viewed using Quick View.

If you can't find the answer to your questions within the pages of this book you may have to call technical support. **"Technical Support Sources"** lists the names, addresses, phone numbers, fax numbers and email addresses for many of the major technical support sources.

The **"Glossary"** includes listings for terms that are not defined explicitly within the topics themselves. It is not intended to be comprehensive, but seeks only to explain potential unknown terms specifically relating the Windows 98, Windows 95 and directly related topics.

The **"Appendix"** covers the Certificates of Authenticity for Windows 95 and 98, both OEM and retail versions.

The **"Index"** is another tool you can use to find information. It is very extensive and is your best source for references to items that may be located under several different listings.

Special Conventions

As you use *WinRef 98 -95*, look for additional information which is broken out of the normal text as *Quick Access, Notes, Tips, Caution, Default Location* and *See Also:*.

Quick Access

Quick Access provides the different methods of access to the current command, module or location listed in order by ease of use. These methods may include mouse, menu and hot key combinations. In many cases there may be several ways to accomplish the same task. The method considered easiest is listed first. Some methods may be listed under several different headings.

Note: In Windows 98 the default setting for opening an item is a double-click; however, it can be changed to a single-click. All the methods that follow are designed for use with a double-click. If you change the default setting in Windows 98 to a single-click you will have to convert some of the methods that follow.

Notes

Notes provide additional information that is related and important to the subject but warrants separation from the text for clarity.

HotTips

 HotTips provide unique methods or implementations of the commands and processes that might not be obvious at first glance.

Caution

Caution provides a warning that certain actions may cause damage to data or your configuration or certain commands may not perform as expected.

Default Location

Default Location provides either the location of the command, folder or module.

See Also

See Also directs you to other sections of *WinRef 98 - 95* which may provide additional information on your subject or other related items.

Typographical Conventions

The following conventions are used throughout this book.

Symbols

All information applies to both operating systems unless one of the symbols below is present.

This symbol indicates that the accompanying text applies ONLY to Windows 95.

This symbol indicates that the accompanying text applies ONLY to Windows 98.

Style Conventions

- **Bold text** is used to emphasize certain words that are important to read or words that you may type.

- *Italic text* is used for books, periodicals, specialized or new terms, variables and to emphasize a particular word or phrase.

- Arial text, with or without an underlined letter, indicates commands that you may select, primarily with the mouse.

Keyboard Conventions

- The names of keyboard keys are shown in a special font, for example, *Enter* or *Tab*.

- If two keys are to be used simultaneously they are show connected with a plus sign (+), for example: *Alt+Tab* means you should hold down the *Alt* key while pressing the *Tab* key.

- If keys are separated by commas, for example *Alt, F, N*, then each key should be pressed individually. In the example above, you would first press and release the Alt key, then press and release the *F* key and then press and release the *N* key.

Mouse

The following standard terminology is used in this guide when working with a mouse. It is assumed that your mouse has been configured with the left button as the primary mouse button. Any reference that requires you to click the secondary button will be referring to "the right mouse button."

- *Point* means to move the mouse until the tip of the pointer is positioned on whatever you want to point to on the screen.

- *Click* means to press and then immediately release the mouse button without moving the mouse.

- *Double-click* means to quickly press and release the mouse button twice.

- *Drag* means to point and then hold down the mouse button, move the mouse to a new position, and then release the mouse button.

Terminology

As you go through the book, you will find that you are told to click a word or icon on a particular "bar." The diagram below identifies these bars:

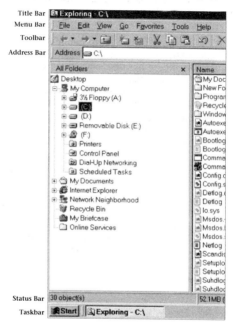

Subject List

In this section you'll find a listing of topics by subject. If you want to learn everything about a particular subject, for example, Communications, File Management or Maintenance, you can look here for all the related topics and feel confident you're thoroughly covering all the areas.

Disk Management

File Management

Graphics

Help

Installation

Maintenance

Multimedia

Navigating

Networking

Optimizing

Printing

Shut Down Windows

Starting Windows

System Configuration

Troubleshooting

Utility Programs

Commands and Features

Commands and Features   **25**

Accessibility Options

Accessibility
Options

The *Accessibility Options* Control Panel tool allows you to change several of the default Windows behaviors including the user interface, sound, and display. Changing these settings can make the computer easier to use for individuals who have special needs.

Some of the accessibility features must have their shortcut key setting turned on for the shortcuts, listed below, to work.

Quick Access

Click , Settings, Control Panel,

then double-click

               Accessibility
               Options

Note: If Accessibility Options is not in the Control Panel, it hasn't been installed. See: "Installing,"p.34 .

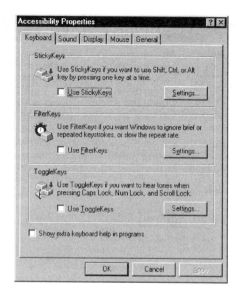

Note: To see if any of the Accessibility Options are turned on, look on the taskbar, where you'll see the appropriate icon(s) displayed.

Keyboard

The *Keyboard* tab provides several features that help the user with keyboard interaction.

StickyKeys

When *StickyKeys* is selected the *Ctrl, Alt* and *Shift* keys act as though they are still depressed even after they are released. They will stay in this state until another key is pressed, other than *Ctrl, Alt* or *Shift*. This feature is beneficial to one who has trouble pressing two keys at once.

Another way to toggle this feature on and off is to:

Tap *Shift* 5 times

Be sure to select the Use shortcut option in Settings to enable this feature. Additional configuration options are also available by clicking Settings.

FilterKeys

When *FilterKeys* is selected Windows ignores brief or repeated keystrokes. This feature is beneficial to one who is slow to release the keys or may tremor while typing. The repeat rate can also be adjusted, see "Keyboard" for more information.

Another way to toggle this feature on and off is to:

Hold down *Right Shift* for 8 seconds

Be sure to select the Use shortcut option in Settings to enable this feature. Additional configuration options are also available by clicking Settings.

ToggleKeys

When *ToggleKeys* is selected the *Caps Lock, Scroll Lock,* and *Num Lock* keys will make a high sound when toggled on and a low sound when toggled off. This feature alerts the user that they have successfully or accidentally pressed these keys.

Another way to toggle this feature on and off is to:

Hold down *Num Lock* for 5 seconds

 If you frequently hit the Caps Lock key accidentally while typing, try turning this feature on. You'll hear the sound, warning you of your mistake.

Be sure to select the Use shortcut option in <u>S</u>ettings to enable this feature. Additional configuration options are also available by clicking <u>S</u>ettings.

Note: No icon appears in the tray, so there is no indicator of whether this feature is turned on or not.

Show extra keyboard help in programs

To take advantage of the additional help features of some programs select, *Show extra keyboard help in programs.*

Sound

The *Sound* tab provides two features that help users, having a hard time hearing the audio warning and information messages, to understand the messages they are receiving.

SoundSentry

When *Sound Sentry* is selected Windows will flash a specified part of the screen to warn you that a sound is being issued from the computer's speaker. You can specify which part of the screen should flash by clicking <u>S</u>ettings.

ShowSounds

When *ShowSounds* is selected a visual representation of the sound, such as a text caption or informative icon, is displayed. It is the equivalent of the effect on television called "close-captioned."

Display

The *Display* tab provides settings that control which colors are used for the screen display. The color scheme that is set up in <u>S</u>ettings overrides any application color scheme.

High Contrast

When *High Contrast* is selected the color scheme that is chosen in <u>S</u>ettings will be the default scheme. These color schemes provide, as options, larger text and contrasting colors, making most items easier to read.

Be sure to select the Use shortcut option in <u>S</u>ettings to enable this feature. Additional configuration options are also available by clicking <u>S</u>ettings.

 Switch between Display Settings: The system's default display settings are still available. You can toggle between your High Contrast settings and the system's settings in Display using the shortcut key combination above. Even if you don't need the High Contrast settings this is still a great way to switch between your two favorite color schemes.

HOt Tip **Improve Display Legibility**: There are many components of the screen display whose size can be changed for better legibility including icons, icon spacing, buttons, menus, title bars, scroll bars, window borders, message boxes, ToolTips, and highlighted items. See Appearance under "Display" for more information on how to change these settings.

HOt Tip **Make Mouse Pointer Easy to See:** The mouse pointer can be hard to see for most anyone. If you want to change the size, shape or movement characteristics of the mouse pointer see the "Mouse" section.

Mouse

The *Mouse* tab provides a feature which allows control of the mouse pointer using the keyboard

Show Mouse Keys

When *Show Mouse Keys* is selected the mouse pointer can be controlled by the numeric keypad keys.

Another way to turn this feature on and off is to:

Left Alt+Left Shift+Num Lock

Be sure to select the Use shortcut option in Settings to enable this feature. Additional configuration options are also available by clicking Settings.

Here's how the keys work on the numeric keypad:

Action	Key(s)
Move Up	8
Move Down	2
Move Right	6
Move Left	4
Move Up Right	9
Move Down Right	3
Move Up Left	7
Move Down Left	1
Single pixel moves	Hold down the *Shift* while using the movement keys.
Large moves	Hold down the *Ctrl* while using the movement keys.
Click	5
Double-click	+
Right-click	– (dash)
Click both	*
Drag	Use the movement keys to point to the object, press *Insert*. Use the movement keys to point to the destination, press *Delete*.
Right-drag	Use the movement keys to point to the object, press the minus-sign (-) then press *Insert*. Use the movement keys to point to the destination, press *Delete*.

HOt Tip **Use Single Pixel Moves for Graphic Work:** Single Pixel Moves is a great feature to have turned on when working on graphical tasks that require precise movements that can't be controlled by the mouse.

General

The *General* tab provides settings that affect the other accessibility features.

Automatic Reset

When *Automatic Reset* is selected, Windows will turn off the Accessibility Options after the computer has been idle for the specified number of minutes. This feature is useful when more than one person is using the same computer.

Notification

The two features in *Notification* provide a warning message when an accessibility feature is turned on and a sound when a feature is turned on or off.

SerialKey Devices

When *SerialKey Devices* is selected, an alternative input device can be connected to one of the serial ports. The serial port and baud rate can be selected by clicking Settings. This feature is beneficial to one who cannot use a standard keyboard or mouse.

Installing

Accessibility Options is not installed by default when you choose the Typical Installation during setup. If it does not appear in the Control Panel you need to install it to enjoy its features. To install Accessibility Options:

1. Click **Start** , Settings, then

   Add/Remove programs in Control Panel.
2. Click on the Windows Setup tab.

3. Select Accessibility Options from the Components list.

4. If you don't have your CAB files available on your hard disk you will need to have your Windows 9x CD or diskettes available.

5. Click OK.

Accessibility Options will now be available in the Control Panel.

 Create User Profiles to meet accessibility needs: If your computer is used by more than one person and not everyone needs the Accessibility Options, create different user profiles to accommodate each persons needs. See "Passwords" (p. 319) for more information.

Note: If you would like more information on Microsoft products and services for people with disabilities call Microsoft Sales Information Center at 800-426-9400 or the text telephone at 800-892-5234. For technical support using the text telephone call 425-635-4948. Microsoft also has information available on their Accessibility and Disabilities web site: www.microsoft.com/enable

..QuicKeys..

Some of the accessibility features available in Accessibility Options must have their shortcut key setting turned on in order for the shortcuts listed below to work.

FilterKeys - Toggle On/Off

Hold down *Right Shift* for 8 seconds

High Contrast - Toggle On/Off

Left Alt+Left Shift+Printscreen

Large Font in Help

Click <u>O</u>ptions on the menu bar, <u>F</u>ont, <u>L</u>arge

or

Alt+O, F, L

Large Text and Icons

Click **Start** , <u>S</u>ettings, Control

Panel, double-click [Display icon], then

Display

Appearance, Scheme, High Contrast,
White/Black (Large or Extra Large)

Mouse Keys - Toggle On/Off

Left Alt+Left Shift+Num Lock

Mouse Size and Appearance

Click **Start** , <u>S</u>ettings,

Control Panel, double-click [Mouse icon]

Mouse

StickyKeys - Toggle On/Off

Tap *Shift* 5 times

ToggleKeys - Toggle On/Off

Hold down *Num Lock* for 5 seconds

Default Location: \Control Panel\Accessibility
Options

See Also: Display; Keyboard; Mouse; Passwords

Add New Hardware

Add New Hardware

Add New Hardware is a Control Panel tool that is used to install the drivers for new hardware devices that you've added to your computer. Windows uses a wizard to lead you through the steps of installation searching for existing hardware. Windows can detect and configure Plug and Play-compliant devices automatically, and can detect many "legacy," or non-Plug and Play devices.

Quick Access

Click ![Start], Settings, Control Panel,

double-click
Add New
Hardware

Installing New Hardware

There are several different installation methods you can use, each one becoming a little more complex, depending on whether or not the device is Plug and Play-compliant and whether it can be recognized by Windows or not.

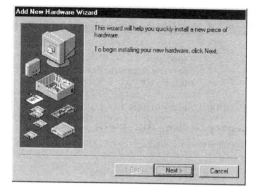

This wizard will help you quickly install a new piece of hardware.

To begin installing your new hardware, click Next.

[< Back] [Next >] [Cancel]

Plug and Play Device

To install a Plug and Play device:

1. Install the device into the computer.

   In most cases you should perform the installation with the power off and the computer unplugged. If the device's documentation recommends otherwise, follow the instructions provided.

2. Start Windows.

   If Windows recognizes the device and has access to the correct driver for the device, it will automatically configure and install it.

3. If the driver is not available, Windows will prompt you to insert a disk with the appropriate driver on it (this could be your Windows CD or a disk from the device manufacturer).

Insert the disk and follow the remaining instructions. You may have to restart your computer so that the changes will take effect.

Note: If you install a Plug and Play device after you've started Windows, follow the instructions below, in "Legacy Device - Automatic Search," to automatically detect and install the device.

Legacy Device - Automatic Search

Windows will recognize most legacy devices and use drivers supplied with Windows. Use the following automatic search feature first. If it doesn't recognize the device or if the manufacturer has supplied a disk with drivers, follow the instructions below for Manual Selection.

1. Install the device into the computer.

   In most cases you should perform the installation with the power off and the computer unplugged. If the device's documentation recommends otherwise, follow the instructions provided.

2. Start Windows.

3. Click **Start**, Settings, Control Panel,

   double-click Add New Hardware.

4. Make sure all other programs are closed, then click Next to begin.

5. Windows 95 prompts you to search for new hardware. Click Yes, then Next.

   Windows 98 does not prompt you to search, just read the warning, then click Next.

6. In Windows 95, read the warning, then click Next.

Windows 98 prompts you to search for new hardware. Click Yes, then Next. Read the next warning and click Next.

Windows begins the search for new devices.

7. If Windows recognizes the device, it will advise you that it did. If you want to see a list of devices it found, click Details.

Click Finish to install and configure the device.

8. If the driver is not available, Windows will prompt you to insert a disk with the appropriate driver on it (this could be your Windows CD or a disk from the manufacturer).

Insert the disk and follow the remaining instructions.

9. If Windows can't find the device, you'll need to select it from a list. Click Next, then continue with step five below in the Legacy Device - Manual Selection section.

Legacy Device - Manual Selection

If the Automatic Search did not work or if the manufacturer has supplied drivers on a disk, use the Manual Selection instructions that follow.

1. Install the device into the computer.

In most cases you should perform the installation with the power off and the computer unplugged. If the device's documentation recommends otherwise, follow the instructions provided.

2. Start Windows.

3. Click **Start**, Settings, Control Panel,

double-click Add New Hardware.

4. Windows 95 prompts you to search for new hardware. Click **No**, then **Next**.

   Windows 98 does not prompt you to search; just read the warning, then click **Next**.

5. In Windows 95, read the warning, then click **Next**.

   Windows 98 prompts you to search for new hardware. Click **No**, then **Next**.

6. Select the type of hardware you are installing, then click **Next**.

7. A list of manufacturers and models is displayed. Select a manufacturer and a model, then click **Next**.

   If you have a disk with the appropriate driver on it, you can click **Have Disk**. Type the drive and path from which the driver will be copied, then click **OK**.

8. If the driver is not available, Windows will prompt you to insert a disk with the appropriate driver on it (this could be your Windows CD or a disk from the manufacturer).

   Insert the disk and follow the remaining instructions.

Note: Additional configuration may be necessary for devices such as the display, keyboard, mouse, modem, printers and network. Each of these devices has its own Control Panel tool that can be used to configure the device. For more information, see the specific section for the device you would like to configure.

Note: If you are unable to properly configure a device using the Add Hardware wizard, you may need to make manual changes to the device's settings using the Device Manager. See Device Manager in the "System" section (p. 438).

 Updated Drivers: Many hardware manufacturers continually update their drivers by correcting errors, adding features and making them more compatible. To make sure you have the latest and greatest driver, after you've completed the initial installation, check the manufacturer's web site and download the newest driver directly into your computer. Instructions for installing the new driver are usually provided on the web site or as a text file in the download.

Removing Hardware Device Drivers

To uninstall or remove a hardware component, see Device Manager in the "System" section (p.438).

Default Location: \Control Panel\Add New Hardware

See Also: Add/Remove Programs; Display; Keyboard; Modems; Network; Printers; System|Device Manager

Add/Remove Programs

Add/Remove Programs

The *Add/Remove Programs* Control Panel tool provides a way to install and uninstall application programs and Windows operating system components. It also provides a procedure to make a startup disk which can be used to boot your computer if it is not booting normally.

Quick Access

Click  , <u>S</u>ettings, <u>C</u>ontrol Panel,

double-click

Install/Uninstall

Using *Install/Uninstall* to install or uninstall your application programs has two benefits. First, it will automatically search your disk media for the Setup.exe or Install.exe program. Second, and more importantly, it will register your program so that in the event you need to remove it, Windows will have all the information necessary to properly do the job.

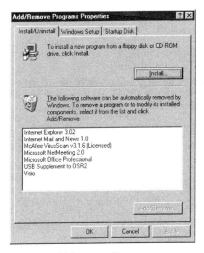

Installing Programs

1. Click **Start**, Settings, Control Panel, then double-click the Add/Remove Programs Icon.

2. Click the Install/Uninstall tab.

3. Click Install.

4. Insert the program's floppy disk or CD into your drive, then click Next.

   Windows will search for the installation program on the media you supplied. Usually this program will be named Setup.exe or Install.exe.

5. If the installation program found is correct, click Finish.

   If the program selected is not correct, use Browse to located the correct installation program.

6. The instructions from this point on will vary according to the program being installed. Follow the instructions to complete the installation.

Note: When a Windows 9x compliant application is installing, it checks to make sure it's not copying an older file over a newer version of the same one. If the file is a shared one, a counter is incremented in the Registry to record the install. Since many programs can share a file, this counter is incremented every time an application that shares this file is installed, and decremented every time an application is uninstalled. Using this counting method, the shared file won't actually get deleted until the last application using the file is uninstalled.

Uninstalling Programs

It's always best to use Install/Uninstall to uninstall your application programs. When an application is installed, it not only copies the program files to its own folder, but may also copy .dll files to other folders, create entries in the Registry, Win.ini, or System.ini, and may create its own .ini file. If an application is installed using Install/Uninstall, Windows records these actions and can then undo them when you use Install/Uninstall to remove the application.

1. Click **Start**, Settings, Control Panel,

   then double-click the Add/Remove Programs icon.

2. Click the Install/Uninstall tab.

3. Select the application program you want to remove from the list.

4. Click Add/Remove.

5. The instructions from this point on will vary according to the application being uninstalled. Follow the instructions to complete the process.

Hot Tip **If Install/Uninstall fails to remove the application**, you have two choices:

1. First, see if there is an uninstall program in the application's folder. If so, run the program.

2. As a last resort, delete the application's folder, then search for entries referencing the application in the Registry, Win.ini, System.ini, Autoexec.bat and Config.sys, then delete them. See the tip below to remove any listing in the Install/Uninstall tab. You may also

have to remove shortcuts that appear on your desktop, in your Start Menu folder, or Startup folder. If you're unsure of the steps to take, calling the application's publisher is probably the best way to find out exactly how to remove the application.

HOt Tip **Insufficient space warning may be wrong:** During the installation process, if Windows warns you that you don't have enough disk space to install the program, you may be getting the message in error. If you think you have enough space, proceed with the installation. Windows won't stop you.

HOt Tip **As a Last Resort, Edit the Registry:** If you find that after you uninstall a program there is still an entry in the list of programs, you can remove the item from the list by modifying the Registry.

CAUTION: *The following instructions involve changing settings in the Registry. If the changes are not made properly, serious problems may result. Be sure to backup your Registry before continuing. See: "Registry" (pg. 351) for more information about backing up and editing the Registry.*

Using Regedit, open the Registry and move to HKEY_LOCAL_MACHINE\ SOFTWARE\Microsoft\Windows\ CurrentVersion\Uninstall.

Click the plus sign (+) next to the Uninstall folder to expand the folder. Find the key for the program you want to delete. Select the key, press *Delete*, then click Yes to confirm the deletion.

The next time you view the list of programs it will be gone.

This procedure can be accomplished much more easily using Tweak UI, one of the Windows 95 PowerToys.

See "PowerToys" (p. 323) for more information.

Note: When an application is installed it may create hidden Mscreate.dir files in each folder it sets up. These files contain the information necessary to properly uninstall the application. If any of these files are deleted, the uninstall program will not delete the empty folder that contained the Mscreate.dir file.

Note: If you receive a message when you start Windows that refers to a program or file that has been deleted, more than likely the problem exists in the System.ini file. To get rid of the message, delete any references to the program or file from System.ini. You can use Notepad or the System Configuration Editor (Sysedit) to edit System.ini. Once the file is open, search for any entries that refer to the program or file in question, then delete them. Save the file. The next time you boot up Windows, the message should be gone.

Windows Setup

When Windows is first installed, you are given the option to install or not install many different Windows components. The choice at that time determines your initial complement of components. If you find that you are missing a component or would like to remove a component you can do so using *Windows Setup*.

Many different components and combinations of components are possible. The components themselves are described in specific sections elsewhere in this book.

Installing a Component

1. Click **Start**, Settings, Control Panel,

   then double-click the Add/Remove Programs icon.

2. Click the Windows Setup tab.

   In Windows 95, the Components list displays immediately; however, in Windows 98 it takes a few seconds to display because Windows 98 actually scans the drive for existing components.

3. Scroll through the Components list to find the component(s) you want to install.

   The components listed can represent one component or several components.

   If there are additional components for a group it will be described in the Description box.

   HOt Tip **The check boxes provide hints** as to what is or isn't installed. If the check box is clear, no components or components within a group are selected. If it is checked and has a shaded background, some, but not all of the components in the group are selected. If it is checked and has a clear background, all the components for that group are selected.

4. If there are multiple components within a group, you can view them by first selecting the component and then clicking Details.

5. To select a component for installation, click the check box next to the component. You must click the <u>check box</u>; clicking the name will select the component, but will not check the check box. You can select as many components as you'd like.

CAUTION: *If you clear a check box that is already checked, that component will be removed. Adding and removing components can take place simultaneously.*

---

6. Click OK to start the install process.

   If the files needed for installation are not available, Windows will prompt you to insert a disk with the appropriate files on it (this could be your Windows CD or a disk from the manufacturer).

   Insert the disk and follow the remaining instructions.

Note: If you have a floppy disk or CD with the appropriate files on it, you can click Have Disk, type the drive and path from which the files will be copied, then click OK. Many of the utility programs that are available in the Windows Resource Kit are installed using this method.

Removing A Component

To remove a component, follow the steps above, but instead of selecting the component with a check mark, clear the check box for the component you want to remove. Click OK to start the process.

You can add and remove components at the same time. Just check and clear the components you want to install or remove.

Startup Disk

There may be a time when your computer will not boot up the way it normally does. This could occur after a crash or lock up of some kind. The *startup disk* allows you to boot directly from a floppy disk. This disk has several diagnostic programs on it that might help you recover from your problems, including Chkdsk, Debug, Scandisk, and Regedit.

You are given the opportunity to create a startup disk when you install Windows. However, if you missed that opportunity or would like to create another one you can do so at any time.

Creating A Startup Disk

1. Click **Start**, Settings, Control Panel,

   then double-click the Add/Remove Programs icon.

2. Click the Startup Disk tab.

3. Insert a floppy disk in your drive, then click Create Disk.

   A warning is displayed advising you that all files will be deleted on the floppy disk.

4. Click OK.

   The startup disk is created.

5. Click OK to close the Add/Remove window.

Note: If you are unable to get into Windows and need to make a startup disk, you can do so from the command folder. At the

MS-DOS command prompt, type: **cd\windows\command**, then *Enter*. Insert a floppy disk into drive a:, then type **bootdisk a:** and press *Enter*.

HOt Tip **Copy to the startup disk any 16-bit drivers you may need**, such as the ones for your CD-ROM, so that you can access any necessary hardware devices when needed.

Note: As an extra precaution, you may want to make two startup disks. Don't forget to try them out before you file them away.

Default Location: \Control Panel\Add/Remove Programs

See Also: Add New Hardware; PowerToys|Tweak UI

Applications

Applications are the programs that you run on the Windows 9x platform.

Quick Access

Click **Start** , Programs, *application*

(some applications may be several levels deep).

or

Double-click application's *file* name (.exe, .com, .bat or .pif).

or

Click **Start** , Run, type the *path* and

executable *file* name (.exe, .com, .bat or .pif), then click OK.

or

In Explorer or My Computer, double-click application's document *file* name.

or

Click, **Start** Programs, MS-DOS Prompt,

type the *path* and application's executable (.exe) *file* name (.exe, .com, .bat or .pif), then press *Enter.*

HOt Tip **Emergency Shutdown**: If your application quits working, locks up or crashes, press *Ctrl+Alt+Delete* to open the Close Program dialog box. Select the program that is not responding, then click End Task. If you are prompted a second time, click End Task again.

Installing, Uninstalling and Location

Applications are generally installed and removed using the Add/Remove Control Panel tool and reside in their own folder, appropriately named after the application. When you install an application you can usually specify the path and folder name that you would like. Consequently the application's location could be anywhere, but will usually reside off the root of your C: drive. The only common folder used by many applications is \Program Files, so if you can't find an application's location, try there.

CAUTION: *Always try to use the Add/Remove Control Panel tool to install and remove applications. This allows Windows to keep track of the program files that are copied to the hard disk, leaving fewer orphaned files on your disk when you remove the application.*

During the installation process a shortcut is usually created which points to the application's executable file (.exe, .com, .bat or .pif), which is the file that starts up the application. This shortcut is placed in the \Windows\Start Menu folder or in a folder within the Start Menu folder. By placing the shortcut in the Start Menu, the application can then be started by clicking

Start, Programs, then the *application* shortcut.

HOt Tip **To set the default location for your applications**, which is where they look for documents and save them, first find the shortcut that's used to start the application. It's usually located on the desktop, or in the Start Menu|Programs folder. Right-click on the shortcut, then select Properties. On the Shortcut tab, change the path in the Start In text box to the one you want to use as the default.

98

HOt Tip **Add your shortcut to the Quick Launch toolbar**. Since the taskbar is accessible at any time, you will always be able to easily launch your application.

HOt Tip **Add a keyboard shortcut** for your most frequently used applications. For example, *Ctrl+Alt+W* for Microsoft Word or *Ctrl+Alt+X* for Microsoft Excel. To add a keyboard shortcut, right-click the program's shortcut in the Start Menu, Programs folder, then click Properties. Click the Shortcut tab, click in the Shortcut key text box and press *Ctrl+Alt+letter*. Now you can start the

Applications   53

application at any time by using your new keyboard shortcut. *Note: Shortcut keys only work if the program being launched is on the desktop or Start menu.*

Hot Tip **Two ways to start your applications automatically**:

1. Place a shortcut to the application in the \Windows\SendTo folder. When an application's shortcut is in the SendTo folder it will launch automatically when Windows starts up.

2. Use the System Agent. The System Agent provides a tool which can be used to set a specific time at which to launch your application. This can be hourly, daily, weekly, monthly, etc. For more information, see "SendTo Folder" (p. 392).

Note: When an application is installed, information relating to the application is stored in the Registry. There are two places you might look for entries:
1. HKEY_CURRENT_USER\Software, which is where entries for the current user are stored and
2. HKEY_LOCAL_MACHINE\SOFTWARE which is where entries relating to the computer hardware are stored.

Switching Between Applications

One of the nice features of Windows is that you can switch between applications without having to close the previous one you were using. In fact, you can have as many applications as you want open all at the same time, at least until you run out of memory.

Having more than one application open at the same time allows you to copy information from one to the other, reference other documents you may be working on and switch from one task to another very easily. Following are several methods you can use to switch between applications.

HOt Tip **Shortcuts to the shortcuts**: When you're in the Save As dialog box for Windows 9x applications, you can right-click in the white space to get the shortcut menu for the folder you are working in. You can also right-click on a folder or an individual file to get its shortcut menu.

..QuicKeys..

Close Application

Click **X** on the title bar

or

Alt+F4

or

Double-click the *application* icon on the title bar

or

Click the *application* icon on title bar, <u>C</u>lose

or

Right-click the *application* button on taskbar, <u>C</u>lose

or

Click <u>F</u>ile on the menu bar, E<u>x</u>it

or

Alt+F, X

Close All Applications

98

Click **Start**, Log Off *user name*

Close Document

Click **X** on the title bar

or

Ctrl+F4

or

Ctrl+W

or

Double-click the *application* icon on menu bar

or

Click the *application* icon on menu bar, <u>C</u>lose

or

Click <u>F</u>ile on the menu bar, <u>C</u>lose

or

Alt+F, C

Close All Documents

Shift+File on the menu bar, then click <u>C</u>lose All

or

Alt, Shift+F, C

Display System Menu for Document

Alt+Hyphen

Go To Beginning of Document

Ctrl+Home

Go To Beginning of Line

Home

Go To End of Document

Ctrl+End

Go To End of Line

End

Insert/Overwrite (toggle)

Insert

New Document

Click 🄳 on the toolbar

or

Click <u>F</u>ile on the menu bar, <u>N</u>ew

or

Right-click *file* name, <u>N</u>ew

or

Ctrl+N

Open Document

Click 📂 on the toolbar

or

Click <u>F</u>ile on the menu bar, <u>O</u>pen

or

Ctrl+O

Open Document With

Select *file*, press *Shift* and right-click the file name, click Open With, select a program, click OK

Print Document

Click 🖨 on the toolbar

or

Click <u>F</u>ile on the menu bar, <u>P</u>rint

or

Right-click *file* name, <u>P</u>rint

or

Ctrl+P

Save Document

Click ![floppy disk icon] on the toolbar

or

Click <u>F</u>ile on the menu bar, <u>S</u>ave

or

Ctrl+S

Select Text

Click, then drag across *text*

or

Shift+arrow key

Select Text to Beginning of Document

Shift+Ctrl+Home

Select Text to Beginning of Line

Shift+Home

Select Text to End of Document

Shift+Ctrl+End

Select Text to End of Line

Shift+End

Start Application

Click ![Start button], <u>P</u>rograms, *application*

(some applications may be several levels deep)

or

Double-click application's executable *file* name (.exe, .com, .bat or .pif)

or

Click ![Start button], <u>R</u>un, type the *path* and executable *file* name (.exe, .com, .bat or .pif), then click OK.

or

Double-click application's document *file* name

or

Click 🏁 **Start** , Programs, MS-DOS prompt, type the *path* and application's executable *file* name (.exe, .com, .bat or .pif), then press *Enter*

Start Application in the Background

Ctrl+double-click application's *file* name or *icon*

Start Application when Windows Starts
(Add to StartUp Folder)

Right-click on blank area of taskbar, Properties, Start Menu Programs, Add, browse to select *file*, Next, double-click StartUp folder, Finish

Start Application with Document

Double-click document *file*

or

Right-click application's document *file* name, Open

or

Select application's document *file* name, click File on the menu bar, Open

Start Application with New Document

Right-click application's document *file* name, New (only if supported by application)

or

Right-click background of window or pane, New, *application*

or

Select application's document *file* name, click File on the menu bar, New

Start Application with Recently Opened Document

Click **Start**, Documents,

select *document*

Switch Between Applications

Click *application* button on taskbar

or

Hold down *Alt, Tab, Tab...*, release *Alt* to open

or

Hold down *Alt, Esc, Esc...*

Switch Between Applications Reversed

Hold down *Alt+Shift, Tab, Tab...*

Switch Between Child Windows

Ctrl+Tab

or

Ctrl+F6 (Microsoft Word)

Switch Between Multiple Windows in the Same Application

(For example, in Notepad, between the Find dialog box and the Notepad work area.)

Alt+F6

Window Menu for Document

Click *program* icon on menu bar or title bar of document menu.

or

Alt+Hyphen

Window Menu - Program, Open

Click *program* icon on title bar

or

Alt+Spacebar

See Also: Add/Remove Programs; Close Program; Desktop; Registry; Run; Shortcuts; Start Menu

Arranging Icons

There are many places where you might choose to *arrange icons*. The Desktop, My Computer, Windows Explorer, Recycle Bin and Network Neighborhood are the most common. The primary reason to arrange icons is so that you can work more easily and quickly with the objects displayed.

Quick Access

Right-click background of *window* or desktop, Arrange Icons, then *sort method*

or

Click View on the menu bar, Arrange Icons, then *sort method*

or

In Explorer, click a *column* heading (Details View)

View

The view selected determines the initial layout of the window pane for every place except the desktop. The views available are Large Icon, Small Icon, List and Details. For more information see "View" (p. 453).

Sort Methods

The *sort methods* (order of the objects) that are available depend on where you are. Some methods are available almost anywhere, while others are very specific.

Common

The following *common* sort methods are used on the desktop and in many of the windows

Auto Arrange · · Automatically arranges icons as they are added or deleted (works only in Large Icon or Small Icon view). When Auto Arrange is off, icons can be relocated anywhere in the window. This is especially useful for the desktop when you may want to organize your icons differently from the standard methods. See "Lining Up Icons" below.

Date · · · · · · · · Sorts by the date last modified.

Name · · · · · · · Sorts by the file or folder's name.

Size · · · · · · · · Sorts by the file size.

Type · · · · · · · · Sorts by the file type.

My Computer

Drive Letter · · · Sorts by the drive letter.

Network Neighborhood

By Comment · · Sorts by the comments associated with the network object.

Recycle Bin

Origin · · · · · · · Sorts by the origin of the file or folder.

Delete Date · · · Sorts by the date the file or folder was deleted.

Lining Up Icons

If you turn off the Auto Arrange method above so that you can organize your icons and arrange them in a way meaningful to you, you may want to tidy them up with the Line Up Icons option. This option will keep your icons in their original location, but line them up using an invisible grid. Every icon will be lined up with the other icons displayed. For more information about the invisible grid, see Appearance in the "Display" section (p. 187).

See Also: Arranging Windows; Desktop; View; Windows Explorer

Arranging Windows

When you want to move or arrange the open windows on your desktop, you have several options from which to choose.

Auto-Arrange

There are three auto-arrange options, all of which are available by right-clicking the background of the taskbar.

Cascade

Cascade begins by placing the first window in the upper left corner of the screen and then proceeds to overlap subsequent windows diagonally down to the right. The title bar is exposed on each window, which allows you to select a window to bring it to the foreground.

Tile (Windows) Horizontally

Tile Horizontally displays each window fully from left to right and arranges the windows one on top of the other, adjusting the distance from top to bottom of each window to accommodate the number of windows displayed.

Tile (Windows) Vertically

Tile Vertically displays each window fully from top to bottom and arranges them from left to right, adjusting the width of each window to accommodate the number of windows displayed.

Note: If windows are minimized and not open they will not be included in the auto arrangement.

Mouse

You can use the mouse to move one window at a time. Here's how:

> Click on the title bar of the window you want to move, drag the window to the new position, then release the mouse button.

 Full Window Drag: If you install Microsoft Plus! or Microsoft Plus! 98 you can set it up to use full window drag. This feature lets you see the entire window, including its contents, as it's dragged, rather than just the frame.

Keyboard

You can also use the keyboard to move a window. Here's how:

> Click on the program icon or press *Alt+Spacebar*, click <u>M</u>ove (the pointer changes to a four-headed arrow), then use the arrow keys to position the window. When the window is where you want it, press *Enter*.

See Also: Arranging Icons; Desktop

Automatic Skip Driver Agent (ASD) is a tool available in the Windows 98 Resource Kit. ASD automatically detects device drivers that fail to enumerate or operations that failed when Windows 98 started up. After two failed attempts, the drivers or operations are disabled by ASD so that they are bypassed on subsequent startups. ASD is then used interactively to display these failures and offer solutions to correct them.

Quick Access

Click , Programs, Accessories, System Tools, System Information, Tools on the menu bar, then Automatic Skip Driver Agent

or

Click , Run, type **ASD**, then click OK

Note: ASD is included in the full Windows 98 Resource Kit and the Windows 98 Resource Kit Sampler. See: "Windows 98 Resource Kit" (p. 487) for more information on installation and additional tools that are available.

If there are drivers or operations that have failed, ASD will list them for your review. Select the operation that failed, then click Details to identify the device and display a possible course of corrective action. Any disabled device can be enabled for the next startup. If the device fails on the next startup,

ASD will again disable the device. The computer will stop responding and will need to be restarted.

All problems that ASD has ever detected are recorded in Asd.log, which is stored in your root folder.

Note: If ASD is run when there are no errors in the Registry, the following message is displayed, "There are no current ASD critical operation failures on this machine."

Default Location: \Windows\Asd.exe

See Also: Windows 98 Resource Kit

Backup

 The Backup utilities offered in Windows 95 and Windows 98 are very different from each other. The two versions were created by different companies, and the 98 version has greater capabilities. Specifically, it:

- Supports a greater number of backup devices
- Permits more explicit backup of the Registry
- Permits differential and incremental backups

MS Backup is not installed by default. To install it, use Add/Remove Programs|Windows Setup (p. 47).

Quick Access

Click **Start**, Programs, Accessories, System Tools, Backup

Or

Click **Start**, Run, type **Backup**, then click OK.

Windows 95 Backup

MS Backup 95 gives you basic back up, restore, and compare capability, as well as basic utilities for formatting and erasing tapes. Backups can consist of: Full System Backup (predefined by the system); selected files; only files that have changed; or sets of files that you have defined and saved.

MS Backup creates two different kinds of files when run:

- **Catalog files,** which list all of the files backed up along with their subdirectories and the backup file where they are stored.

- **Data files,** which are compressed versions of the files selected for back up.

Note: Because of their proprietary format, these files must be written to a standard DOS diskette or floppy drive, not to a network drive.

CAUTION: *Files backed up to a network drive are sometimes unrecoverable.*

Compatible tape drives:

One of the weaknesses of the Windows 95 Backup utility is the small number of drives with which it is compatible.

Connected through the primary floppy disk controller: QIC 40, 80, and 3010 tape drives made by Colorado Memory Systems, Conner, and Iomega; Wangtek in hardware phantom mode only.

Connected through a parallel port: Colorado Memory Systems QIC 40, 80 and 3010.

Not Compatible: Archive drives, Irwin Accutrak tapes and drives, Mountain drives, QIC Wide tapes,

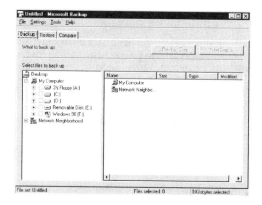

QIC 3020 drives, SCSI tape drives, Summit drives, Travan drives, any drive connected to a secondary floppy disk controller or an accelerator card.

 Quick Compatibility Check: Use Redetect Tape Drive on the Tools menu in Backup to check your tape's/drive's compatibility. If the media is detected successfully, you should be OK; if not,

- Check the list of compatible/incompatible drives above
- Clean the tape drive head
- Check the electrical connection
- Run Redetect again with a new tape

Note: The first time you open MS Backup in Windows 95, it automatically creates a backup set called "Full System Backup." If you want to back up your registry and other necessary files, you must use this

file set. Clicking your hard disk icon to
select it for backup will not copy all of
these files.

The Backup Dialog Box

The Backup Dialog Box contains three tabs:
Backup, Restore and Compare. All three tabs share
the same menus - File, Settings, Tools and Help.

File menu

On each tab, the File menu contains commands to
Open a backup set, Close, Save, Save As, Page
Setup, Print, Exit.

Settings Menu

File Filtering: Allows the user to exclude files
from the backup by file type.

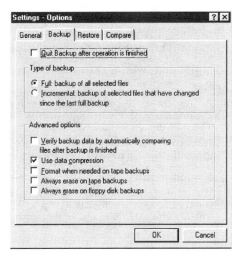

Drag and Drop: Allows the user to select options for backing up by dragging files to the Backup icon.

Options: The Options dialog box contains four tabs that allow the user to set a number of defaults:

General

The General tab contains only 2 check boxes: Turn on audible prompts and Overwrite old status log.

Backup

The Backup tab contains three sections. The first lets you set a default to quit Backup when the operation is finished.

In the second section, Type of Backup, the user determines whether the backup to be run will be full or incremental.

The third section, Advanced Options, lists options for automatic functions: compare, data compression, format backup tape if needed, and erasure of old tapes or floppies.

Restore

The Restore tab also contains three sections: The first lets you set a default to quit Backup when the process is finished.

The second section allows you to determine the destination for restored files - the original locations, an alternate location, or in a single directory in an alternate location.

The third section, Advanced Options, gives you the choices for automatic compare, and whether and when files should be overwritten in the restore process.

Compare

The Compare tab contains only two sections: Automatically quit Backup upon completion, and Location of Compare. The location options are Original Location, Alternate Location or Alternate location, single directory.

Tools Menu

The Tools menu allows you to format or erase a tape, or to Redetect the tape drive.

Help

Backup has its own specific Help section, accessible through this menu.

Backing Up Your Files

Back Up Selected Files

1. Click the Backup tab in the Backup dialog box.
2. Click the plus sign (+) next to the drive(s) you want to back up.
3. Select the files or folders you want to back up by clicking the box next to the name.
4. Click Next Step.
5. Click the icon for the drive or file where you want to store the backup.
6. Click Start Backup.
7. Type a name for the backup, and if you want to password protect it, click Password Protect.

   When the backup is finished, an "Operation Complete" message will pop up. Click OK to close the message, then OK to close the Backup window.

Incremental Backup

An incremental backup is one which includes only files that have changed since the last backup. Most backup software uses the Archive attribute to determine which files to include, and consequently backs up new files and renamed files also.

MS Backup for Windows 95, on the other hand, uses the date on which a previously backed-up file was changed. For this reason, files which were created or renamed after the last backup will not be included in the incremental backup.

1. Click the Backup tab, Settings, Options
2. On the Backup tab, click Incremental, then OK.
3. Click the *files* you want to back up, then Next Step.
4. Click the *destination* for your backup.
5. Click File, Save As...
6. Type a name for your backup set, then Save.
7. Click Start Backup.

Restoring Your Files

1. Click the Restore tab
2. Select the drive that holds the backup you want to restore.
3. In the right window pane, click the backup set you want, then Next Step.
4. In the left window pane, click the boxes next to the folders you want to restore.
5. When your selection is complete, click Start Restore.

Comparing Your Files

1. Click the Compare tab in the Backup dialog box.

2. In the left pane, select the drive or folder containing the backup set you want to Compare from.

   - Clicking a folder selects all the files inside it; to select a specific file, click the box next to it in the right pane.

3. Click Next Step.

4. Select the folders/files from that backup set that you want to compare.

5. Click Start Compare.
   A screen will pop up showing you the progress of the Compare process. When it has finished, an "Operation Complete" notice will pop up.

6. Click OK, then OK to close the Backup dialog box.

Other Backup Alternatives

Hewlett-Packard issued a more fully-featured version of the Windows 95 applet called Colorado Backup for Windows 95. It supports a greater number of HP drives and controllers, allows scheduling of unattended backups, and other enhancements.

98 Windows 98 Backup

Windows 98 Backup is a limited version of Seagate's Backup Exec. It supports a larger number of backup devices than the 95 version, but still includes only certain tape drives. If yours isn't listed, try the "any tape backup" setting - it may work.

The Windows 98 Backup dialog box is simpler to use than the earlier version, and has optional Wizards to guide you through the backup and restore processes. It also provides a link to Seagate for more information.

The Backup Dialog Box

The dialog box contains 2 tabs, Backup and Restore. They share five menus: Job, Edit, View, Tools, and Help.

Backup tab

1. In the Backup Job box, type the name of your backup job, or select one from the drop down list.

2. Under What to Back Up, click either All selected files or New and changed files.

   Select drive in the left pane by checking the box (all files on the drive) or clicking the plus sign (+) expanding it; select folders or files in the right pane.

3. Under Where to Back Up, choose the destination for your backup.

4. Under How to Back Up, click Options.

Restore

The Restore tab has corresponding sections:

1. Select the drive/folder/file from which to restore in the Restore From section.

2. Select What to Restore from the left and right panes.

3. Indicate Where to Restore by selecting from the drop down list.

4. Indicate How to Restore by clicking Options.

The Options dialog box

Options opens a dialog box with six tabs: General, Password, Type, Exclude, Report and Advanced.

General

The General tab has 3 sections:

Compare: check whether to compare original and backup files.

When backing up to media: Select No Compression, Compress to Save time, or Maximum compression to save space.

If the media already contains backups – append, overwrite or let me choose during backup.

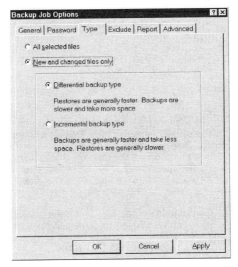

Password

If you choose to protect the Backup job with a password, you can set up the password here.

Type

Click All selected files or New and changed files only; if you choose New and changed, you can also select whether the backup is incremental or differential.

Exclude

Allows you to exclude specified types of files from your backup.

Report

A report is automatically generated when you run Backup. On this tab you can check boxes to determine contents of the report.

Advanced

Click the box if you want the Registry included in your backup.

Menus

Job

The Job menu contains commands similar to the usual File menu: New, Open, Save, Save As, Delete, Options and Exit. The Options command opens the Options dialog box described previously. The most recently run jobs will be displayed on the menu as well.

Edit

Commands on the Edit menu are available when either the left or right pane is active. This menu allows you to select or deselect disks, folders and files for backup.

View

View allows you to toggle on/off the Toolbar, Status Bar, and Job Details. You can select List View or Details View. Clicking Selection Information brings up information on the number of files and bytes. Refresh updates the screen.

Tools

The commands listed in this menu will bring up the Backup Wizard or Restore Wizard; Select a Media device, or choose whether to view or print the report. The Preferences command gives you access to three check boxes – Show startup dialog, include registry in backup/restore processes, and Show number and size of files before operations.

Help

The Help menu opens Backup-specific help.

Default Location:
\Program Files\Accessories\Backup

See Also: Emergency Recovery Utility; Long File Name Backup; Registry

Battery Meter

If you have a portable computer running on batteries, a battery icon is displayed on the taskbar. If the computer is running on AC current, the plug icon is displayed. There are two ways to find out how much power you have left: the *Battery Meter* and the tool tip display.

Quick Access

Double-click on the taskbar,

the Battery Meter is displayed.

or

Hold the pointer over and

the tool tip is displayed

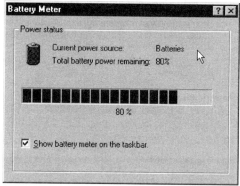

Note: If the battery icon is not displayed on the taskbar, the Show battery meter on taskbar option is probably not selected. You'll find this option in the Power tool dialog box in the Control Panel.

Low Battery Warning

When the battery gets low, a warning message will be displayed.

To enable the low battery warning message:

click on the taskbar and select

Enable low battery warning. After you select it, there should be a ✓ in front of the selection.

Note: You should enable the low battery warning as most portable computers will drain their batteries fairly steadily and then drop rapidly at the end of their charge.

Bootlog.txt

The *Bootlog.txt* file records the successful or unsuccessful loading of programs at start up. The log is originally created during Setup when the operating system is first started. Reviewing this file can sometimes help when you're trying to troubleshoot a startup problem.

If, at any time, you feel you are having problems during the system startup, you can create a boot log.

Boot the computer to the Startup Menu ("Starting Windows 95..."), press **2** to select Logged.

Viewing the Boot Log

To view the boot log, use Logview or Notepad to open the file named *Bootlog.txt*, or click on the file name in the right pane of explorer. The file is located in your root folder.

There are several sections of the boot log that you can examine. The following table lists the sections, errors and corrective action.

Section and Errors	Corrective Action
Loading real-mode drivers:	
No XMS memory	This section should contain the following entry: loadsuccess = c:\windows\himem.sys If not, verify that the file exists and is in CONFIG.SYS
Incorrect MS-DOS version (message displays when the driver loads)	If drivers or programs worked in the past but now generate this error, make sure this section contains the following entry: loadsuccess = c:\windows\setver.exe
Windows 9x will not start on a SCSI hard drive	Make sure this section contains the following entry: loadsuccess = c:\windows\setver.exe
IFSHLP.SYS message occurs	Make sure this section contains the following entry: loadsuccess = c:\windows\ifshlp.sys

Loading VxDs:	
	Make sure this section contains entries that look like this: loading vxd = ios loadsuccess = ios
Cannot access D??SPACE drives	Make sure this section contains the following entry: loadsuccess = c:\dblspace.bin
Sharing violations occur	This may occur if the Vshare VxD failed to load. The entry would appear as follows: loadfailed = vshare
System-critical Initialization of VxDs:	
System-critical initialization error occurs	Make sure this section contains entries that look like this: syscritinit = ios syscritinitsuccess = ios
Device Initialization of VxDs:	
	Make sure this section contains entries that look like this: deviceinit = ios deviceinitsuccess = ios

Successful VxD Initialization:	
	Make sure this section contains entries that look like this:
	initcomplete = ios
	initcompletesuccess = ios

The following table lists the types of entries that would appear describing the system startup process.

Entry	Description
Error	Errors logged during startup
Fail	Indicates failures occurring during startup
Dynamic load success	VxDs loaded dynamically
INITCOMPLETESUCCESS	VxDs loaded successfully
LoadStart, LoadSuccess, Loading Device, Loading VxD	Loading processes
LoadFailed	Component failed to load
SYSCRITINIT, SYSCRITINITSUCCESS	System initialization actions
DEVICEINIT, DEVICEINITSUCCESS	Device initialization actions

Dynamic load device, Dynamic init device	Dynamic loading and initialization of devices
Initing, Init Success, INITCOMPLETE Init, InitDone	Initialization actions
Status	Indicator of current status

Note: Most actions in the boot log are followed by a matching entry, for example: the first entry could be LoadStart = GDI.EXE followed by LoadSuccess = GDI.EXE. If no matching entry follows, the attempt was unsuccessful.

Default Location: c:\Bootlog.txt

See Also: Logview; Startup Menu

Boot-Up

See: Starting Windows (p. 427)

Briefcase

See: My Briefcase (p. 287)

Cabinet (CAB) Files

Cabinet (CAB) files are the compressed files Windows 9x uses during the installation process and subsequently, whenever you install a new Windows component not previously installed.

During the install process, Windows will look for the appropriate CAB file on the CD-ROM or floppy disks and extract the files it needs from the CAB file. Not all files are extracted during the installation process, only those necessary for the components selected during the install.

Windows will need to access the CAB files three times after the initial installation:

1. When installing applications using Install in the Control Panel's Add/Remove Program tool. (Sometimes applications require a Windows system file that wasn't previously installed.)
2. When installing Windows components using Windows Setup in the Control Panel's Add/Remove Program tool.
3. When you are trying to replace a damaged or corrupt Windows system file.

Using CAB Files from a Hard Drive

Every time Windows needs to access the CAB files you'll need to have the original installation CD-ROM or floppy disks available. This is not always convenient. If you have the hard disk space, it's much more convenient to copy the files to your local or network hard disk and access them there.

This is a two step process. First, you will copy the files to the hard disk and second, make changes to the Registry so that Windows can find them.

Copying the CAB Files

Before you copy the CAB files to your hard disk, make sure you have approximately 120 MB of space available, then follow the directions below:

1. Create a folder in your \Windows folder called CABS.

2. Using Microsoft Explorer, copy all the *.cab files from the \Win98 or \Win95 folder on your Windows CD-ROM into the CABS folder.

   If you are using diskettes rather than a CD-ROM, the process is more time consuming. You will have to copy the CABs from each and every diskette.

Changing the Registry

After you've copied your CAB files to your local or network hard drive, you need to change the path in your Registry to point to that location. Then whenever Windows needs to extract a file from one of the CABS, it knows exactly where to go find the CABS. Follow the steps below to change the path.

> **CAUTION:** *The following instructions involve changing settings in the Registry. If the changes are not made properly, serious problems may result. Be sure to back up your Registry before continuing. See: "Registry" (p.351) for more information about backing up and editing the Registry.*

1. Using Regedit, open the Registry and move to HKEY_LOCAL_MACHINE\SOFTWARE\Microsoft\Windows\CurrentVersion.

2. Click on the Setup folder.

3. In the panel on the right, right-click on the SourcePath item, then select Modify.

4. Type the new path to your CABS folder, for example: **c:\windows\cabs**, then click OK.

Be sure to include the ending backslash; otherwise, it won't work.

Note: If you don't change the registry to point to the CAB file location, you will need to point to the location each and every time Windows needs to extract a file. To do this when you are using Windows Setup in the Control Panel's Add/Remove Programs, select the components you want to install, then click the Have Disk button. Now use the function and move to the folder that contains the CAB files.

Finding a File in the CABS

Since the system files are contained in the compressed CAB files, the system file names cannot be viewed directly in Microsoft Explorer or My Computer. Use the Find command as described below to locate a specific file.

1. Using Microsoft Explorer, navigate to the location of your CAB files. If you're looking on the CD-ROM, the files are in the \Win98 folder or \Win95 folder. If you've copied them to a hard drive and don't know where they are, or don't know if they've been copied to the hard drive, use the Find command to find them. Search for the *.cab files on the drive in question.

2. Right-click on the folder containing the CAB files, then select Find.

3. In the Named text box type *.cab.

4. Click the Advanced tab, then type the *name* of the file you are looking for in the Containing text box.

5. Click the Find Now button to start the search.

6. After you've located the CAB file containing the file you are searching for, use the Extract command, documented below, to extract the file from the CAB.

Hot Tip **The easiest way to find files and view the contents** of CAB files is to use the Cabinet Viewer. The Cabinet Viewer is installed automatically with Windows 98, but not with Windows 95. To obtain it for Windows 95, you can install the Microsoft Windows 95 PowerToys which includes the programs. See "Cabinet Viewer" (p. 87) and "Power Toys" (p. 323) for more information.

Extracting System Files from CABS

To extract a system file from one of the CAB files, use the Cabinet Viewer or the Extract command. The Extract command is run from the MS-DOS command line. If you know which CAB file contains the file you want to extract, you can specify it in the command. If you don't, you can have Extract look for it. See: "Cabinet Viewer" (p. 87) and "Extract" (p. 194) for more information.

See Also: Cabinet Viewer; Copying Files & Folders; Extract (MS-DOS); Find; PowerToys; Starting Windows

Cabinet Viewer

The *Cabinet Viewer* is a tool that allows you to view the contents of the compressed CAB files as you would any other files using the standard shell functions.

The Cabinet Viewer is automatically installed as part of the default Windows 98 installation; however, to use it with Windows 95 you will need to download a set of utilities from Microsoft's web site, called the PowerToys, and then install it. See: "PowerToys" (p. 323) for more information.

Using the Cabinet Viewer

To use the Cabinet Viewer:

1. Navigate to the folder containing your CAB files. You can use My Computer, Microsoft Explorer, or Network Neighborhood to do so.

2. Locate the CAB file you want to view, then double-click it.

   The Cabinet Viewer window will open displaying the contents of the CAB file.

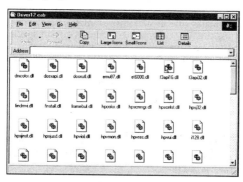

Extracting Files

To extract files from the CAB files:

1. Select the file you want to extract.

2. Click <u>F</u>ile on the menu bar, then Extract.

or

> Right-click the file, then click **Extract**.
>
> A browse dialog box is displayed.

3. Using the browser, navigate to the location you want the file to be extracted to, then click OK.

> The file is extracted and saved in the new location.

Default Location:
\Windows\System\ShellExt\Cabview.dll

See Also: Cabinet (CAB) Files; Extract (MS-DOS); PowerToys

Calculator

Calc

The *Calculator* is an accessory that you can use to perform simple arithmetic as well as complex scientific and statistical calculations. You can work in one of two views, Standard or Scientific. The Calculator will remember the

Standard View

view last used when you open it the next time. The Calculator can be used with either the mouse or the keyboard or a combination of the two. See "Keyboard Equivalents" below.

Quick Access

Click , Programs, Accessories,

then 🖩 Calculator

To change to the Scientific View, click View on the menu bar, then Scientific

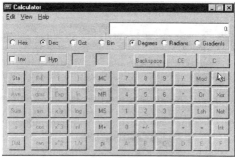

Scientific View

Hot Tip **To find out quickly what a button does** on the Calculator, right-click the button, then click What's This?

Performing a Calculation

To perform a simple calculation follow these steps:

1. Click the C (Clear All) button or press *Esc* to clear any previous entries.

2. Type in the first number for your calculation or use the mouse and click the number buttons to make your entry.

   The number should appear in the Calculator's display window.

3. Depending on what calculation you want to make, click + to add, - to subtract, * to multiply, or / to divide.

4. Enter the next number in the calculation.

5. Continue entering any remaining operators and numbers.

6. Click = when you are finished.

HOt Tip **Entering Numbers from the Keypad:** The numbers across the top of your keyboard can always be used when entering numbers; however, to enter numbers and operators using the numeric keypad you must press *Num Lock*.

HOt Tip **To use your calculations in other applications** just use the standard Windows Copy and Paste commands.

Performing a Statistical Calculation

To perform a statistical calculation follow the steps below:

1. Click <u>V</u>iew on the menu bar, then click <u>S</u>cientific.

2. Click the C (Clear All) button or press *Esc* to clear any previous entries.

3. Type in the first number for your calculation, or use the mouse and click the number buttons to make your entry.

   The number should appear in the Calculator's display window.

4. Click **Sta** to open the Statistics Box, and then click **Dat**.

   Your entry is displayed in the Statistics Box.

5. Enter your additional data. Be sure to click **Dat** after each entry.

6. After you've entered all your data click one of the three statistics buttons: **Ave**, **Sum** or **s**.

   The result will appear in the Calculator's display.

Hot Tip **To display a number from the Statistics Box in the Calculator**, select the number, then click Load.

Hot Tip **To delete one entry in the Statistics Box**, select the number, then click CD (clear datum). To delete all entries, click CAD (clear all data).

Hot Tip **To calculate the inverse of one of the statistical functions**, select Inv, then click the statistical function key. Inv will clear itself after the calculation is performed.

Performing a Scientific Calculation

To perform a scientific calculation follow the steps below:

1. Click <u>V</u>iew on the menu bar, then click <u>S</u>cientific.

2. Click the C (Clear All) button or press *Esc* to clear any previous entries.

3. Select a number system: Hex, Dec, Oct or Bin.

4. Type in the first number for your calculation or use the mouse and click the number buttons to make your entry.

   The number should appear in the Calculator's display window.

5. Depending on what calculation you want to make click + to add, – to subtract, ∗ to multiply, / to divide or any other operator.

6. Enter the next number in the calculation.

7. Continue entering any remaining operators and numbers.

8. Click = when you are finished.

Keyboard Equivalents

If you prefer using the keyboard rather than the mouse with the Calculator, the following keyboard equivalents can be used.

Button	Key
%	%
(	(
)	)
∗	∗
+	+
+/-	F9
-	-
.	. or ,
/	/
0-9	0-9
1/x	r
=	Enter
A-F	A-F
And	&
Ave	Ctrl+A
Back	BackSpace
Bin	F8
Byte	F4
C	Esc
CE	Del
cos	o

Button	Key
Hex	F5
Hyp	h
In	n
Int	;
Inv	i
log	l
Lsh	<
M+	Ctrl+P
MC	Ctrl+L
Mod	%
MR	Ctrl+R
MS	Ctrl+M
n!	!
Not	~
Oct	F7
Or		
Pl	p
Rad	F3
s	Ctrl+D
sin	s
sqrt	@

Dat	Ins		Sta	Ctrl+S
Dec	F6		Sum	Ctrl+T
Deg	F2		tan	t
dms	m		Word	F3
Dword	F2		Xor	^
Exp	x		x^2	@
F-E	v		x^3	#
Grad	F4		x^y	y

Default Location: \Windows\Calc.exe

Canceling Selections

See: Selecting Files & Folders (page 388)

Capturing Screens

See: Clipboard|Capturing Screens (page 111)

CD Player

Cdplayer

Windows 9x includes the *CD Player* as part of its multimedia tool set. The CD Player is used to control audio CDs. It has all the standard controls you would expect, such as play, pause, stop and eject, as well as some advanced controls. Use the controls as you would on an actual electronic device.

Quick Access

Insert an audio CD in the CD-ROM drive (works only if AutoPlay is enabled)

or

Click , Programs, Accessories,

Multimedia, CD Player

or

98

Click , Programs,

Accessories, Entertainment, CD Player

CD Player dialog box, shown with <u>V</u>iew, <u>T</u>oolbar enabled.

HOt Tip **Create a shortcut for the CD Player** and place it on your desktop, then you can quickly access it when you need it.

If you create a shortcut from the file it won't include the special parameter /play. Be sure to add it on the end of the command line so that your CD will start playing as soon as you double-click the shortcut. Here's an example:
\windows\cdplayer.exe /play

Create a shortcut to a favorite track by including it in the command line that you use for your Target in the shortcut. Here's an example:

\windows\cdplayer.exe/play f:\ track03.cda.

Finish up by renaming the shortcut to the name of the song.

Default Location: \Windows\Cdplayer.exe

See Also: CD-ROM Drive

CD-ROM Drive

 CD-ROM discs have become standard in the industry for delivery of software. Most new computer systems are now shipped with CD-ROM drives installed. The main advantage of CD-ROM discs is the amount of storage space that is available on them—650 megabytes, the equivalent of more than 450 floppy disks. An entire application can now be delivered on one disc, which allows the user to install the software in about a third of the time.

Multimedia has benefitted most from CD-ROM technology, allowing publishers to deliver images, audio and video that, in the past, could not fit on a single floppy disk.

Using a CD-ROM Drive

A CD-ROM drive is used similarly to a hard or floppy drive. It appears along with the other drives in My Computer and Explorer; however, it does have a distinctive icon as shown above.

When there is no disc in the drive, the appropriate drive letter is displayed below the icon. When a disc is in the drive, the title of the disc is displayed next to the drive letter in Explorer and My Computer.

The CD-ROM drive is accessed by double-clicking the icon or right-clicking the icon, and then clicking Open.

Hot Tip **To eject a disc from your CD-ROM drive** without having to touch the drive, right-click the CD-ROM icon, then click Eject.

Hot Tip **Create a shortcut to your CD-ROM drive on your desktop**. In the shortcut Properties, change the Target to Explorer /e, /root, x:\ where x is the CD-ROM drive letter. Be sure to delete the drive designation in the Start in text box before saving your changes. Now when you use the shortcut to access your CD-ROM drive, Windows 9x displays your files and folders using the two-pane Explorer view. If you don't change the Target as shown above, Windows 9x will either launch the program specified in the Autorun.inf file, or display your files and folders in a single-pane Explorer view.

Hot Tip **Create a Dedicated Music Drive:** If you have an extra CD-ROM drive, consider dedicating it to music. You can specify which drive should be used for music by opening the Control Panel, double-clicking Multimedia, then clicking the CD Music tab. Change the CD-ROM drive letter to your dedicated drive, then click OK to save your changes. Now Media Player, CD Player, and other programs will use this drive as the default.

AutoPlay

When a disc is inserted into the drive, it is automatically detected. If the disc contains data and is enabled for AutoPlay (has an Autorun.inf file on the disc), the designated program in the Autorun.inf file will begin to run.

Audio CDs don't have Autorun.inf files, so if no file exists, Windows 9x executes the default action for the corresponding file type. An audio file's default action is Play, so Windows 9x launches the CD Player application. See "CD Player" (pg. 94) for more information on playing audio CDs.

> **Hot Tip** **To temporarily disable the AutoPlay feature**, hold down the *Shift* key while inserting the disc into the CD-ROM drive. Release the *Shift* key after the drive's indicator light goes out.

Disabling AutoPlay for All Discs

AutoPlay is enabled for all data and audio discs by default. To disable AutoPlay for all discs and retain disabled as a default, follow these steps:

1. Click **⊞ Start** , Settings, Control Panel.

2. Double-click , then click the Device Manager tab.

3. Double-click the CD-ROM entry in the list. A list of CD-ROM drives is displayed.

4. Double-click the desired drive to open its Properties, then click the Settings tab.

5. In the Options panel, clear the check box for Auto insert notification.

   If the Options panel does not have a check box for Auto insert notification, you can make the change in the Registry.

CAUTION: *The following instructions involve changing settings in the Registry. If the changes are not made properly, serious problems may result. Be sure to backup your Registry before continuing. See: "Registry" (p. 351) for more information about backing up and editing the Registry.*

Using **Regedit**, open the Registry, click <u>E</u>dit on the menu bar then <u>F</u>ind.

Type **AutoInsertNotification**, then click Find Next.

Double-click the entry's name to open the edit window, then change 01 to 00.

Click OK to save the change.

6. Click OK, then OK again to finish.

7. You will be prompted to restart your computer. You can do so immediately or wait until later; however, your changes will not take effect until you do restart.

   To enable AutoPlay, just follow the steps above, selecting Auto insert notification as the default.

Disabling AutoPlay for Audio CDs

AutoPlay is enabled for audio CDs by default. To disable AutoPlay for just audio CDs and retain it as a default, follow these steps:

1. Double-click , click <u>V</u>iew on the menu bar, then <u>O</u>ptions.

2. Click the File Types tab, then select the AudioCD entry in the Registered file types list.

3. Click the <u>E</u>dit button, **Play** should be listed in bold under <u>A</u>ctions.

4. Click the <u>S</u>et Default button; Play will change from bold to normal type.

5. Click <u>C</u>lose, then <u>C</u>lose again to finish.

To enable AutoPlay as the default, just follow the steps above, clicking <u>S</u>et Default to make the action, **Play**, bold again.

> **Assign Your Own Letter to the CD-ROM Drive:** Windows 9x normally assigns the next logical drive letter to your CD-ROM drive; however, if you would like to assign it a specific letter, here's how:
>
> 1. Open the Control Panel and double-click the System icon.
>
> 2. Click the Device Manager tab, then double-click the CD-ROM entry in the list.
>
> 3. Double-click the drive you want to work with, then click the <u>S</u>ettings tab.
>
> 4. In the Reserved drive letter panel, select the desired drive letter from the Start drive letter list. The same letter will display in the End drive letter list.
>
> 5. Click OK to save your changes.

HOt Tip **To improve the performance of your CD-ROM drive**, you need to change two settings.

1. Right-click My Computer, click Properties, Performance tab, File System, then the CD-ROM tab.

2. Move the sliding bar all the way to the right for Supplemental Cache Size, then select Quad Speed or Higher from the Optimize access pattern for drop-down list.

These changes will increase the size of the cache for your CD-ROM drive.

Using a CD-ROM Drive in MS-DOS Mode

The 32-bit, protected-mode CD-ROM file system (CDFS) drivers have replaced the 16-bit real-mode drivers used in MS-DOS, providing superior performance; however, there are times when it will still be necessary to use the real-mode drivers.

The two most common times are:

1) when you are installing Windows 9x from MS-DOS or

2) running an MS-DOS program that requires access to the CD-ROM drive.

In both cases, the real-mode drivers must be available when you start your computer in MS-DOS mode.

The two files that need to be available are **Mscdex.exe** which is located in the \Windows\Command folder and is run from the Autoexec.bat or the Dosstart.bat file, and the real-mode device driver that was included with your CD-ROM drive, which is run from the Config.sys file. Follow the instructions from the manufacturer to complete the installation of the drivers.

Note: If you do not have the device driver for your CD-ROM drive (usually delivered on a floppy disk), you may need to contact the manufacturer to obtain it. If you need it fast, most companies will allow you to download the drivers from their web site.

Hot Tip **Copy both real-mode drivers to your startup disk** so that in case you can't boot into Windows 9x, you will still be able to access your CD-ROM drive from MS-DOS.

98

Hot Tip **Access the CD-ROM Drive from the Emergency Startup Disk:** The Emergency Startup Disk (ESD) includes generic, real-mode ATAPI CD-ROM and SCSI drivers that can be used to access CD-ROM devices when running Windows 98 from the ESD. These drivers will not work with all CD-ROM drives, but offer a solution in an emergency.

See Also: Add New Hardware; CD Player; CD-ROM File System (CDFS)

CD-ROM File System (CDFS)

The *CD-ROM File System* (CDFS) is a 32-bit protected-mode driver that was introduced with Windows 95. It replaces the 16-bit real-mode drivers, Mscdex.exe, and the manufacturer's driver supplied with the CD-ROM drive. CDFS offers improved performance over the real-mode 16-bit drivers. It has a dynamic cache that is both larger and smarter than the one used by Mscdex and is optimized for CD-ROMS.

Multimedia presentations especially benefit from the read-ahead features of the cache, which offers smoother playbacks than earlier versions.

See Also: CD-ROM Drive

Character Map

Charmap

The *Character Map* is a tool you can use to copy special characters, foreign language characters, symbols and graphics and insert them into a document. This full set of ANSI characters are contained within the fonts that you have available but are not easily accessible from the keyboard. Character Map allows you to preview these characters in advance and then copy them to the clipboard for use wherever you need them.

Quick Access

Click **Start**, Programs, Accessories,

then Character Map

Note: If the Character Map is not available on the menu, it hasn't been installed. See: "Installing the Character Map" below.

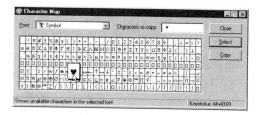

Hot Tip **To enlarge a specific character** so that you can see it better, just click the character and hold down the mouse button.

Using the Character Map

To use the Character Map:

1. Click , Programs, Accessories,

   Character Map

2. Select the font you want using the Font drop-down list box.

   Its special characters will be displayed.

3. Look at the Characters to copy text box to see what it contains. If you just opened the Character Map it will be clear. If you had previously selected a character, it may still be there. To clear it, select the characters and press *Delete*.

4. Click the character you want to use, then click Select.

   The character is displayed in the Characters to copy text box. You can select additional characters if you'd like. Each one will be added to the end of the others in the Characters to copy text box.

CAUTION: *If you change fonts while selecting several characters at a time, all characters will be affected. You can't mix fonts in one selection.*

5. Once you've select the character(s) you need click <u>C</u>opy.

   The characters are copied to the Clipboard.

6. Open or move to the destination document, position the insertion point, then use the <u>P</u>aste command to copy the character into the document.

HOt Tip **To select characters faster,** just double-click them.

HOt Tip **Need to draw a box?** Try using the Terminal font box drawing characters.

HOt Tip **Looking for a copyright** (©)**or trademark** (™) **symbol?** You'll find them here in the Character Map.

Note: The display in the lower right of the Character Map window lists the keystrokes you could use to produce the character without using the Character Map. Remember to use the numbers on the numeric keypad, not the row of numbers across the top of your keyboard, when using this method.

CAUTION: *If you try to use the Character Map to copy and paste characters into non-Windows applications it may not work. It all depends on how well Windows can translate the ANSI character into an IBM extended character. If it doesn't work, you will have to enter the character directly using the appropriate* ***Alt*** *+ code combination for the IBM extended character.*

Installing Character Map

If the Character Map does not appear on the Accessories menu, you will have to install it. To install the Character Map:

1. Click **🏁 Start**, Settings, Control Panel
   then 🔳
   Add/Remove
   Programs

2. Click on the Windows Setup tab.

3. Select the Accessories option from the Components list, then click the Details button.

4. Scroll down, find 🗺 Character Map, then select it.

5. If you don't have your CAB files available on your hard disk, you will need to have your Windows 9x CD or diskettes.

6. Click OK.
   Character Map will now be available on your Accessories menu.

Default Location: \Windows\Charmap.exe

See Also: Clipboard; Fonts

Checklinks, ChkInks

See: Link Check Wizard (p. 262)

Clipboard

Clipbrd

The *Clipboard* is a temporary storage area in memory that facilitates the exchange of data between applications. Whenever you Cut or Copy objects or data, the information is stored in the Clipboard. The information stays there until something else is cut or copied, which replaces the contents of the Clipboard, or the computer is shutdown. It can only hold the information from one cut or one copy at a time.

The information stored in the Clipboard can be pasted (transferred) into other applications or different parts of the same application. Since the information is not removed from the Clipboard when you paste, you can paste the same information as many times as you want.

The Clipboard accepts data from internationally aware applications while preserving all the language formatting characteristics. This facilitates the exchange of information without the loss of the rich text data.

HOt Tip **Copy from the Character Map:** If there are specific symbols or characters you use often from the Windows Character Map, you can use the Copy button within the Character Map dialog box, to copy a selected character or series of characters to the Clipboard. You can then paste the character(s) into the application you are working with.

Clipboard Viewer

If you want to see what's in the Clipboard you can use the Clipboard Viewer to view its contents.

Quick Access

Click **Start** , Programs,
Accessories, System Tools, Clipboard
Viewer.

or

Click **Start** , Programs, Accessories,

Clipboard Viewer

Note: If the Clipboard Viewer is not on the
menu it hasn't been installed. See: "Installing the Clipboard Viewer" below.

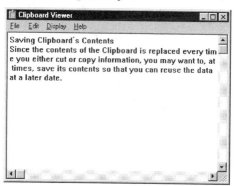

Saving Clipboard's Contents

Since the contents of the Clipboard are replaced every time you either cut or copy information, there may be times when you want to save its contents so that you can reuse the data at a later date.

To save the contents of the Clipboard:

1. Within Clipboard Viewer, click File on the menu bar, then Save As.
2. Navigate in the Save As dialog box to the folder in which you want to save the file, then type a file name using the extension .clp.
3. Click OK. The file is saved.

The Clipboard file format .clp is not easily read by other applications. The best way to use these files is to read the file back into the Clipboard. Once the file is in the Clipboard you can paste it into just about any application.

To open a file in the Clipboard:

1. Click File on the menu bar, then Open.
2. Navigate in the Open dialog box to the location of the file, then select the *file* name.
3. Click OK. The file is opened in the Clipboard.

CAUTION: *When a .clp file is opened in the Clipboard, anything that is in the Clipboard will be replaced with the contents of the file.*

Clearing the Clipboard

The Clipboard uses memory to store your information. If you've copied a large object or a lot of data to the Clipboard you may need to recover that memory so that you can run other programs.

When you are in the Clipboard Viewer you can clear the Clipboard using the following steps:

1. Click Edit on the menu bar, then Delete.
2. Click Yes to clear the Clipboard.

HOt Tip **Clear the Clipboard without Clipboard Viewer:** If you need to clear the Clipboard but do not have the Clipboard Viewer open, copy a single character from your application to the Clipboard. It won't completely clear the Clipboard but it will reduce the amount of memory used to almost nothing.

Note: If you've copied a rather large item to the Clipboard, you may receive a Windows message asking whether you want to keep the current contents of the Clipboard. If you answer Yes, the contents will be retained; if you answer No the contents will be erased.

HOt Tip **Quick View Plus:** If you need to copy data from files that you can't open because you don't have the original application, consider an add-on software product called Quick View Plus. Quick View Plus lets you open a file and then copy data from the file into the Clipboard. See Quick View for more information about Quick View Plus.

Display Options

The Clipboard Viewer stores its information in different formats. The views available to you under *Display* depend on the format of the original data. By changing the view, you can prepare the data for transfer to other applications that might require a different format. Selecting Auto will always return the data to its original format. Following are some of the display options that may be listed:

DataObject	Embed Source
Object Descriptor	Native
Rich Text Format	OwnerLink
Picture	OLE Private Data
DIB Bitmap	Locale
Bitmap	OEM Text
Palette	

Installing the Clipboard Viewer

The Clipboard Viewer is not installed by default when you choose the Typical Installation option. If it hasn't already been installed you can install it by following the next few steps:

1. Click , Settings, Control Panel,

   then double-click ![Add/Remove Programs]

2. Click the Windows Setup tab.

3. Select Accessories in the Components list box, then click the Details button.

4. Select Clipboard Viewer, then click OK.

5. Click OK again.

   If you originally installed Windows using a CD-ROM or floppy disk(s), you may be prompted to insert one of the disk(s) into your computer.

6. The Clipboard Viewer is now installed.

Capturing Screens

The Clipboard can be used to capture the entire screen or the active window. The images can then be pasted as a bitmap into other applications or saved as a file.

To capture the entire screen:

Print Screen

To capture the active window:

Alt+Print Screen

or

Shift+Print Screen

 To print a captured screen, copy the screen to the Clipboard, paste it into Paint or WordPad, then use the Print command to print the screen.

Default Location: \Windows\Clipbrd.exe

See Also: Character Map; ClipTray; Copy; Copying Files & Folders; Cut; Moving Files & Folders; Paste; Quick View; Scraps

---

98 ClipTray

ClipTray is a tool available in the Windows 98 Resource Kit. It allows you to store blocks of text and assign names to those blocks. The text can be retrieved through the ClipTray menu and placed in your Clipboard. Once in the clipboard, the text can be pasted anywhere you like.

Quick Access

To access the ClipTray menu:

Right-click , in the System Tray of the taskbar. Cliptray

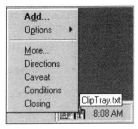

*The above Quick Access method assumes that
ClipTray is already up and running.* If you
plan to use ClipTray often, add a shortcut
for ClipTray to your Startup folder so that it
will be open and ready when you need it.
You'll see its icon in the System Tray on the
taskbar if it's active.

If you don't think you'll use it that often, create a
shortcut on your desktop or somewhere else that's
convenient.

Note: ClipTray is included in the full Windows 98 Resource Kit and the Windows
98 Resource Kit Sampler. See: Windows
98 Resource Kit (p. 487) for informa-

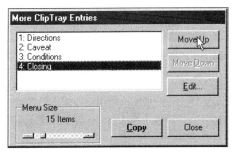

tion on installation and additional tools
that are available.

Using ClipTray

To use ClipTray:

1. Right-click in the System Tray of the
   taskbar

2. Select one of the entries in the bottom
   panel. Once an entry is selected, the text
   for that entry is copied into the Clipboard
   and is available for use.

3. If you don't see the entry you want, click
   More and the full list of entries becomes
   available.

4. Select the entry you want from the list,
   then click Copy. The dialog box will close.

 Prioritize Entries: If you use some entries more often than others and you
want to move those entries up higher on
the list, just select the entry you want to
move, then click Move Up.

 Change Number of Entries: You can
change the number of entries that appear in the ClipTray menu by moving
the slider control for Menu Size one way
or the other.

Adding a New Entry

When you first open ClipTray it will be empty. To
build a list of the most common text you use,
you'll need to add some entries. Here's how:

1. Double-click in the System Tray of
   the taskbar.

or

Right-click **Cliptray** (icon) in the System Tray of the taskbar, then click **A**dd.

If you are using multiple ClipBook text files, be sure you have selected the correct one before you add new entries. See "Using Multiple ClipTray Text Files" below.

2. Type the *name* for the entry, then press *Tab.*
   This name will show up on the ClipTray menu.

3. Type or paste in the *text* for the entry, click **A**dd, then **C**lose.

Editing an Entry

If you need to make changes to either the name or the text of an entry, here's how:

1. Right-click **Cliptray** (icon) in the System Tray of the taskbar, click **O**ptions, then **E**dit.

2. Select the *name* of the entry you want to edit from the drop-down list, then click **Edit Current**.

3. Change the *name* or the *text*, then click **Save**.

4. Click **OK** to close the ClipTray Editor.

Deleting an Entry

If you need to delete an entry from the list follow these steps:

1. Right-click **Cliptray** (icon) in the System Tray of the taskbar, click **O**ptions, then **E**dit.

2. From the drop-down list, select the *name* of the entry you want to delete, then click Delete.

3. Click <u>Y</u>es to confirm the deletion, then OK.

Preview Mode

ClipTray is set up to copy the text from your selected entry directly onto the Clipboard. If you want to see the text it's copying as it copies, turn Preview Mode on. Here's how:

Right-click in the System Tray of the taskbar, click <u>O</u>ptions, then <u>P</u>review Mode.

A check mark is now present next to the menu item.

To turn Preview Mode off, repeat the steps above.

Using Multiple ClipTray Text Files

You may want to create different ClipTray text files to accommodate varying needs. For example, one for legal clauses, another for sales letters and yet another for personal use.

Creating a New File

To create a new file:

1. Right-click Cliptray in the System Tray of the taskbar, click <u>O</u>ptions, <u>F</u>ile, then Open/Create.

2. Navigate to the folder in which you want to save the file (the default folder is My Documents), type the file name in the file name text box, then click <u>O</u>pen.

3. Click Yes to confirm the creation of the file.

The new file will now appear in a list of available ClipTray text files.

Opening a Different File

To open an existing file:

1. Right-click ![Cliptray icon] in the System Tray of the taskbar, click Options, then File.

   A list of available ClipTray text files displays.

2. Click the file you want to use.

HOt Tip **To see the name of the current text file**, hold the mouse pointer over the ClipTray icon in the System Tray of the taskbar—the file name will display as a ToolTip.

Default Location:
\Program Files\Win98RK\Cliptray.exe

See Also: Clipboard; Windows 98 Resource Kit

Clock

See: Regional Settings (p. 349)

Close Program

The *Close Program* dialog box is used to close a program or application that has quit responding or has locked up. This process is designed so that only the offending program need be closed, allowing you to continue running other programs you have open.

CAUTION: *When you use Close Program to close a program you will more than likely lose any recent changes you have made in the program.*

Here's how to use Close Program:

1. After exhausting the standard methods of closing the program, press *Ctrl+Alt+Delete*. The Close Program dialog box is displayed.

2. In the display area, Windows lists all the programs that are currently open. Select the program that has [**Not responding**] next to it, then click End Task

   If you press *Ctrl+Alt+Delete* a second time or click Shut Down, all open programs including Windows 9x will be closed.

3. A confirmation message is displayed warning that you may lose data if you continue. This message may take a few seconds to display, so be patient.

   Click End Task to complete the process.

CAUTION: *If you try to restart the offending program after a you've used Close Program to close it you may find it continues to act abnormally. If this is the case you will need to restart Windows and try again.*

See Also: Shut Down

Closing Files or Windows

The process of *Closing Files or Windows* is common throughout Windows. When you close a file or Window you may also be closing the associated application. When attempting to close a file that has not been saved, most applications will provide an additional prompt for you to save it.

Quick Access

> Click **X** on the title bar

or

> Double-click *document* icon

or

> Click <u>F</u>ile on the menu bar, <u>C</u>lose

or

> Double-click *program* icon

or

> *Alt+F4*

or

> *Alt+Spacebar, C*

See Also: Shutdown

Context Menu

See: Shortcut Menu (p. 397)

Control Panel

Control Panel

The *Control Panel* is a folder that contains command, control and configuration programs that you can use to change the hardware, software and system settings for Windows

The programs that appear in the Control Panel may vary depending on the hardware or software you have installed. For example, if you are communicating across a network you will see the icon for Network management, or if you have a PCMCIA card installed you will see the icon for PC Card (PCMCIA); otherwise, the icons will not be displayed.

Hot Tip **To have Windows display a description** for each of the icons in the Control Panel, open Windows Explorer then click on the Control Panel icon in the left pane of the window. A list of the icons and their descriptions will appear in the right pane of the window.

Quick Access

Click **Start**, Settings, then

Control Panel

Or

Double-click 🖥 My Computer, then

double-click 📁 Control Panel

The Windows 98 Control Panel

The Windows 95 Control Panel

98

Note: If you are using Windows 98 or Internet Explorer 4.x, the Control Panel has two hyperlinks available on the left side of the window. Microsoft Home connects you to the home page on Microsoft's web site and Technical Support connects you specifically to Microsoft's technical support area.

To open any of the programs in the Control Panel, just double-click the appropriate icon.

Each of the programs in Control Panel is different and detailed enough to warrant its own section in this book. To find out more information about each of them, just look it up alphabetically by name.

Hot Tip **Simplify Your View:** If there are tools in your Control Panel that you don't use on a regular basis you can *move* them to another folder which will simplify your view. The Control Panel files (.cpl) are located in the \Windows\System folder. Make sure the location you move them to is a safe location, you never know when you might need one of these files.

You can also use the Control.ini file to control whether the tools load. To prevent a tool from loading, open the \Windows\Control.ini file with Notepad. There should be a heading called [don't load]; if not, create one at the beginning of the file. Under this section heading, type the name of the .cpl file you don't want to load followed by =no. Save the file and exit. Following is an example:

```
[don't load]
snd.cpl=no
joystick.cpl=no
midimap.drv=no
```

Hot Tip **Create a Shortcut to Control Panel**: If you find yourself opening the Control Panel often, create a shortcut on your desktop so you can open it in one step. To create a shortcut, open Explorer, click the Windows folder, right-click Control.exe, drag it to your desktop, then select Create Shortcut(s) Here. In the shortcut's Properties, add *Ctrl+Alt+C* in the Shortcut key text box, and you'll be able to open the Control Panel at any time.

Hot Tip **Extra Control Panel Folder:**
You can create an additional Control Panel folder by giving the folder a specific name. To do this, right-click your Desktop, select New and then Folder. Type the following name for the folder: **Control Panel. {21EC2020-3AEA-1069 -A2DD-08002B30309D}.**

When you press _Enter_ to save the name, only Control Panel will be displayed for the name, the rest will be hidden. You can now drag this new folder to your Start button, Office toolbar or anywhere you would like. If you create this new folder in the Start Menu folder, the Control Panel will operate as a cascading menu. If you drag it to the Start button, it will open the Control Panel window rather than cascade.

Hot Tip **Create a Shortcut to a Control Panel Tool:** If you only use one or two programs in the Control Panel regularly, create a shortcut by dragging the specific icons to the desktop or to your Start Menu folder. If there are several programs you use, create a folder in the Start Menu called Control and then copy the programs into the folder.

..QuicKeys..

Close Utility Window

Click ❌ on the title bar

or

Click OK

or

Click Cancel

or

    Alt+F4

or

    Esc

Open

Click **Start**, Settings, Control Panel

or

Double-click ,
My Computer

double-click
Control Panel

or

Ctrl+Esc, S, C

Default Location: \Control Panel

See Also: Desktop; Start Menu; System Policies

Copying Disks

A disk can be copied to another disk of like kind using the Copy Disk command. For example, a 3½ diskette can be copied to another 3½ diskette, but cannot be copied to a 5¼ diskette. The Copy Disk command makes an exact duplicate of the original, including the disk's Label.

Note: Disks can also be copied using the MS-DOS Diskcopy command.

Quick Access

From My Computer or Explorer

Right-click the *drive* icon, then click Copy Disk...

From My Computer

Select the *drive* icon, then click File on the menu bar, Copy Disk...

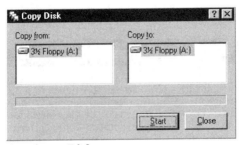

Copying a Disk

To copy a disk:

1. Insert the disk you want to copy from (source) into the disk drive.

2. In the Copy Disk dialog box, select the Copy from *drive*, in the left window.

3. If the Copy to disk (destination) is different, select it. If it's the same, you don't have to make a selection.

4. Click Start.

5. After the data has been copied from the Copy from disk, you may be prompted to insert the Copy to disk. Insert the Copy to disk, then click OK.

Hot Tip **Use Copy Disk to Back up Original Disks**: When you make backup copies of original disks, always use the Copy Disk command. Many install programs refer to the Label on the disks during the install process, so you'll want make sure the Label is copied with the data to your backup disks. Using any other method to copy the data will not copy the Label.

See Also: Copying Files & Folders; Xcopy & Xcopy32

Copying Files & Folders

Files and folders can be copied to other areas of the same drive or to different drives. When a file or folder is copied, the original is left undisturbed and a copy or duplicate is created at a new location. During the copying process, the data is temporarily stored in the Clipboard. Following are several methods that can be used in My Computer or Windows Explorer to copy files and folders:

Drag and Drop

Ctrl+drag *file(s)* or *folder(s)* to the *destination* on the same drive.

or

Drag *file(s)* or *folder(s)* to the *destination* on a different drive.

or

Right-click *file(s)* or *folder(s)* and drag to the *destination*, then click <u>C</u>opy Here.

or

Ctrl+Shift, click *file(s)* or *folder(s)* and drag to the *destination*, then click <u>C</u>opy Here

HOt Tip **End Drag and Drop Confusion:** When you use the drag and drop method to *copy* a file or folder, a plus sign (+) will be displayed with the pointer as it is placed over the destination.

- If an arrow ⬐ is displayed, you are creating a *shortcut* to the file or folder rather than a copy.

- If nothing is displayed with the pointer you are *moving* the file or folder.

HOt Tip **Quick Cancel:** If you're in the middle of using the drag and drop method and you want to cancel your action, just press *Esc* before you drop.

HOt Tip **Right -Click and Drag:** When working with folders, right-click and drag the folder—you will be given a choice between copying and moving.

CAUTION: *If you drag and drop an executable (.exe) file, you will end up with a shortcut to that file rather than a copy of the file. Be sure to hold down the Ctrl key while dragging the file and a copy will be made.*

HOt Tip **Easy Copies Between Windows:** If you are using My Computer or Explorer, and find it troublesome to position and size multiple windows to facilitate your copy procedure from one window to another, try this:

- Open the window you want to copy to, then minimize it.

- Next, open the window you want to copy from, click or right-click the file or folder you want to copy, then drag it to the minimized window on the taskbar.

- Hold it over the button for a moment until the window becomes active; you can now navigate to where you want to copy the file or folder to and complete the copy.

Copy and Paste

Right-click *file(s)* or *folder(s)*, click <u>C</u>opy, right-click the destination, then click <u>P</u>aste

or

Select *file* or *folder*, click on the toolbar.

move to the destination,

then click

or

Select the *file* or *folder*, click

on the toolbar, move to the destination,

then click

or

Select the *file* or *folder*, press *Ctrl+C*, move to the destination, then press *Ctrl+V*

or

Select the *file* or *folder*, click <u>E</u>dit on the menu bar, <u>C</u>opy, move to the destination, click <u>E</u>dit, then <u>P</u>aste

Hot Tip **Mix and Match Commands**: You can combine the Copy or Paste commands from the menu, toolbar or shortcut menus. For example, you could use the Copy command from the shortcut menu, and then use the Paste command from the toolbar.

Note: When you **copy** a folder, its entire contents, including all files and folders, are copied.

If you **drag** a folder to another folder of the **same** name, the folder is copied into the destination folder, it does not replace it.

To **replace** a folder of the same name, drag the folder to the parent folder or drive.

See Also: Cutting Files and Folders; Moving Files & Folders; Selecting Files & Folders; Undo; Xcopy & Xcopy32

Country Settings

See: Regional Settings (p. 349)

Crash Protection

There are many conditions and reasons that could contribute to a lock-up or system crash. By performing the standard maintenance procedures on your system you are taking the first step toward preventing problems. No matter what, however, you should take the following actions so that in the event you do encounter a crash, you will have the greatest possible chance to recover your system.

- Backup your data
- Backup your Registry files
- Create a Startup disk
- Copy your CD-ROM drivers to your Startup disk
- Backup your system and configuration files using the Emergency Recovery Utility

Store this information in a secure, safe place. If you do have a problem, you will have everything necessary to replace or recover your system.

See Also: Add/Remove Programs; Add/Remove Programs|Startup Disk; Backup; CD-ROM Drive; Emergency Recovery Utility; Registry

Creating Files & Folders

Files and folders can be created on your desktop, in My Computer, or in Windows Explorer. You do not have to be in an application to create files or folders. Here are two methods you can use:

Quick Access

Right-click an open area of the background, click <u>N</u>ew, then click the type of file or folder you want to create.

or

In My Computer or Windows Explorer, click <u>F</u>ile on the menu bar, <u>N</u>ew, then click the type of file or folder you want to create.

The file types that appear on the menu are dependent on the applications that have been installed on your computer.

See Also: Deleting Files & Folders

Currency Format

See: Regional Settings (p. 349)

Cutting Files & Folders

The *Cut* command comes in handy when you are moving files or folders from one location to another. When files and folders are cut, the original is not removed from its source folder until it is pasted into another location. Once the paste is completed, however, the original is removed from its location. During the copying process the data is temporarily stored in the Clipboard. If you decide to cancel the process, just return to the window from which you made the cut, then press *Esc*.

Following are several methods that can be used in My Computer or Windows Explorer to Cut and Paste files and folders:

Cut and Paste

Right-click *file(s)* or *folder(s)*, click C<u>u</u>t, (Cut in Win98) right-click the destination, then click <u>P</u>aste

or

 Select *file* or *folder*, click on the toolbar,

move to the destination, then click

or

Select the *file* or *folder*, click
on the toolbar,
move to the destination, then click

or

Select the *file* or *folder*, press *Ctrl+X*, move
to the destination, then press *Ctrl+P*

or

Select the *file* or *folder*, click <u>E</u>dit on the
menu bar, Cu<u>t</u> (Cut in Win98), move to the
destination, click <u>E</u>dit, then <u>P</u>aste

or

Select the *file* or *folder*,

Type *Alt+E, T* (98) or *U* (95) to cut

Move to the destination, then *ALT+E, P* to
paste.

> **HOt Tip** **You can mix the Cut and Paste commands** from the menu, toolbar or shortcut menus. For example, you could use the Cut command from the shortcut menu and then use the Paste command from the toolbar.

See Also: Copy; Copying Files & Folders; Move;
Moving Files & Folders; Selecting Files & Folders;
Undo; Xcopy & Xcopy32

Date Format

See: Regional Settings (p. 349)

Date/Time

The time is displayed on the right side or bottom
of the taskbar, depending on the position of the
taskbar. The initial settings are entered using the
Date/Time tool in the Control Panel.

Time is displayed on the taskbar.

To view the date, place the mouse pointer on the time display on the taskbar and wait for the date to display.

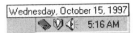

Note: If the Time is not displayed on the taskbar, make sure the Show Clock checkbox is selected in the properties for the taskbar. To view the taskbar properties, right-click the taskbar, then select Properties.

Quick Access

Double-click the time display on the taskbar.

or

Right-click the time display on the taskbar, then click Adjust Date/Time.

or

Click **Start**, Settings, Control Panel,

then double-click

Date/Time

or

Double-click , Control Panel,

My Computer

then double-click

Date/Time

Date/Time   133

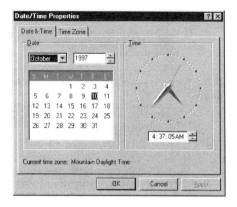

All of the above the above access methods display the Date/Time Properties window. There are two tabs: *Date & Time* and *Time Zone*.

Date & Time

The *Date & Time* tab contains the settings for month, year, day and time. To make changes to the date or time select the Date & Time tab, then use the following instructions:

Month

> To change the *month*, click on the drop down box for the month, then select the current month.

Year

> To change the *year*, use the arrows on the spin box for the year and increment or decrement the year.

Day

To change the *day*, click on the appropriate day on the calendar.

Time

To change the *time*, in the time box below the clock, select either the hour, minutes, seconds or am/pm by double-clicking the value, then type over the selection or use the arrows to increment or decrement the value.

When you are finished making adjustments to the date or time click OK to save your changes.

CAUTION: *Windows uses the date and time setting to record when files are created and modified. If your date or time is not set properly, your files will not be date and time stamped accurately.*

HOt Tip **To make sure your computer is set to the correct time**, try one of the freeware utilities available on the Internet. These utilities will calibrate your clock to the time maintained by various atomic clocks located around the world.

AtomTime95 (Atmtm14a.zip) and Dimension 4 (D4time41.zip) are both available on Windows Magazine's web site which is located at http://www.winmag.com/Win95/software.htm.

Time Zone

The *Time Zone* tab provides a way for you to set the time zone to one which reflects the area in which you live or are staying. There are two ways to change the time zone:

Click the drop down list box at the top of the tab, then select the appropriate time zone.

or

Click on the map in the area you desire; the highlighted time zone will move to the newly selected area and change the time zone in the drop down list box.

HOt Tip Be sure to **select the check box to automatically adjust your clock** for daylight savings time, then you won't have to change it manually when the time change occurs.

HOt Tip **To calculate the time in another time zone,** use the Greenwich Mean Time (GMT) adjustment and determine the difference between the time zones. Add or subtract the appropriate number of hours from your local time.

..QuicKeys..

Change Date Format

Click  , Settings, Control Panel,

double-click , Date

Change Time Format

Click **Start** , Settings, Control Panel,

Double-click , Time

Show Clock

Right-click blank area of taskbar, Properties, Show Clock

View Date

Place mouse pointer on time display on taskbar and wait for date to display

View Time

Time is displayed on the taskbar

View Time in Another Time Zone

Double-click time display on taskbar, Time Zone

or

Click **Start** , Settings, Control Panel,

Double-click , Time Zone

Default Location: \Control Panel\Date/Time

See Also: Regional Settings

Defragmenter

See: Disk Defragmenter (p. 170)

Deleting Files & Folders

There are many ways you can delete files and folders. Some have permanent results, while most only temporarily store the items in the Recycle Bin.

Quick Access

98

Select the *file* or *folder*, then

click on the toolbar

or

95

Select the *file* or *folder*, then click
on the toolbar

or

Drag the *file* or *folder* to the

or

Right-click the *file* or *folder*, then click
<u>D</u>elete

or

Select the *file* or *folder*, click <u>F</u>ile on the
menu bar, then <u>D</u>elete

or

Select the *file* or *folder*, <u>D</u>elete

Hot Tip **To Delete or Not to Delete?** If there's ever a question about whether you should delete a file, don't delete it. Instead, move it into a holding folder and then see if it affects your operations. If no problems seem to come up in the next month or so, it's probably safe to delete the file.

Hot Tip **Identifying Files:** If you encounter a file that you can't identify such as .exe, .dll or .ocx, and you want to know more about it, open Windows Explorer, right-click the file, click P<u>r</u>operties, then the Version tab. Normally, you should find listed the company name that created the file, the product it's associated with and the version number.

Hot Tip **Deleting .tmp files**: Orphaned temporary (.tmp) files can accumulate quickly in the \Windows\Temp folder. You can safely delete any files dated prior to today's date. Depending on the applications you use, you may have other .tmp files on your disk. Use the Find command to locate and delete them.

Hot Tip **Other files you can safely delete** to recover disk space are .___, .old, .bak, .00x, .prv and .txt.

Hot Tip **Delete Unneeded Video Files**: Video files (.avi) usually take up quite a bit of disk space. To reclaim some disk space, use the Find command to locate .avi files and delete any you don't need. The \Windows\Help folder contains 7 MB of these video files that you can delete for starters.

Hot Tip **Delete Unneeded Zip Files:** If you're done with your zipped files (.zip), use the Find command to locate and delete them.

Windows 9x prompts you to confirm your deletion whenever you use the Delete commands or the Delete button. The message you will see depends on whether you are deleting a document or an executable file.

If it's a document, the message is simply "Are you sure you want to send '*file name*' to the Recycle Bin?" If it's an executable, the message contains a warning "The file '*file name*' is a program. If you remove it, you will no longer be able to run this program or edit some documents. Are you sure you want to move it to the Recycle Bin?"

If you drag and drop a file onto the Recycle Bin, no message is displayed, since Windows 9x assumes you wouldn't be doing this unintentionally.

HOt Tip **Turn off Delete Confirmation message**: If you don't want to see the confirmation messages when you delete, you can turn them off in the Recycle Bin Properties. Right-click the Recycle Bin icon, click Properties, clear the checkbox for Display delete confirmation dialog, then click OK.

HOt Tip **Delete Files Permanently:** If you want to delete files or folders permanently, hold down the *Shift* key while deleting them. The files or folders will not go to the Recycle Bin, but will be permanently removed from the disk drive at the time of deletion. Note that if you use the *Delete* key in the numeric keypad and *Num Lock* is activated, the file will still go to the Recycle Bin. To avoid this problem, release the *Num Lock* or use the other *Delete* key.

Note: When you delete files in Windows 9x you don't free up any disk space because you've only moved the file to the Recycle Bin. In fact, the Recycled Bin actually uses another 280 bytes for each file to store information about the file. You will free up space only when the Recycle Bin is emptied.

CAUTION: *If you delete files from the MS-DOS prompt, the files are not moved to the Recycle Bin.*

Hot Tip

To quickly erase all files on a floppy disk, create a shortcut on your desktop that contains the following command:

deltree /y a:.

Name the shortcut something like Clean Up A:. Now, whenever you want to clean up a floppy disk, insert the disk in drive a:, then double-click the new shortcut.

Recovering Deleted Files

The easiest and most common way to recover files is to use the Restore command in the Recycle Bin. See "Recycle Bin" for more information on restoring files.

If the file you want to recover is not in the Recycle Bin, there is one more method you can try: the Undelete command. This will only work if the file has not been written over by another file.

Undelete.exe is an MS-DOS command and is not supplied with Windows 9x. To use it you will have to copy it from your previous version of MS-DOS, or from another computer that is still running MS-DOS, to your Windows 9x hard drive. The basic syntax for the command is:

Undelete *drive*:*path**filename.extension*

To execute this command you will need to shut down Windows and restart the computer in MS-DOS mode. At the MS-DOS command line, type the command and press **Enter**. If the file is recoverable the name will be displayed with a "?" for the first character. Follow the instructions on the screen and replace the "?" with the first letter of the file name. The file can then be used as any other file. You can get more information on the

Undelete command from MS-DOS Help by typing Undelete /? at the MS-DOS command line.

 Undo a Deletion: If you delete a file or folder and you realize you made a mistake, you can immediately use the Undo command to reverse the process. For more information see "Undo" (p. 449)

Deleting Duplicate Files

Duplicate files can take up valuable disk space. If you want to find and remove duplicates, you can do so using the Find command. The next few steps show you how:

1. Click **🏁 Start**, Find, Files or Folders.

2. Type *. and a common file extension you use, such as doc or xls. It should look like this: *.doc.

3. Click the Find Now button. Your entire hard disk is searched and the results are displayed.

4. Click the Name column header to sort the list by name.

5. Look for duplicates by scrolling through the list. Use the file size and date modified to determine which one to delete. If you need to view the contents of the file, use Quick View.

6. When you find a duplicate, delete it by right-clicking the file, then Delete.

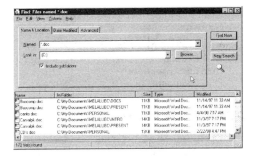

Delete Previous Versions of Windows:
If you've upgraded from Windows 3.x
and elected to overwrite your previous
version of Windows, Windows 9x setup
prompts you to save your previous version of Windows and system files. If you
did, Windows 9x created two files
W9xundo.dat and W9xundo.ini. These
files contain your previous version of
Windows and are stored in your root directory. When you feel that you no longer need the ability to restore your
previous version of Windows, you can
safely delete them and in the process recover approximately 15 megabytes of
disk space.

Identifying Unwanted Programs

Every once in a while it pays to look for programs
that you no longer need or want. These programs
and associated files are just taking up valuable disk
space. Following is a method for identifying and
locating those unwanted programs:

1. Create a folder on your desktop called Shortcuts.

2. Click **Start**, Find, Files or Folders.

3. In the Named text box, type ***.exe *.com**, then click Find Now.

4. Click Edit on the menu bar, then Select All.

5. Drag the files and drop them on the Shortcuts folder you created on the desktop. A shortcut will be created for each program file.

6. Open the Shortcuts folder and execute each program by double-clicking each program file.

If you decide you don't want the program anymore, you can look at the Shortcut tab in the Properties for the file and find out where it's located. You can then delete the program and any associated files. It's always recommended that you use the Add/Remove Programs tool in the Control Panel to remove programs if possible, rather than just deleting the files.

CAUTION: *If you don't know for sure what the program is, it's always safer to leave it than delete it.*

CAUTION: *You may end up with hundreds of shortcuts depending on how many programs you have installed. Be sure to delete all these shortcuts when you are finished, otherwise they will be taking up valuable disk space.*

Check CAB files: If you think you have a file that could be deleted, but want to make sure it's not a Windows system file, use the Find command and search the CAB files to make sure. See "Cabinet (CAB) Files"(p. 84) for more information.

See Also: Creating Files & Folders; Cutting Files and Folders; Recycle Bin|Restoring Files & Folders; Quick View; Undo

Desktop

The *Desktop* is your main work area, your base of operations. When you first start Windows, your screen is filled with a background color or graphic and the icons that represent commonly used applications, utilities, and folders. By using one of the icons or the Start menu all programs can be accessed from the Desktop.

The Windows 98 Desktop

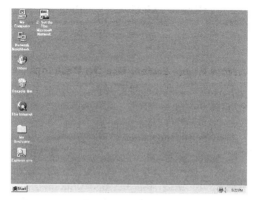

The Windows 95 Desktop

HOt TiP **Create shortcuts to your favorite programs** on your desktop so that you can access them quickly and easily.

Many actions can be taken from the Desktop, including changing its appearance, manipulating windows, and arranging icons. Following are some of the actions you can take:

..QuicKeys..

Appearance

Right-click background of desktop, Properties, Appearance

or

Click , Settings, Control Panel,

double-click ![Display], Appearance

Applications, Switch Between

Click *application* button on taskbar

or

Hold down Alt, Tab, Tab…

Arrow Keys - Enable Use On Desktop

Ctrl+Esc, Esc, Shift+Tab

Colors

Right-click background of desktop, Properties, Appearance

or

Click ![Start], Settings, Control Panel,

double-click , Appearance

Display

Folders, Close All Parent

Shift+click [X],

Folders, Show All Open

Right-click background of taskbar, Tile (Windows) Horizontally, Tile (Windows) Vertically or Cascade (Windows)

Icons, Arrange

Right-click background of desktop, Arrange Icons, then *sort method*

Icons, Line Up

Right-click background of desktop, Line up Icons

Icons, Move

Drag to new *location* (with auto arrange off)

Properties

Right-click background of desktop, Properties

or

Click **Start** , Settings, Control Panel,

double-click 🖥️
Display

Screen Saver

Right-click background of desktop,

Properties, 🖥️ Screen Saver
Display

or

Click **Start** , Settings, Control Panel,

double-click 🖥️ , Screen Saver
Display

Shortcut, Create

Right-click and drag *object* to desktop, Create Shortcut(s) Here

or

Right-click background of desktop, New, Shortcut

Sounds

Click **Start** , Settings, Control Panel,

double-click 🔊
Sounds

Wallpaper

Right-click background of desktop, Properties, Background

or

Click **Start** Settings, Control Panel,

double-click 🖥️ , Background
Display

Window, Close Current

Click **✖** on the title bar

or

Double-click *program* icon on title bar

or

Alt+F4

or

Click *program* icon on title bar, <u>C</u>lose

or

Right-click *program* button on taskbar, <u>C</u>lose

or

Click <u>F</u>ile on the menu bar, E<u>x</u>it

or

Alt+F, X

Windows, Cascade

Right-click blank area of taskbar, <u>C</u>ascade (Windows)

Windows, Minimize All

Right-click blank area of taskbar, <u>M</u>inimize All Windows

or

Ctrl+Esc, Alt+M

Windows, Tile Horizontally

Right-click blank area of taskbar, Tile (Windows) <u>H</u>orizontally

Windows, Tile Vertically

Right-click blank area of taskbar, Tile (Windows) <u>V</u>ertically

Windows, Undo Minimize All

Right-click blank area of taskbar, <u>U</u>ndo Minimize All

HOt Tip **To easily send files or folders to the desktop**, create a shortcut in the SendTo folder with the following Command line:

C:\Windows\Desktop

Once the shortcut is created, you can send files or folders to the desktop by using the Shortcut menu. Right-click the file or folder, click SendTo, then Desktop.

HOt Tip **Turn off the Resize Flicker:** Every time you maximize or minimize a window, you will see a kind of flicker as the window finds its home. This flicker is designed to give you a visual indication of where the window is going. If you want to turn off this effect you can do so in the Registry.

CAUTION: *The following instructions involve changing settings in the Registry. If the changes are not made properly, serious problems may result. Be sure to backup your Registry before continuing.*

Use Regedit to open the Registry, then navigate to \HKEY_CURRENT_USER\ Control Panel\Desktop\WindowMetrics. Click Edit in the menu bar, New, then String Value. Type **MinAnimate** for the name and press *Enter* twice. In the Value Data text box type **0**, then click OK.

HOt Tip **Quick Access to the Desktop:** When you have several windows open it is often difficult to access your desktop. The usual way to do so is to minimize all your windows and then make a selection. Here's another way that you can gain access to the icons on your desktop without minimizing everything:

Right-click Start, Open, double-click Programs and then double-click Startup. Now, create a shortcut by clicking File on the menu bar, New, then Shortcut. In the command line text box type:
c:\windows\explorer /root,
Click Next, type in **Desktop** for the name of the shortcut and then click Finish.

To make sure this Explorer window starts out minimized and out of the way, right-click the Desktop shortcut file, click Properties, Shortcut and then select *Minimized* from the Run drop-down list box. Click OK to save your change.

The next time you start Windows, a new button will appear on your taskbar. You will be able to select it at any time, no matter how many windows you have open, and have complete access to every icon on your desktop.

A second way is to click Start, Run, type a period in the command line, then click OK. The desktop folder is displayed.

A third option is to install one of the Power Toys, DeskTop Menu. See "Power Toys" (pg. 323) for more information.

98

Windows 98 and Internet Explorer 4.x make displaying the desktop easy with a feature called Quick Launch. Enable Quick Launch by right-clicking a blank area of the taskbar, Toolbars, Quick Launch. Then you can just click the desktop icon on the taskbar at any time.

Hot Tip **Eliminate Unwanted Taskbar Buttons:**
If you have unwanted minimized buttons on your taskbar, or an open window when you first start Windows, there are two places you can check to remove the offending programs from the load sequence.

The first place to look is in the Startup folder, located in the \Windows\Programs folder. Using My Computer or Windows Explorer, view the contents of the folder and determine if the program exists there. If so delete it.

If it does not exist in the Startup folder, use Notepad to open the Win.ini file. It's located in the \Windows folder. At the top of the file in the [Windows] section you will find two commands: load= and run=. Delete any unwanted programs from these lines and any spaces that occur in between the programs. Save the file and restart Windows.

Hot Tip **Change Speed at Which Menus Open:** If you want to increase or decrease the speed at which your menus open you can do so in the Registry.

CAUTION: *The following instructions involve changing settings in the Registry. If the changes are not made properly, serious problems may result. Be sure to backup your Registry before continuing.*

Use Regedit to open the Registry, then navigate to \HKEY_CURRENT_USER\ Control Panel\Desktop. Double-click the MenuShowDelay string. Type the new delay time you wish to use (the default is 500 milliseconds represented by a 5), then click OK.

Hot Tip **Separate Standard Icons from Personal Icons:** Move all your standard icons such as, My Computer, Network Neighborhood, Recycle Bin, etc. to the right side of the desktop. As you add new icons to your desktop they will appear on the left side, automatically maintaining separation from your standard icons. Auto Arrange must be turned off for this to work.

Hot Tip **Remove Standard Icons:** If you want to remove some of the standard icons on your desktop that do not have the delete command available on the short-cut menu, you can do so in the Registry.

CAUTION: *The following instructions involve changing settings in the Registry. If the changes are not made properly, serious problems may result. Be sure to backup your Registry before continuing.*

Use Regedit to open the Registry and navigate to \HKEY_LOCAL_MACHINE\ SOFTWARE\Microsoft\Windows\ CurrentVersion\explorer\Desktop\ NameSpace.

There may be several key numbers listed under the NameSpace folder. As you select a number in the left pane, the name of the icon it represents is displayed in the right pane. When you find the one you want to delete, select the number, right-click the number, then click Delete. You might want to record the key number before you delete it so that you can recreate it if necessary.

Hot Tip **Change from Plain Folder Icon:** If you want to change the icon for a new folder to something other than the default plain folder, create the folder somewhere else, then drag it to your desktop. A shortcut is created for the folder and in its properties you can change the icon.

98

When you change the icon in Windows 98, a pallet is displayed from which you can choose a variety of different icons.

Default Location: \Windows\Desktop

See Also: Applications; Arranging Icons; Arranging Windows; Display; Shortcuts; Taskbar

Detlog.txt

Every time the hardware detection routine runs in Windows it creates and records what's transpired in a log file called *Detlog.txt*. If Windows does not recognize a new device that you've added to your system, it logs information about the process in Detlog.txt. Viewing this log may provide information that could help you with the installation of a new device.

A new Detlog.txt file is created every time the detection routine is run and any previous version is renamed to Detlog.old. The detection routine is run during setup and also when using the Add New Hardware Control Panel tool.

Detlog.txt is a text file that can be viewed with Logview, Notepad, or WordPad.

Default Location: \detlog.txt

See Also: Logview

Device Drivers

See: Add New Hardware (p.37); Section 5-Glossary (p. 541); System|Device Manager (p.438)

Device Manager

See: System|Device Manager (p. 438)

Dial-Up Networking

Dial-Up Networking

Dial-Up Networking (DUN) is used to establish and store information about your modem connections to other computer systems such as the Internet, your office, or home. It also is used to actually dial the number of the system you are connecting to and make the connection. Once a connection is made, data can be transferred and applications can be run.

Quick Access

98

Click , Programs, Accessories, Communications, then Dial-Up Networking

Click , Programs, Accessories,

then Dial-Up Networking

Note: If Dial-Up Networking does not appear on your menu, it hasn't been installed yet. To install Dial-Up Networking use the Control Panel tool Add/Remove programs. On the Windows Setup tab you'll find the Communications category. Dial-Up Networking is a component of that category.

Making A New Connection

Make New Connection

To make a connection to another computer system, you record the name of the connection, the modem you will use and the phone number of the system you are connecting to. Once that is completed you are ready to dial up your connection.

It's much easier to create a new connection if your modem is already installed and operating correctly. The instructions that follow assume you have your modem already installed. If you don't have your modem installed, you will be led through additional dialog boxes to install your modem. For more information on installing a modem see "Add New Hardware," (p. 37).

To make a new connection:

1. Click , Programs, Accessories, (Communications), then Dial-Up Networking.

2. Double-click the Make New Connection icon.

3. Click in the first text box and type the name of the computer you want to connect to.

4. Select an installed modem from the drop-down list box, then click Next.

5. Type the area code and telephone number of the computer you are connecting to.

6. Select the appropriate country code, then click Next.

7. Click Finish to complete the process.
   A new icon displays in the Dial-Up Networking folder with the name you assigned.

To edit the information in a connection, right-click the connection icon, then select Properties. A dialog box will open. You can then make the changes you need to make.

Dialing A Connection

My Connection

After you have created a connection for the computer you want to call, you can use the connection icon to dial up your connection.

To dial up your connection:

1. Click Start, Programs, Accessories, (Communications) then Dial-Up Networking.

2. Double-click the connection icon you want to use.

3. Type in your Username and Password if necessary.

4. Change the Dialing From location if necessary, then click Connect.

Your computer will dial the computer you are calling and establish a connection.

`HOt Tip` **Set Up Multiple Dialing Locations**: If you dial out from different locations, which may require that you dial a number to get an outside line, or if you periodically use a calling card, you can set up multiple dialing locations by clicking the Dial Properties button on the Connect To dialog box.

`HOt Tip` **Eliminate a Step:** If you have to respond to Dial-Up Networking's Connect button every time you try to connect to your ISP, you can eliminate the step easily. Click Start, Programs, Accessories, (Communications), Dial-Up Networking, Connections on the menu bar, then Settings. On the General tab, clear the option labeled "Prompt for information before dialing."

`HOt Tip` **Create an additional Dial-Up Networking folder** by giving the folder a specific name. To do this right-click your Desktop, select New and then Folder. Type the following name for the folder:

Dial-Up Networking.{992CFFA0-F557-101A-88EC-00DD010CCC48}.

When you press *Enter* to save the name, only Dial-Up Networking will be displayed for the name, the rest will be hidden. You can now drag this new folder to your Start button, Office toolbar or anywhere you would like.

Default Location:

\Windows\Start Menu\Programs\
Accessories\Dial-Up Networking

\Windows\Start Menu\Programs\
Accessories\Communications\Dial-Up
Networking

See Also: Add New Hardware; Modems

Dialog Box

A *dialog box* is a tool that you can use to type or select information for Windows 9x to use for a particular purpose.

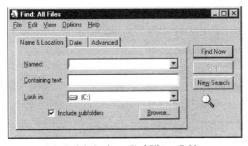

A typical dialog box - Find Files or Folders

Navigating

Dialog boxes have several different components, but most will have one or more places to type or select information and one or more command buttons. When there is more than one button, one of them will always have a darker outline than the others. This is the button that is active and will execute when the *Enter* key is pressed.

The *Tab* key will move the focus from one object to another. Holding down the *Shift* key while using *Tab* will move in reverse order.

Following are a few methods you can use to move through a dialog box:

Move through Objects (within a tab)

> Click *object*

or

> *Tab*

Move through Objects in Reverse

> Click *object*

or

> *Shift+Tab*

Move through Tabs

> Click *tab*

or

> *Ctrl+Tab*

Move through Tabs in Reverse

> Click *tab*

or

> *Ctrl+Shift+Tab*

Close the Dialog Box

> Press *Esc* (Does not work in all dialog boxes)

or

Press *Alt+F4*

or

Click ⊠

or

Click <u>F</u>ile on menu bar, <u>C</u>lose

or

ALT+F, C

or

Double-click upper left icon

or

Right-click upper left icon, <u>C</u>lose

or

Click OK or Cancel

Dialog Box Elements

Usually there are several different elements contained within a dialog box. Each element has its own particular use and works in a specific manner. The following table lists and provides details about each of the elements:

Name	Definition	Example
Check box	A square box that when selected has a check inside it, and when cleared is empty. More than one check box can be selected at a time.	

Combo box	A text box and a list box combined. This element not only allows you to select an item, it also lets you type in a new item.	
Command Button	A rectangular button that executes a command. If the button label ends with ellipsis points, more information will be need before the command is executed.	
Drop-down arrow	Used with the combo box and drop-down list box, this element indicates that a list is available, and can be accessed by clicking on the drop-down arrow.	

Drop-down combo box	Functions like the combo box; however, its default state is closed. Clicking the down arrow displays the list.	
Drop-down list box	Functions like the list box (see below). However, its default state is closed. Clicking the down arrow displays the list.	
Group Box	A related set of options, usually enclosed with a frame.	
Label	The text that describes an element or object.	
List box	A type of box that contains a list of items from which the user can select.	

Option button	A round button that, when selected, turns off or excludes all other buttons in the group.	○ None ● Coarse ○ Fine ○ Line art ○ Error diffusion
Slider	A control that changes the value, within a continuous range, by sliding it back and forth.	Desktop area — Less —— More 800 by 600 pixels
Spin box	Text box in which the user can type or use the up and down arrows to change the value.	5 : 30 : 01 AM
Tab	A label and selection control for separate pages within a dialog box.	Install/Uninstall W
Text box	A box in which the user can type text.	Computer name:
Title	The title of the dialog box. Generally, it matches the command that launched it.	Keyboard Properties

Unfold button	A command button that enlarges the current dialog box or displays more options.	

Hot Tip **Dialog Box Shortcut Menu:** You can right-click on the command line in any dialog box to display a shortcut menu with the following options: Undo, Cut, Copy, Paste, Delete and Select All.

Help

If you need help while you are in a dialog box, there are three possibilities from which you might choose, depending on how the dialog box was designed.

- Some boxes have a menu bar on which appears a Help menu option,
- Other boxes have a Help button located somewhere within them.
- If there is a ? in the upper right corner, you can click it, then click the object you would like help on.

Dir (MS-DOS)

Dir is an internal MS-DOS command that displays a list of the subdirectories and files in the current or specified directory. Dir displays both the short 8.3 file name and the long file name.

Hot Tip **Print a Directory List**: If you need to print a list of the subdirectories and files produced by the Dir command, use the following command:

dir [drive:][path] /o:n > prn

/o:n - sorts the items in order by name

> prn - redirects the output to the printer

If you want to capture the list for future use, change the destination, prn, to a file name.

Hot Tip **Use Wildcards:** Wildcards can now be used with the Dir command more effectively than in previous versions of MS-DOS. For example, **dir *r.*** will show only files and folders that end in the letter "r" and **dir *r*.*** will show all files and folders that contain the letter "r".

Command

Dir [*Drive:*] [*Path*] [*Filename*] [/**p**] [/**w**] [/**a**[[:]attributes]] [/**o**[[:]sortorder]] [/**s**] [/**b**] [/**l**] [/**v**] [/**4**]

 Examples: Dir or Dir *.exe or Dir *. or Dir /b

Options:

Drive: .... Specifies the drive you want to display.

Path .... Specifies the path to the directory or file you want to display.

Filename .... Specifies the file you want to display.

attributes	D =	Directories
	H =	Hidden files
	S =	System files
	R =	Read-only files
	A =	Files ready for archiving
	– =	Prefix meaning "not"

sortorder	N =	Name (alphabetical)
	E =	Extension (alphabetical)
	G =	Group directories first
	A =	Last Access Date (earliest first)
	S =	Size (smallest first)
	D =	Date and time (earliest first)
	– =	Prefix used to reverse order

/A:*attributes* ....Displays files with specified attributes.

/B ....Uses a bare or minimal format only showing directories and files without headings or summaries.

/L ....Uses lowercase letters for file names.

/O:*sortorder* ....List the files in sorted order.

/P ....Pauses after each screen full of information.

/S.............................Displays files in the specified directoryand all its subdirectories.

/V ....Uses verbose format
                               which adds allocated size,
                               last date accessed, the file
                               attribute, total bytes allo-
                               cated, total disk space,
                               and percentage space in
                               use to the default format.

/W ....Uses the wide list format.

/Z ....Eliminates the long file
                               name column.

98

/4 ....Displays four digit years.
                               Ignored if combined with
                               /v.

Notes: Options can be used together. For exam-
            ple, dir /b/z/l will list only the 8.3 char-
            acter file names in lowercase.

See Also: My Computer; Network Neighborhood;
Windows Explorer

Disconnect Network Drive

When you need to remove a network drive mapping, you can do so using the Disconnect Network Drive option. This function is available in Windows Explorer, My Computer or Network Neighborhood.

Quick Access

Click ![icon] on the toolbar.

or

Right-click *drive* icon, then click Disconnect

or

Click **Tools** on the menu bar, then Disconnect Network Drive (Windows Explorer)

or

Alt+T, then *D* (Windows Explorer)

or

Click **File** on the menu bar, then Disconnect (Network Neighborhood)

or

Alt+F, then *D* (Network Neighborhood)

The dialog box displays all the network computers you are currently connected to.

To disconnect:

1. Select the appropriate drive mapping from the Drive list box.

   If you want to select more than one drive mapping at the same time, hold down the *Ctrl* key while you make your selections.

2. Click OK to save your changes.

The drive mappings will no longer appear in Windows Explorer or My Computer.

See Also: Map Network Drive; My Computer; Network Neighborhood; Windows Explorer

Disk Defragmenter

Defrag

The *Disk Defragmenter* is a tool used to reorganize the order in which files are stored on your hard drives. When files are saved they are stored in small units called *clusters*.

Initially these clusters will be all together side by side in one area of the hard disk. As the file is modified, additions to the file may not be able to be stored next to the first clusters since other files may have used that space. After a period of time, depending on how often you modify your files, pieces of a given file will be scattered all over the disk; in other words, fragmented. When Windows tries to open a file, it has to go to several places on the drive to assemble the various pieces so that it can present the file as one piece. Since Windows has to go to several places instead of just one, it takes longer to open the files. This causes a performance problem, but it can be easily fixed using the Disk Defragmenter.

The Disk Defragmenter reorganizes the files on the disk, putting the fragmented pieces of each file all in one place. It also consolidates the free space so that future defragmentation is less likely. This can speed up disk access by as much as 300%, depending on how often the defragmenting process is run.

Quick Access

Click **🏁 Start**, Programs, Accessories, System Tools, Disk Defragmenter

or

Right-click a *drive* icon, Properties, Tools, then Defragment Now

Running Disk Defragmenter

After starting the Disk Defragmenter using one of the Quick Access methods above, you are ready to configure the Disk Defragmenter for operation.

1. If you have started the Disk Defragmenter from the System Tools menu, you will be asked to select the drive you want to work with. Select the *drive* using the drop-down list box.

2. The Disk Defragmenter will examine the disk to see if it needs to be defragmented. The percentage of fragmentation and a recommendation to defragment or not to defragment the drive will be displayed.

   If the Disk Defragmenter does not recommend defragmentation, you can still run the process with no adverse affects.

3. Click Select Drive if you want to work with a different drive.

4. Click <u>S</u>ettings or Advanced (see below) to change any of the default settings.

5. Click Start to start the defragmenting process.

6. The display will show you the progress that is taking place. If you want to see the activity in detail, click Details. Running in the Details view will cause the process to take longer to complete. The fastest execution is with Details off and the window minimized.

7. You can Pause or Stop the process any time.

Hot Tip **First Things First:** For best results, always delete any unnecessary files, empty the Recycle Bin and run ScanDisk before running the Disk Defragmenter.

Note: The Disk Defragmenter can be run as a background operation; however, it will affect performance. Use the Pause or Stop commands if it is interfering too much with your other operations.

Note: The Disk Defragmenter can be run with DoubleSpace or DriveSpace drives, although it will not work with other compressed drives such as Stacker or SuperStor. It's even more important to defragment compressed drives since they store data in smaller increments than uncompressed drives. This means they will become fragmented sooner.

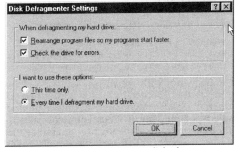

The Windows 98 Settings dialog box

Settings provides you with a method to change the defaults for the Windows 98 Disk Defragmenter. The default settings provide the most complete and thorough defragmentation; however, you can change them if you think it will be advantageous.

Note: In Windows 98 your choices are fewer than in Windows 95's Advanced Options, but there is also new functionality.

Rearrange program files so my programs start faster

This setting will reorganize program files, placing all the files associated with a particular application in the same location on your drive. The applications that have received this treatment will run at optimum speed since all their programs can be quickly accessed from one location.

In Windows 98 a process called *Task Monitor* monitors the programs that you use and records in a log file the disk access patterns during their start up.

These log files are stored in the \Windows\Applog folder. The format of the log file name is *application.lgn*, where *application* is the name of the application and *n* is the drive letter on which the application resides. Here are a few examples:

Word.lgc	Log for Word, located on drive C.
Excel.lgd	Log for Excel, located on drive D.
Notepad.lgc	Log for Notepad, located on drive C.

The frequency with which you access these programs is also recorded in the log files. When you run the Disk Defragmenter, it calls a program called Cvtaplog.exe. This program compiles the information from all the log files and builds a file for each drive called Applog.dtn. The Disk Defragmenter uses the instructions in these files to organize the program files in a sequence which helps them to load and start faster.

Check the drive for errors

If this option is checked, the Disk Defragmenter will check the drive for errors before it starts. If it finds any errors it will stop and recommend that ScanDisk be run.

I want to use these options

Select the first option if you want the current settings to be used only one time. If you want the current settings to become the new defaults, select the second option.

Advanced Options

Windows 95 uses the label *Advanced Options* rather than Settings for the setup of the Disk Defragmenter. The default settings provide the most complete and thorough defragmentation. The Advanced Options allow you to change these settings if you think it will be advantageous.

Full defragmentation

Full defragmentation reorganizes the files so that each file is in stored in one contiguous unit and all free space is consolidated in one place.

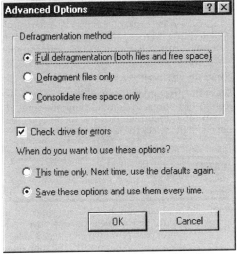

The Windows 95 Advanced Options dialog box

Defragment files only

Defragment files only reorganizes the files so that each file is in stored in one contiguous unit; however, it does not consolidate the free space. The process will take less time to run, but the files you save in the future will be more likely to become fragmented.

Consolidate free space only

Consolidate free space only consolidates the free space; however, it does not defragment existing files. The files you save in the future will remain unfragmented longer but existing files will become more fragmented.

Check drive for errors

If this option is checked, the Disk Defragmenter will check the drive for errors before it starts. If it finds any errors, it will stop and recommend that ScanDisk be run.

When do you want to use these options?

Select the first option if you want the current selection of options to be used only one time. If you want the current options to become the new defaults select the second option.

CAUTION: *Do not use previous MS-DOS versions of DEFRAG with Windows 9x because you may encounter unexpected adverse results.*

Note: You should run the Disk Defragmenter on a regular basis to keep your disk drive operating at peak performance. Check it at least once a week to begin with, and then more or less depending on whether or not the Disk Defragmenter thinks it's necessary.

Hot Tip **To automatically defragment your drives** on a regular basis, consider purchasing Microsoft Plus! It has a scheduling agent called System Agent that allows you to set up a specific time to automatically run the Disk Defragmenter.

Hot Tip **Create a Shortcut for Defrag** and place it in your Startup folder so that your hard disk is defragmented every time you start your computer. The command you would put in your Shortcut, to start Defrag, defragment your C drive and close Defrag automatically would look like the following:

   c:\Windows\Defrag.exe c: /noprompt

Command

Defrag [*drive:* |/all] [/F|/U|/Q] [/Noprompt] [/Concise|/Detailed]

Options:

Drive: ....Specifies the drive(s) you want to defragment

/All ....Defragment all local nonremovable drives

/F ....Defragment files and consolidate free space

/U ....Defragment files only

/Q ....Consolidate free space only

/Concise..........Hide details during operation (default)

/Detailed.........Show details during operation

/Noprompt .....Do not stop and display confirmation messages

Notes:

1. Defrag.exe is a Windows-based command and does not have an MS-DOS-based equivalent.

2. Defrag.exe can be run in the <u>R</u>un dialog box or from a shortcut.

3. Defrag.exe can be used in MS-DOS batch files or from the command line by prefacing it with the *start* command. Here's an example:

    start /w defrag c:

    The start /w command used in this example allows the batch file to stop and wait for Defrag to finish running; otherwise, the batch file would try and continue as soon as Defrag was launched.

Default Location: \Windows\Defrag.exe

See Also: Recycle Bin; ScanDisk

Disk Drives

..QuicKeys..

Available Disk Space

Select drive icon
(information will appear in the left window pane).

or

Right-click *drive* icon, Properties,
General tab.

or

Select *drive* icon, click File on the menu bar,
Properties, General tab.

Connect Network Drive

Select *drive* icon, click on the
toolbar

or

Right-click *drive* icon, Map Network Drive

or

In Windows Explorer, click Tools on the
menu bar, Map Network Drive

or

Alt+T, M (Windows Explorer)

or

In Network neighborhood, click File on the
menu bar, Map Network Drive

or

Alt+F, M (Network Neighborhood)

Defragment

Click ![Start], Programs, Accessories,

System Tools, Disk Defragmenter

or

Right-click a drive icon, Properties, Tools
tab then Defragment Now

Disconnect Network Drive

In Windows Explorer, My Computer or Network
Neighborhood,

Click  on the toolbar

or

Right-click *drive* icon, Disconnect

or

In Windows Explorer, click <u>T</u>ools on the menu bar, <u>D</u>isconnect Network Drive

or

In Explorer, *Alt+T, D*

Format Drive

Right-click *drive* icon, For<u>m</u>at

Properties

98

Select the *drive*, click on the toolbar

Or

95

Select the *drive*, click on the toolbar

or

Right-click *drive*, P<u>r</u>operties

or

In My Computer or Network Neighborhood, Alt+double-click *drive*

or

Select the *drive*, *Alt+Enter*

or

> Select the *drive*, *Shift+F10, R*

or

> Select the *drive*, click <u>F</u>ile on the menu bar, <u>P</u>roperties

Rename

Double-click , right-click the *drive* icon,

click <u>P</u>roperties, click the General tab,

at the Label field type the new *name*, then click OK

View Contents of Drive

In Explorer or My Computer, double-click *drive* icon

View Drives

Double-click

Disk Space

The total capacity of a drive as well as its used and free space can be viewed in both My Computer and Windows Explorer. The totals are displayed both numerically and graphically on the General tab of the Properties for the drive.

Quick Access

98

Select *drive* in My Computer or Windows Explorer (information will appear in the left window pane).

or

Right-click the *drive* in My Computer or
Windows Explorer, then click P<u>r</u>operties,
General.

or

Select the *drive* in My Computer or Windows Explorer, click <u>F</u>ile on the menu bar,
then P<u>r</u>operties, General.

HOt Tip **Size a Group of Files or Folders:** If you
want to find out how much space is
taken up by one or more files or folders
select them by holding down the *Ctrl*
key then clicking each file or folder.
Once they are selected, use the Quick
Access methods above to display the
space utilization. The display will list
the number of files, folders and the
amount of space they are using.

HOt Tip **To view the disk space on all your
drives at once**, hold down the *Ctrl* key
and click each drive icon. One dialog
box will open but each drive's information will be displayed on its own tab.

Cleaning Up Your Drives

If you are running out of disk space, consider one
or more of the following:

- Empty the Recycle Bin and adjust its
  maximum size.
- Delete temporary files.
- Delete duplicate files.
- Delete unnecessary files.
- Delete unnecessary shortcuts.
- Delete unnecessary e-mail.

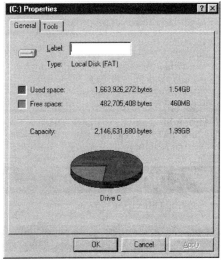

The Drive Properties Dialog Box.

- Clear the Internet Explorer History folder and adjust its maximum number of days to keep history.
- Remove Internet Explorer Favorites.
- Remove temporary Internet files.
- Remove Windows components you don't use.
- Remove programs you don't use.
- Remove online services.
- Use DriveSpace to compress your files.
- Repartition your hard disk into smaller units.
- Format your hard disk using FAT 32.

Please see the specific sections for more information regarding the actual procedures.

CAUTION: *Do not let your free disk space get below 20 MB. Windows 9x needs this free space to use for virtual memory. Windows "swaps" programs and data from RAM to the hard disk dynamically, consequently, if you're short on disk space your system performance will suffer.*

See Also: Add/Remove Programs; Deleting Files & Folders; FAT; Recycle Bin; Shortcuts; System\Virtual Memory

Disks, Copying

See: Copying Disks (p. 124)

Disks, Renaming

See: Renaming Disks (p. 366)

Display

Display

Display is a Control Panel tool that lets you specify the properties that control the look and feel of your system's desktop. These include the background, fonts, colors, screen saver, and screen resolution.

Quick Access

Right-click background of the desktop, then Properties

or

Click , Settings, Control Panel, then

double-click

Display

Background

You can select either a Pattern or Wallpaper from the list boxes. In Windows 98, the Pattern list box is accessed through the Pattern button. Your choices are previewed in the simulated screen above. If you need to find a source elsewhere on your drive, use the Browse function and locate the

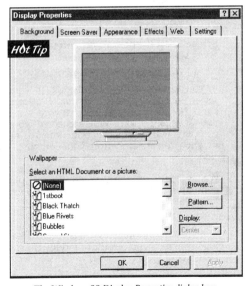

The Windows 98 Display Properties dialog box.

file. Three additional Display options, Tile, Center, and Stretch (Windows 98 only), control how the wallpaper is positioned on the screen.

> **Hot Tip** **Pattern vs. Wallpaper:** If you are using a Pattern, be sure to select None for Wallpaper.

Screen Saver

A screen saver is a moving graphical image that displays on your screen after a specified idle period. On the Screen Saver tab you can turn the screen saver on and off, and control which images are displayed.

Enabling the Screen Saver

To turn a screen saver on, select one from the Screen Saver list box. To turn off the screen saver, select None.

Password Protection

If you choose to password protect your screen saver, select the Password Protected check box, then establish a password using the Change button. When enabled your computer will be protected from others using it, when you are away from your computer.

Wait Period

Wait specifies in minutes how long your computer remains idle before Windows launches the screen saver.

Settings

The Settings button gives you access to a dialog box which you can use to modify the appearance of the screen saver you've selected.

Energy Saving

Allows you to take advantage of any energy saving capabilities your monitor may have.

Appearance

The appearance of your desktop is something that you live with day in and day out. The Appearance tab provides several tools that you can use to control the color combinations and fonts that are used for the display.

Scheme

There are many schemes, or combinations, involving different colors, fonts and sizes that have been developed. These are listed in the Schemes list box and can be selected for use.

Item

An Item such as Desktop (background), Icon or Menu Bar can be individually controlled. To change an item, select it from the Item list box. When the item is selected it will automatically make active the properties that you can change. You can then make changes to its size, color or font.

 Name Your Own Appearance Scheme: If you create a unique combination of elements that you would like to save, click Save As and you can assign a name to your combination that will appear in the list of Schemes.

Effects

On the *Effects* tab you can change the default icons for the items on your desktop to ones that better suit your tastes.

Other visual effects can also be enabled or disabled, such as large icons, color, animation, and smoothing.

 Web

The *Web* tab lists channels that you are subscribed to and any Active Desktop items. If the check box next to the item is not selected, the item will not appear on the desktop.

Settings

On the *Settings* tab you can specify the number of colors, resolution, and font size used for your display.

Color Palette

The Color Palette is determined by the capabilities of your video adapter and monitor. The higher the quality, the more colors you can use.

Desktop Area

The Desktop Area determines the resolution used and is restricted by the capabilities of your video adapter and monitor. Changing the Desktop Area to a higher resolution allows you to display more objects on your desktop, but also makes the images smaller.

Is Your Type Too Small to Read? If you change your screen to a higher resolution and the type is too small to read, use Font Size to make the type larger.

Font Size

Using Font Size you can change the size of the fonts used for common window elements. The default is Small. If you need to enlarge them, select Large or Other. Other lets you customize the font size as a percentage of the normal size. (Font Size is under Advanced Properties in Windows 98)

Advanced Properties

If your adapter or monitor have specific properties that can be set, you can access them through the Advanced Properties button.

See Also: Accessibility Options

Documents Menu

 Windows 9x tracks your most recently used documents and displays their names under the *Documents* menu, which is located on the Start menu. When you select Documents from the Start menu you see the last 15 documents you've used. When a new document is opened, regardless of the application, it is added to the list—the oldest one in the list disappears.

Quick Access

Click **Start**, Documents

To open one of the documents in the list, just select it. Windows 9x will automatically open the associated application as well as the document you selected. Each item in the list is actually a shortcut to the document. Windows 9x stores these shortcuts in the \Windows\Recent folder.

Clearing Documents

You may want to clear some or all of the documents from the Documents menu to make it easier to read, or for security reasons.

Clearing All Documents

To clear all documents from the Documents menu:

> Right-click a blank area of the taskbar, click Properties, then the Start Menu Programs tab. In the Documents Menu panel at the bottom, click the Clear button.

or

> Click ![Start], Settings, Taskbar, then the tab.
> In the Documents Menu panel at the bottom, click the Clear button.

Clearing All Documents Using a Batch File

Another way to clear all documents from the Documents menu is to use a batch file. This method has certain advantages over the one described above. For example, the shortcut for the batch file can be placed on the desktop or Start Menu for easier access. It could also be placed in the \Windows\Start Menu\Programs\Startup folder so that all documents are cleared when Windows 9x starts up. Some people prefer this for security reasons; that way no one will be able to see what they've recently worked on.

Follow these steps to create the batch file:

1. Using Notepad, create a new file and type in the following command:
   echo y | del c:\windows\recent*.*

2. Save the file as \Batch\ClrDocs.bat (you may have to create the folder if it doesn't exist).

3. Close the document, then navigate to the \Batch folder using My Computer or Microsoft Explorer.

4. Right-click the batch file name, click Properties, then the Program tab.

5. Select Minimized from the Run drop-down list, then select the Close on exit check box.

6. Click OK to save your changes. A shortcut is created for the batch file.

   At this point you may want to rename the shortcut to something more descriptive, for example, Clear Documents.

7. Now you can copy this shortcut to wherever you want. If you are using user profiles, see the Note below.

Clearing Individual Documents

To selectively clear individual documents from the Documents menu:

1. Use My Computer or Microsoft Explorer to navigate to the \Windows\Recent folder.

2. Select the shortcuts you want to remove, then delete them.

Note: If you are using user profiles, the document shortcuts will be located in the \Windows\Profiles*User*\Recent folders. Where *User* is the individual's user name. You will need make the appropriate path changes in any batch files that reference these files.

Default Location: \Windows\Recent

See Also: Start Menu

Drive Converter

See: FAT|Converting Drives to FAT32 (p. 196)

Emergency Recovery Utility (ERU)

The Emergency Recovery Utility (ERU) is a program that you can use to back up important files that might be needed in case of a system failure. The files that are backed up are:

Autoexec.bat	Config.sys
Win.ini	System.ini
Protocol.ini	User.dat
System.dat	Io.sys
Command.com	Msdos.sys

The program file Eru.exe is located on the installation CD. You can run the program from there or copy it to your local hard drive.

> **Hot Tip**
>
> **To run ERU from your local hard drive**, create a folder named ERU on your drive then copy the four files from \Other\Misc\Eru on your installation CD to your new folder. Create a shortcut on your desktop for Eru.exe and then you'll be ready to run it whenever you want.

Note: ERU is only available for Windows 95. Windows 98 has a new program called *ScanReg* that replaces ERU. See Registry Checker (p. 357) for more information.

Backing Up Files

To back up your configuration files to a floppy disk or another hard drive follow these steps:

1. Double-click Eru.exe, then click Next.

2. If you want to back up the files to a floppy disk in drive a: click Next, otherwise, click Other Directory, then Next and designate your directory.

3. Insert a disk in drive a: and click OK.

4. To back up all the files click Next.
   To select only certain files click Custom.

   The recovery programs and backup files are copied to the disk.

Note: If there is not enough space on the destination disk, ERU will back up the smallest files first. The files that don't fit won't get backed up. You can, however, use the Custom option to selectively back up files to more than one disk.

Restoring Files

To restore your backup files to their original locations follow these steps:

1. Start your computer in MS-DOS mode.

2. Insert the disk with the backup on it into the drive. Type *a:*, then press *Enter* to change to you're a: drive.

3. Type *erd* and press *Enter*.

4. Press *Y* and then *Enter*.
   The files are restored to their original locations.

CAUTION: *If you back up your files to a network drive, you must be able to access the network drive in MS-DOS to be able to run the restore program.*

Default Location: \Other\Misc\Eru\Eru.exe

See Also: Backup; Registry|Backing Up The Registry; Registry Checker

Explorer

See: Windows Explorer (p.488)

Extract (MS-DOS)

Extract is used to extract a system file from one of the compressed CAB files. This command is run from the MS-DOS command line. If you know which CAB file contains the file you want to extract you can specify it in the command. If you don't, you can have Extract look for it.

The Extract command is copied to your \Windows\Command folder during the installation process; however, if you need to get a fresh copy it is in the \Win98 or Win95 folder of your CD-ROM, or on Disk 1 if you're using diskettes.

Command

Extract.exe [/y] [/a] [/d | /e] [/l *dir*] cabinet [filename ...]

or

Extract.exe [/y] source [newname]

Extract.exe [/y] /c source destination

Options

Cabinet .... Cabinet file, with two or more files, from which file(s) are to be extracted.

Filename .... Name of the file(s) that are to be extracted.

Source .... Cabinet file with only one file.

Newname .... New filename to give the extracted field.

/A or /All .... Process all cabinet files using the cabinet chain starting with the first cabinet file specified.

/C .... Copy a cabinet file without extracting its contents. Use to copy files from DMF formatted diskettes.

/D .... Display a cabinet directory without extract its contents.

/E .... Extract all files from a cabinet file. Use instead of *.*.

/L *dir* .... Location to place the extracted files. The default is the current directory.

/Y .... Eliminate overwrite prompt for existing files.

Notes:

1. The /c and /a switches cannot be used together.

2. Extract will not overwrite a file that is in use. If you receive an "Access Denied" error while overwriting or deleting a file, you need to restart your computer to the Command Prompt Only (F8 during the startup). The extraction will now work since the files are no longer in use.

3. If you are extracting files from CABs on a local or network drive and receive an error message indicating that you have corrupt CAB files, just replace the CAB files on your drive with a fresh copy from your CD-ROM.

Default Location:
   \Windows\Command\Extract.exe

See Also: Cabinet (CAB) Files; Cabinet Viewer; Starting Windows

FAT

The *FAT* (File Allocation Table) is a database of all the storage space on your disk. There are two systems currently in use, FAT16 and FAT32.

The FAT groups data into units called clusters. When a drive is formatted, the FAT uses different cluster sizes depending on the size of the drive partition and which version of FAT is used. One of the main advantages of using FAT32 is that it uses a significantly smaller cluster size than FAT16. Under FAT16, each cluster occupies 32 K for a 2 GB drive; under FAT32, each cluster uses only 4 K. The following table illustrates the difference between FAT16 and FAT32.

Drive Size	FAT16 Cluster Size	FAT32 Cluster Size
< 32 MB	512 bytes	Not Supported
32-63 MB	1 K	Not Supported
64-127 MB	2 K	Not Supported
128-255 MB	4 K	Not Supported
256-259 MB	8 K	Not Supported
260-511 MB	8 K	Not Supported
512 MB - 1 GB	16 K	4 K
1 - 2 GB	32 K	4 K
2 - 8 GB	Not Supported	4 K
8 - 16 GB	Not Supported	8 K
16 - 32 GB	Not Supported	16 K
32 - 2048 GB	Not Supported	32 K

FAT16 was the default for Windows 95; however, if you have installed OEM Service Release 2 (OSR2) for Windows 95 or you are using Windows 98, you can use either FAT16 or FAT32. To find out what version of Windows you are running see "Versions, Windows" (p. 451)

Advantages of FAT32

Use of Space

Since FAT32 uses smaller cluster sizes, it can store more data in the same amount of space, thereby increasing the available disk space on your system. For example, on a 2GB disk drive using FAT32, a 2KB file would use 4KB of space, whereas using FAT16 it would use 32KB. Thus, FAT 32 uses 28KB less space. If you apply this concept across your drive you can easily see that using FAT32 can save a significant amount of space. You can expect to gain 15 to 25% on most drives, and in some cases up to 50%.

Manages Larger Disks

FAT16 is limited to 65,535 clusters. Because of this limitation, it can only be used to format partitions up to 2GB. FAT32, however, can be used for partitions up to and exceeding 2GB.

Note: When using some applications you will find that they do not display the correct amount of free space over 2 GB. This is a limitation of the application and may be corrected in updated versions of the application.

Reliability

When using FAT16, the system files have to be located at the beginning of the drive. If that area of the drive is damaged, the drive becomes useless, since the system files cannot reside there. FAT32 allows the system files to be written to any part of the disk drive, so if there is damage in one area, the system files can be moved to another.

Improves Performance

Since FAT32 uses fewer resources than FAT16, applications will respond at least 50% faster when using FAT32.

CAUTION: *Older disk utilities that have not been updated to work with FAT32 will not work with disks using FAT32; however, all the utilities supplied with Windows 98 and Windows 95 OSR2 such as FDISK, Format, ScanDisk, and Disk Defragmenter have been updated. DriveSpace does not support compression on FAT32 drives.*

Partitioning Drives

If you are setting up a system from scratch and would like to use FAT32, you can partition your disk drives using FDISK. The following steps show you how:

1. Create a startup disk on an existing system by inserting a blank 3½" disk into your drive, click **🏁 Start**, Settings,

   Control Panel, double-click Add/Remove Programs, click the Startup Disk tab, then Create Disk.

   or

   Create a startup disk by starting the Windows installation process and continuing until the creation of the startup disk is complete, then cancel the installation.

2. Reboot your computer using the startup disk.

3. At the first screen, type **2** (Start computer without CD-ROM support).

4. At the MS-DOS command prompt, type **fdisk**, then press *Enter*.

5. If you have a disk drive that is larger than 512MB, a screen appears notifying you that it can be partitioned using FAT32.

   If the drive cannot be partitioned using FAT32, or if your Windows 95 version does not support FAT32, the FDISK Options screen displays.

6. Type **Y**, then *Enter* to enable large disk support.

7. Type **1** (Create DOS Partition or Logical DOS Drive), then press *Enter*.

8. Type **1** (Create Primary DOS Partition), then press *Enter*.

9. Type **Y**, then press *Enter* to create a partition at the maximum size.

   To create more than one partition see "FDISK (MS-DOS)" on page 206.

10. Press *Esc* to exit FDISK.

The drive is now partitioned using FAT32.

Depending on your needs, you can continue by formatting the drive or restarting the installation process.

Note: FDISK will only partition disks larger than 512MB using FAT32; additionally, the boot partition cannot be larger than 7.8GB.

Converting Drives To FAT32

If you already have a system up and running and would like to convert from FAT16 to FAT32, follow the next steps:

1. Click [🅁 Start], Programs, Accessories, System Tools, then Drive Converter.

2. After reading the introduction, click Next.

   The Drive Converter will list all the drives in your system. If a drive is too small to convert (less than 512MB) it will be identified.

3. Select the drive you want to convert, then click Next.

   The Drive Converter scans your drive looking for incompatible utilities, then offers you a chance to backup your disk drive.

4. If you need to back up your disk drive, click **Create Backup** and Microsoft Backup will launch.

5. Click <u>N</u>ext, to continue.

An informational screen is displayed, notifying you that your system will restart in MS-DOS mode and that the process may take several hours to complete.

6. Click <u>N</u>ext to start the conversion process.

Your system will restart in MS-DOS mode. Run the DOS version of ScanDisk, then begin the conversion process. As it completes each stage of the conversion, it checks off the appropriate step so that you are aware of its progress. When the conversion is finished, your system restarts and the Disk Defragmenter is launched.

7. When the Disk Defragmenter is complete, click <u>F</u>inish.

The conversion from FAT16 to FAT32 is now complete.

Hot Tip **To find out whether your drive is using FAT32,** double-click My Computer, right-click the drive you want to check, then click <u>P</u>roperties. If the drive is using FAT32 it will show Local Disk (FAT32) for the Type. If it is using FAT16 it will show Local Disk (FAT).

FAT32 Conversion Information: You can find out approximately how much disk space you will gain by converting to FAT32 prior to actually converting. To do this, download a special utility called Fat32win.exe, which is the FAT32 Conversion Information program.

1. Using your Internet browser, navigate to Microsoft's web site: http://www.microsoft.com/ windows98/info/fat32.htm.

2. Download the FAT32 Conversion Information program.

3. Execute the program by double-clicking the file name.

4. Select the drive you want to evaluate, then click Scan. The additional space to be gained after conversion will be displayed.

CAUTION: *If you plan to set your system up to dual-boot between different Windows platforms, you don't want to use FAT32. FAT32 is incompatible with MS-DOS 6.x, Windows 3.x, early versions of Windows 95 (prior to OSR2), and Windows NT. These platforms will not be able to recognize a drive formatted using FAT32.*

See Also: Backup, Disk Space; FDISK (MS-DOS); Formatting Disks; Version—Windows.

Favorites

Favorites is available in Windows 98 from the menu bar in My Computer, Microsoft Internet Explorer, Network Neighborhood, and Windows Explorer. The list of Favorites is also available from the Start menu. It lists destinations such as Web sites and folders that you frequent on a regular basis. Favorites provides a method to add and organize destinations, whether they be on your local drives, network drives, or on the Internet.

Once a destination is added as a favorite, it displays on a list at the bottom of the Favorites menu, either by itself or within a folder. When you select an entry from the Favorites list, Windows moves you directly to the destination. This makes it easy to return to destinations without having to remember the path or address.

Note: Favorites is only available in Windows 95 from within Microsoft Internet Explorer.

Quick Access

Click Favorites on the menu bar

or

Click 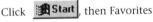, then Favorites

Add To Favorites

The first option on the Favorites menu, available from the menu bar, is *Add To Favorites*. Use this to add a site or folder location to the list of favorites at the bottom of the menu.

To add a favorite:

1. Using Microsoft Internet Explorer, My Computer, Network Neighborhood, or Windows Explorer move to the destination that you want to make a favorite.

2. Click Favorites on the menu bar, then Add To Favorites.

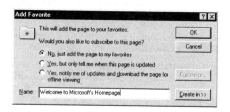

3. Select one of the three subscription options.

   If the destination is not a Web site, the default is No. If the destination is a Web site, the other two options are available. These options control the type of subscription you want to maintain. The first notifies you when the content on the Web page changes. The second notifies you and downloads pages from the site according to a schedule that you determine.

4. If you want to modify the default Name, type in your changes. This name is displayed on the Favorites menu.

5. To place your favorite in a particular folder click Create in. You can select an existing folder or create a new one.

6. Click OK to create the favorite. The new favorite appears on the Favorites menu.

Note: Each item on the Favorites menu is just a shortcut that points to the destination you have specified. All of these shortcuts are stored in the folder called Favorites which is in the \Windows folder.

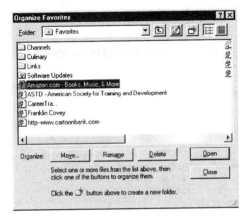

Organize Favorites

Windows provides a dialog box called *Organize Favorites* to make it easy to rearrange and organize your favorites. You may find the need to create folders for different topics so that you can organize your favorites within those folders.

To organize your favorites:

1. Select the shortcut you want to manipulate.
2. Use Move, Rename, or Delete to perform the action you want.
3. Click Close to close the dialog box.

Hot Tip **To create a new folder** click [icon] on the toolbar or right-click the background, select New, then Folder.

Hot Tip **Organize Favorites List**: Since the entries in the Favorites list are nothing more than shortcuts, you can organize them using My Computer or Windows Explorer. Just navigate to \Windows\Favorties and do your work there.

Default Location: \Windows\Favorites

See: My Computer; Network Neighborhood; Start Menu; Windows Explorer

FDISK (MS-DOS)

FDISK is an MS-DOS command that is used to partition your hard disk drives. A hard disk has to be partitioned before any formatting or installation processes take place. FDISK can be used to partition disks using FAT16 or FAT32. See "FAT" for more information. FDISK can be used to:

- Create DOS partition or Logical DOS Drive
- Set active partition
- Delete partition or Logical DOS Drive
- Display partition information

When FDISK is launched, a series of menus and options are displayed which perform the processes listed above.

Using FDISK

If you are setting up a system from scratch and would like to use FDISK to partition your disk drives, follow the steps below:

1. Create a startup disk on an existing system by inserting a blank 3½″ disk into your drive, click **🏴 Start**, Settings, Control Panel, double-click Add/Remove Programs, click the Startup Disk tab, then Create Disk.
   or
   Create a startup disk by starting the Windows install process and continuing until the creation of the startup disk is complete, then cancel the installation.

2. Reboot your computer using the startup disk.

3. At the first screen, type *2* (Start computer without CD-ROM support).

4. At the MS-DOS command prompt, type **fdisk**, then press *Enter*.

5. If you have a disk drive that is larger than 512 MB, a screen appears notifying you that it can be partitioned using FAT32.

   If the drive cannot be partitioned using FAT32 or your Windows 95 version does not support FAT32, the FDISK Options screen displays.

6. Type *Y*, then *Enter* to enable large disk support, or *N* if you want to use FAT16.

7. Type *1* (Create DOS Partition or Logical DOS Drive), then press *Enter*.

8. Type *1* (Create Primary DOS Partition), then press *Enter*.

   If a primary partition already exists you will have to delete the existing primary before creating a new one. Follow the FDISK options to perform the deletion before continuing.

9. Type *Y*, then press *Enter* to create a partition at the maximum size. When the process is complete, press *Esc* to exit FDISK. You can ignore the following steps.

   If you do not want your entire disk partitioned as one partition type *N*. You are then asked to specify the size of the partition in megabytes or by percentage. After you type in your entry, press *Enter*, then continue with step 10.

10. Press *Esc* to return to FDISK Options menu, then press *1* (Create DOS Partition or Logical DOS Drive), then press *Enter*.

11. Type *2* (Create Extended DOS Partition), then press *Enter*.

   The remaining space available is displayed. You can accept the entry or type in another value. If you are creating more than two partitions continue with step 10 and 11 until all disk space is used.

   After making your entry press *Enter*.

12. Press *Esc* to create the logical drive, then *Enter*.

13. Once all logical drives have been assigned press *Esc* to return to the FDISK Options menu.

14. Press 2 (Set active partition), then *Enter*.

15. Type the number of the partition you want to be active (partition you will boot from), usually 1, then press *Enter*.

16. Press *Esc* to return to the FDISK Options menu.

17. To view the partition information press 4, then *Enter*.

18. Press *Esc* to return to the FDISK Options menu.

19. Press *Esc* twice to exit FDISK.

Depending on your needs, you can continue by formatting the drive or restarting the installation process. See "Formatting Disks" or "Installation" for more information.

CAUTION: *When you use FDISK to partition a drive, all existing information is destroyed. It is not recoverable. Additionally, if a partition is deleted, all existing information is destroyed.*

CAUTION: *If you are partitioning a disk that was previously partitioned with a third party partitioning program manufactured by Disk Manager, Storage Dimensions, SpeedStor, Priam, or Everex, do not use FDISK to partition your disk. Use the same program that was used to partition the disk to make any changes. These programs manipulate the BIOS and communications with the hard-disk controller and are not compatible with FDISK. To find out whether one of these programs was used, search for one of the following files: Dmdrvr.bin (Disk Manager), Sstor.sys (SpeedStor), Hardrive.sys (Priam), and Evdisk.sys (Everex). If any of these files exist, the disk was probably not formatted with FDISK. Another clue is to look for device= entries in the Config.sys which may show one of these drivers being loaded.*

Command

Fdisk [/status] [/x]

Parameters:

/Status ......Displays the partition information.

/X ....Ignores extended disk-access support. If you receive disk access or stack overflow messages when executing FDISK use this switch.

Notes:

1. A low format on the drive must take place before running FDISK. Most drives today are already low level formatted at the factory. If you need to low level format a drive be sure to check with the manufacturer before doing so—you risk damage to your drive if the process is performed improperly.

2. The maximum size of a partition is determined by whether you use FAT16 or FAT32. FAT16 has a 2 GB limitation. FAT32 has no limitation.

3. To use FAT32 the drive must be at least 512 MB in size.

Default Location:
\Windows\Command\Fdisk.exe

See Also: FAT; Formatting Disks

File and Folder Properties

File and Folder Properties describe the characteristics of, and control the access to, files and folders. Each file and folder has its own set of properties.

Quick Access

> Right-click the *file* or *folder*, then click Properties.
>
> (This method works in My Computer, Network Neighborhood, Windows Explorer, and open dialog boxes of most applications.)

or

> Select the *file* or *folder*, click File on the menu bar, then Properties.

General

All file types have *General* information available. This includes information in addition to what is listed in the detail view of My Computer or Explorer, which lists Size, Type and date Modified. General information provides:

Filename

> Displays the name of the file or folder.

Type

> Displays the type of file for example, Microsoft Word or Microsoft Excel.

Location

> Displays where the folder or file is located.

Size

> Displays the size of the file or the contents of a folder.

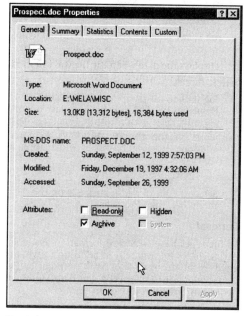

Contains

Displays how many folders and files are contained in a folder.

MS-DOS Name

Displays the eight-character folder or filename with a three-character extension assigned for use in MS-DOS. MS-DOS and some network systems do not support long filenames and therefore need to use this format.

Created

Displays the date that the folder or file was created.

Modified

Displays the date when the file was last modified and subsequently saved.

Accessed

Displays the date the file was last opened without any modifications having been made.

Attributes

Attributes control how the folder or file is used, viewed and whether it is marked for backup. Following are the four attributes used:

Hidden

Hides the file or folder and prevents it from being deleted or copied.

 To view hidden files in either My Computer or Explorer, select **View** from the menu bar, **Options**, then the **View** tab. Select **Show all files** the hidden files will now be displayed when using My Computer or Explorer.

Read-only

Specifies that no one can write to this file or folder. Marking a file Read-only significantly reduces the chances that it will accidentally be deleted. The file can still be deleted, it just requires an additional confirmation during the deletion procedure.

Archive

Indicates that the file or folder has been changed since the last time it was backed up.

System

Indicates that the file or folder is needed for the operating system to work. Never delete any system file.

Viewing Multiple Files

If you select several files the attributes are handled differently:

- A blank box in front of an attribute means that none of the files has that attribute set.

- A check mark in the box in front of an attribute means that all of the files have that attribute set.

- A gray box with a gray check mark in front of an attribute means that one or more, but not all, of the files have that attribute set.

To remove this attribute from those files that have it, click the attribute. The check mark disappears.

To set this attribute for all the selected files, click the attribute twice. A check mark should appear in the box.

If you choose OK and redisplay the file or folder properties, the change will show up everywhere it should.

Summary

If a file has properties of its own, items from the file's properties are displayed in the Summary. This may include items such as: Author, Keywords, Comments, Title, and Subject.

Statistics

If a file has properties of its own, items from the file's properties are displayed in Statistics. This may include items such as: Created, Modified, Accessed, Last Saved, Revision Number, Pages, Paragraphs, Lines, Words, and Characters.

Version

Some files, such as application executables (.exe) and dynamic link libraries (.dll), contain Version information in the Properties. This may include: File Version, Description, Copyright, Company Name, Internal Name, Language, Original Filename, Product, Name, Product, and Product Version.

To view the details for the items in the Item name list, click on an Item in the list and the Value will display in the Value list to the right.

See Also: Section 4 - File Types; View|File Types

File Associations

See: Section 4 - File Types (p. 515); View|Options or Folder Options|File Types (p. 469)

File Attributes

See: File & Folder Properties|Attributes (p. 213)

File Manager

Winfile

The Windows 3.x *File Manager* still exists in Windows 98 and Windows 95; however, there are two reasons why you may not want to use it:

1. **File Manager does not use the Recycle Bin**. When you delete a file from within File Manager the file is deleted and does not get moved to the Recycle Bin.

2. **File Manager does not recognize long file names**, which can make working with long file names difficult.

Quick Access

Click **Start**, Run, type **Winfile**, then click OK.

or

Double-click Winfile.exe

HOt Tip **If you plan to use File Manager** on a regular basis, create a shortcut to it.

Note: File Manager will not display more than 2 GB of free space.

Default Location: \Windows\Winfile.exe

See Also: Explorer; My Computer; Shortcuts

File System Properties

See: System|Performance (p. 439)

File Types

See: Section 4 - File Types (p. 515); View|Options or Folder Options|File Types (p. 469)

File Version

See: File & Folder Properties|Version (page 215)

Files

..QuicKeys..

Arrange Icons

Right-click background of window, Arrange Icons, then *sort method*

or

Click View on the menu bar, Arrange Icons, then *sort method*

or

Click a *column* heading (Details View)

Attach to E-Mail Message

Drag *file* to attachment area of e-mail message

Close

Click

or

double-click *document* icon

or

Click File on the menu bar, Close

Copy

Select *file*, click on the toolbar

or

Select *file*, click on the toolbar

or

Ctrl+drag *file* to *destination* on same drive

or

Right-click *file* and drag to *destination*, Copy Here

or

Ctrl+Shift, click *file* and drag to *destination*, Copy Here

or

Drag *file* to *destination* on a different drive

or

Right-click *file*, Copy

or

Select *file*, *Ctrl+C*

or

Select *file*, click Edit on the menu bar, Copy

Copy Using Send To

Select *file*, *Ctrl*+right-click, Send To, *destination* on same drive

or

Right-click *file*, Send To, *destination* on a different drive

Create

Right-click the desktop or the background, click New, then the file *type*

or

Click <u>F</u>ile on the menu bar, New, then the file *type*

or

95

Alt+F, W, then click the file *type*

or

98

Alt+F, N, then click the file *type*

Cut

98

Select *file*, click on the toolbar

or

95

Select *file*, click on the toolbar

or

Right-click *file*, Cu<u>t</u>

or

Select *file*, *Ctrl+X*

or

Select *file*, *Shift+F10, T*

Delete

Select *file*, press click on the toolbar

or

Select *file*, click on the toolbar

or

Drag *file* to

or

Right-click *file*, <u>D</u>elete

or

Select *file*, click <u>F</u>ile on the menu bar, <u>D</u>elete

or

Select *file*, *Delete*

Delete (no recovery)

Select *file*, *Shift+Delete*

or

Select *file*, *Shift* then drag *file* to

Deselect

Click *file*

or

Press any arrow key

Find

F3

or

Click <u>T</u>ools on the menu bar, <u>F</u>ind

or

Win+F (Microsoft Natural Keyboard)

Find File Containing Text

F3, Advanced

or

Click <u>T</u>ools on the menu bar, <u>F</u>ind, Advanced

Move

Shift+drag *file* to *destination* on a different drive

or

Right-click *file* and drag to *destination*, <u>M</u>ove Here

or

Ctrl+Shift, click *file* and drag to *destination*, <u>M</u>ove Here

Move Using Send To

Right-click *file*, Send <u>T</u>o, *destination* on same drive

or

Select *file*, then *Shift*+right-click, Send <u>T</u>o *destination* on a different drive

New

Click <u>F</u>ile on menu bar, Ne<u>w</u>

Open

Double-click *file*

or

Right-click *file*, <u>O</u>pen

or

Right-click *file*, Op<u>e</u>n With

or

Select *file*, click <u>F</u>ile on the menu bar, <u>O</u>pen

Paste

Click on the toolbar

or

Click on the toolbar

or

Right-click *destination*, <u>P</u>aste

or

Ctrl+V

Print

Right-click *file*, <u>P</u>rint

or

Select *file*, click <u>F</u>ile on the menu bar, <u>P</u>rint

Properties

Select the *file*, click on the toolbar

or

Select the *file*, click on the toolbar

or

Right-click *file*, P<u>r</u>operties

or

Alt+double-click *file*

or

Select the *file*, *Alt+Enter*

or

Select the *file*, *Shift+F10*, *R*

or

Select the *file*, click File on the menu bar, Properties

Quick View

Right-click the *file*, then Quick View

or

Select the *file*, click File on the menu bar, then Quick View

or

Drag a *file* to an open Quick View window

Rename

Right-click *file*, Rename

or

Click *file* name, pause, click again

or

Click *file* icon, then *file* name

or

Select *file*, *F2*

Restore from Recycle Bin

Double-click Recycle Bin, right-click *file*, Restore

or

Double-click Recycle Bin, select *file*, click File

on the menu bar, Restore

Select

Click *file*

or

>   Right-click the *file* (this will also display the
>   shortcut menu)

or

>   Use the arrow keys to move to the *file*

or

>   Type the first letter of *file* name

Select All

>   Click <u>E</u>dit on menu bar, Select A<u>ll</u>

or

>   *Ctrl+A*

Select Multiple Non-Sequential

>   *Ctrl*+click *file*

or

>   *Ctrl+Space Bar* on *file*

Select Multiple Sequential

>   Click first *file*, *Shift*, then click last *file*

or

>   Arrow to first *file*, *Shift*, then arrow to last
>   *file*

Select Multiple to Beginning of List

>   Click *file*, *Shift+Ctrl+Home*

Select Multiple to End of List

>   Click *file*, *Shift+Ctrl+End*

Shortcut Menu

>   Right-click *file*

or

>   Select *file*, *Shift+F10*

Shortcut Menu - Alternate

>   *Ctrl*+right-click *file*

or

Select *file*, *Ctrl+Shift+F10*

Sort Files

Right-click background of window, Arrange Icons, then *sort method*

or

Click View on the menu bar, Arrange Icons, then *sort method*

or

Click a *column* heading (Details View)

Undo Last Action

Click on the toolbar

or

Click ⟲ on the toolbar

or

Click Edit on menu bar, Undo *action*

or

Right-click the background of a window, pane or the desktop, then select Undo *action*

or

Ctrl+Z

Files, Copying

See: Copying Files & Folders (p. 126)

Files, Creating

See: Creating Files & Folders (p. 130)

Files, Cutting

See: Cutting Files & Folders (P. 131)

Files, Deselecting

See: Selecting Files & Folders (p. 388)

Files, Moving

See: Moving Files & Folders (p. 279)

Files, Renaming

See: Renaming Files & Folders (p. 367)

Files, Selecting

See: Selecting Files & Folders (p. 388)

Find—Computer

Find–Computer is used to search for shared computers that reside on your network. When the computer is located, it lists all the shared folders it finds on that computer.

Quick Access

Click **Start**, Find, Computer

or

Ctrl+Win+F, (Microsoft Natural Keyboard)

or

In Explorer, click Tools on the menu bar, Find, Computer

or

Alt+T, F, C (Explorer)

or

Right-click Network Neighborhood, Find Computer

To search for a particular computer, type the name of the computer in the Named text box. Wildcard characters such as "*" or "?" cannot be used; the name must be typed in exactly.

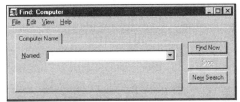

The Find Computer dialog box

Find Now

Use the Find Now button to start the search for the computer meeting your search criteria.

To browse the shared files and folders on the computer that was found, double-click the computer's name in the list or right-click it, then click Open.

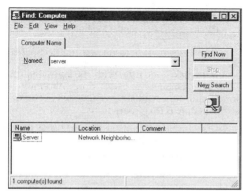

Result of Find Computer search.

New Search

Use the New Search button to clear all existing search criteria and prepare for a new search.

See Also: Find - Files or Folders; Find - On the Internet; Find - People; Network Neighborhood

Find Fast

Find Fast

Find Fast is actually a Microsoft Office utility. It indexes the contents of all Microsoft Office documents and uses these indexes to speed up text searches within these documents. The indexes are automatically updated and maintained. Find Fast can have an adverse affect on Windows, decreasing the performance of Windows itself.

If Find Fast is being used you'll find it in your Startup folder. To keep Find Fast from running, remove it from the Startup folder and restart your computer.

Find Fast creates three hidden files in the root of your hard disk: _ofidx.ffa, ofidx.ffl, and ofidx.ffx. It updates these files every time Windows is started and on a regularly set schedule. The default schedule is every two hours.

Find Fast can be customized to your needs using the Find Fast Utility in the Control Panel.

Default Location: \Control Panel\Find Fast

See Also: Find - Files or Folders

Find - Files or Folders

 Find - Files or Folders is used to search for files or folders when you're not sure where they might be on your drives. Using several different criteria including file name, file extension, file type, file size, date modified or created, and text contained in the file, the search can be quite specific.

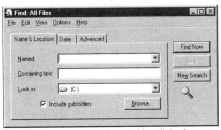

Windows 98 Find Files or Folders dialog box

Quick Access

Click **Start**, Find, Files or Folders

or

Win+F (Microsoft Natural Keyboard)

or

In Explorer, click Tools on the menu bar, Find, Files or Folders

or

Right-click a folder, then Find

or

In Windows Explorer, **Alt+T, F, F**

or

F3

or

Click on a blank area of the taskbar, then press **F3**

Name & Location

The *Name and Location* tab lets you specify a file name or a partial file name. Type the file name in the Named text box. Wildcard characters such as "*" or "?" can be used, for example: *.exe or 9801??.doc The "*" replaces multiple characters, whereas, the "?" replaces one character.

HOt Tip **Use Quotes for Multi-word Names:** If the file or folder name is composed of more than one word be sure to enclose the words in quotes, for example: "My Documents," otherwise, only the first word is used in the search.

HOt Tip **Search for More than One File:** To search for more than one file at the same time, type the file names in Named text box separated by a space.

Hot Tip **Drop Down Box Lists Most Recent Searches:** If you want to repeat a particular search, use the drop-down list box to display and then select your most recent searches.

The <u>C</u>ontaining Text option is most useful when the only thing you know about a file is a string of text that is contained in the file. Type in the text string you want to search for using as many words as you need. This option appears on the Name & Location tab in Windows 98. In Windows 95 it appears on the Advanced tab.

The <u>L</u>ook in text box lets you specify a drive and/or path in which to search. You can type in the drive and path, use the drop-down list box to select an available drive, or click the Browse button to navigate to the folder you want to search. Using this option to narrow your search will cut your search time significantly.

Hot Tip **To search more than one drive at a time**, type the drive letters separated by semicolons in the Look in text box, for example: C:;D:;F: If this is a search you perform frequently, consider saving the search using the Save Search feature described below.

Hot Tip **To search all drives simultaneously** including floppy, local hard drives, and mapped network drives select My Computer from Look in's drop-down list box.

Hot Tip **Get rid of all unnecessary temporary files**—search by *.tmp and then delete them.

Date (Modified)

The *Date (Modified)* tab lets you specify files or folders that have been created or modified within a date range, during the previous *x* months, or *x* days. The default setting is all files. To enter your criteria select the appropriate option button and change the dates or numbers.

Advanced

The *Advanced* tab lets you select files of a specific type, files that contain particular text strings or files of a certain size.

Of type:

The drop-down list contains the common types of files. If you need to search for a type that's not listed, use the Named text box on the *Name & Location* tab and type and "*" and the file name extension, for example: *.dif

Containing Text

Containing Text is most useful when the only thing you know about a file is a string of text that is contained in the file. Type in the text string you want to search for using as many words as you need. This option appears on the Advanced tab in Windows 95. In Windows 98 it appears on the Name & Location tab.

Size

The Size is option is extremely helpful in locating large files that you may what to delete.

Use the first drop-down list to indicate At least or At most then specify the size.

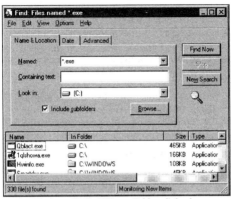

Windows 98 Find Files or Folders dialog box

CAUTION: *The search criteria contained in the three different tabs is used together to determine what files are displayed. If your criteria are too specific, you may not find any matches. Check under each tab to make sure you are not inadvertently excluding possibilities.*

Find Now

Use the Find Now button to start the search for all files or folders meeting your search criteria.

You can use the files listed in the results window just as if they were in My Computer or Windows Explorer. You can double-click a file to open or execute it, or right-click it to access the options on the shortcut menu. You can also use Quick View, from the shortcut menu, to view the contents of many different documents.

Hot Tip You can **open the parent folder for any file** by selecting the file name, clicking <u>F</u>ile on the menu bar, then Open Containing Folder. A My Computer window will display listing the contents of the parent folder.

Hot Tip **Optimize Column Width:** If you find that you can't see enough data in a column, or if you're seeing too much, double-click the lines separating the column headings. The columns will automatically size themselves to the data they contain. You'll know you're on the right line and ready to double- click when your pointer becomes a ✛ .

New Search

Use the New Search button to clear all existing search criteria and prepare for a new search.

Save Search

You can save the search criteria by clicking <u>F</u>ile on the menu bar, then <u>S</u>ave Search. An icon named for your search criteria is placed on your desktop, for example:

Files named
@.com.fnd

When you want to look at the results of the search, just double-click the icon and your results are displayed.

Save Results

You can save the results of a search by selecting <u>S</u>ave Results, which is under <u>O</u>ptions on the menu bar, and then clicking <u>F</u>ile on the menu bar, S<u>a</u>ve Search. An icon is place on your desktop named for your search criteria, for example:

Files named
@.com.fnd

Files named
@.com.fnd

When you want to look at the results of the search, just double-click the icon and your results are displayed.

HOt Tip You can **find file names that are contained in compressed files** created by PKZIP or compatible programs. Search for files named *.zip, listing the specific file you are looking for in Containing text. Don't use wild cards in Containing text, and be sure that Case Sensitive is <u>not</u> selected in the <u>O</u>ptions menu.

HOt Tip **To change the default Look In directory** to something other than the current folder, for example "c:\", here's how:

CAUTION: *The following instructions involve changing settings in the Registry. If the changes are not made properly, serious problems may result. Be sure to backup your Registry before continuing. See: "Registry" for more information about backing up and editing the Registry.*
---

1. Use **Regedit** to open the Registry, and move to : HKEY_CLASSES_ROOT\Directory\shell\find.

2. Select ddeexec, then double-click Default in the right window pane. In

Find - Files or Folders **235**

the <u>V</u>alue data text box, change both
"%I" entries to the path you want,
for example,

    [FindFolder("c:\", c:\)].

3.   Click **OK** to save your changes. From
this point forward, the default directory will be "c:\" whenever you
right-click a folder and select <u>F</u>ind.

See Also: Find—Computer; Find—On the
Internet; Find—People; Microsoft Explorer, My
Computer; Quick View

Find - On the Internet

When you select *Find - On the Internet* it launches
Internet Explorer, then dials-up your Internet Service Provider. Once it makes a connection,
Internet Explore provides a page from which you
can select a search category and type in the text
you want to search for. Upon executing the
search, by clicking the Search button, Internet Explorer proceeds to look for what you've asked.

Quick Access

Click ![Start] , <u>F</u>ind, On the <u>I</u>nternet

or

Click <u>T</u>ools on the menu bar, <u>F</u>ind, On the
<u>I</u>nternet (Explorer)

or

Alt+T, F, O (Explorer)

See Also: Find Files or Folders; Find Computer;
Find People

Find - People

Find - People is used to search for individuals, companies, or organizations in your own personal address books such as Microsoft Outlook, Microsoft Outlook Express and Microsoft Exchange, as well other directories that are available on the Internet. (*Find - People* is not available unless you are using one of these programs or IE.) Using several different criteria including name, e-mail address, address, phone, and other information the search can be quite specific.

Quick Access

Click ![Start] , Find, People

or

Ctrl+Win+F, P (Microsoft Natural Keyboard)

or

Click Tools on the menu bar, Find, People (Explorer)

or

Alt+T, F, P (Explorer)

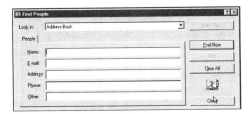

Look In

Using the drop-down list box select your Address Book or any of the available directory services on the Internet.

Note: If the directory you selected is on the Internet, you can click the Web Site button to view the directory service.

People

Type your search criteria into any number of the fields listed on the People tab. The more criteria entered the more specific your search will be.

Find Now

Use the Find Now button to start the search for all people meeting your search criteria. All entries that match you selection criteria will be listed in an expanded window.

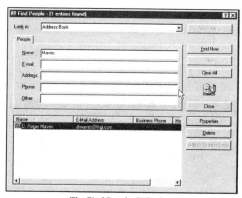

The Find People dialog box

Properties

To Edit or Remove an Address Book entry, select an entry from the list of names produced with the Find Now command, then click on the Properties button to open the entry in the Address Book. You can now make changes to the entry.

Add to Address Book

If you use Find People to locate a person on the Internet you can add them to your personal Address Book. Just select the entry, then click the Add to Address Book button.

Clear All

Use the Clear All button to clear all existing search criteria and prepare for a new search.

See Also: Find—Files or Folders; Find—Computer; Find—on the Internet

Folder Attributes

See: File & Folder Properties|Attributes (p. 211)

Folders

..QuicKeys..

Arrange Icons

> Right-click background of window, Arrange Icons, then *sort method*

or

> Click View on the menu bar, Arrange Icons, then *sort method*

or

> Click a *column* heading (Details View)

Calculate Folder(s) Size

Select *folder(s)*, right-click any *folder*, Properties (Size will be a total of all folder(s) selected.)

Close

Click

or

Alt+F4

Close All Folders On Drive

In Explorer, double-click the ***drive*** icon to close the tree, then press *F5*

Close All Parent

Shift+click

Copy

98

Select *folder*, click on the toolbar.

or

95

Select *folder*, click on the toolbar.

or

Ctrl+drag *folder* to *destination* on same drive.

or

Right-click *folder* and drag to *destination*, Copy Here.

or

Select *file*, *Ctrl+Shift* , and drag to *destination*, Copy Here.

or

Drag *folder* to *destination* on a different drive.

or

Right-click *folder*, <u>C</u>opy.

or

Select *folder*, *Ctrl+C*.

or

Select *folder*, click <u>E</u>dit on the menu bar, <u>C</u>opy.

Copy Using Send To

Select *folder*, *Ctrl*+right-click, Send <u>T</u>o, *destination* on same drive.

or

Right-click *folder*, Send <u>T</u>o, *destination* on a different drive.

Create

Right-click on the desktop or in the background, click <u>N</u>ew (New), <u>F</u>older.

or

In Explorer, click <u>F</u>ile on the menu bar, <u>N</u>ew (New), <u>F</u>older.

or

98

Alt+F, N, F

or

95

Alt+F, W, F

Cut

Select *folder*, click on the toolbar

or

Right-click, Cut

or

Select *folder*, *Shift+Delete*

or

Select *folder*, click on the toolbar

or

Right-click, Cut

or

Select *folder*, *Shift+F10, T*

or

Select *folder*, *Ctrl+X*

Delete

Select *folder*, press click on the toolbar

or

Select *folder*, click on the toolbar

or

Right-click *folder*, <u>D</u>elete

or

Select *folder*, press *Delete*

or

Select *folder*, click <u>F</u>ile on the menu bar,
<u>D</u>elete

Delete (no recovery)

Select *folder*, Shift+Delete

or

Shift then drag *folder* to

Recycle Bin

Find

F3

or

Click <u>T</u>ools on the menu bar, <u>F</u>ind

or

Win+F (Microsoft Natural Keyboard)

Move

Drag *folder* to *destination* on same drive

or

Right-click *folder* and drag to *destination*,
<u>M</u>ove Here

or

Shift+drag *folder* to *destination* on a different drive

or

Right-click *folder*, Cu<u>t</u>, right-click on *destination*, <u>P</u>aste

or

Select *folder*, *Ctrl+X*, move to *destination*,
Ctrl+V

or

Select *folder*, click <u>E</u>dit on the menu bar,
<u>C</u>opy, move to *destination*, click <u>E</u>dit on
menu bar, <u>P</u>aste

Move Using Send To

Right-click *folder*, Send <u>T</u>o, *destination* on same drive.

New

Right-click in background, New, <u>F</u>older

or

Click <u>F</u>ile on the menu bar, <u>N</u>ew, <u>F</u>older.

or

98

Alt+F, N, F

or

95

Alt+F, W, F

Open

Double-click *folder*.

or

Right-click *folder*, <u>O</u>pen

or

Select *folder* in right pane, click <u>F</u>ile on the menu bar, <u>O</u>pen (Windows Explorer).

Open All Folders On Drive (Windows Explorer)

Select the *drive icon*, then press * on the numeric keypad.

Paste

Right-click *destination*, <u>P</u>aste.

or

Ctrl+V

Properties

98

Select the *folder*, click on the toolbar.

or

95

Select the *folder*, click on the toolbar.

or

Right-click *folder*, P<u>r</u>operties

or

Alt+double-click *folder*

or

Select the *folder*, *Alt+Enter*

or

Select the *folder*, *Shift+F10, R*

or

Select the *folder*, click <u>F</u>ile on the menu bar, P<u>r</u>operties

or

Select the folder, *Alt+F, R*

Rename

Right-click *folder*, Rena<u>m</u>e

or

Click *folder name*, pause, click again

or

Click *folder icon*, then *folder* name

or

Select *folder*, *F2*

Select

Click *folder*

or

Type the first letter of *folder* name

Select All

Click <u>E</u>dit on menu bar, Select A<u>ll</u>

or

Ctrl+A

Select Multiple Non-Sequential

Ctrl+click *folder*

or

Hold down *Ctrl,* arrow to folder, *Space Bar* to select folder

Select Multiple Sequential

Select first *folder, Shift,* then click last *file*

or

Arrow to first *folder, Shift,* then arrow to last *folder*

Shortcut Menu

Right-click *folder*

or

Select *folder, Shift+F10*

Sort Folders

Right-click background of window, Arrange <u>I</u>cons, then *sort method*

or

Click <u>V</u>iew on the menu bar, Arrange <u>I</u>cons, then *sort method*

or

Click a *column* heading (Details View)

Undo Last Action

 Click on the toolbar

or

 Click on the toolbar

or

Click <u>E</u>dit on menu bar, <u>U</u>ndo *action*

or

Right-click the background of a window,
pane or the desktop, then select, <u>U</u>ndo *action*

or

Ctrl+Z

View Contents

Double-click *folder*

or

Right-click *folder*, <u>O</u>pen

or

Select *folder*, click <u>F</u>ile on the menu bar,
<u>O</u>pen

View Parent Folder

 Click on the toolbar

or

 Click on the toolbar

or

Backspace

Folders, Copying

See: Copying Files & Folders (p. 126)

Folders, Creating

See: Creating Files & Folders (p. 130)

Folders, Cutting

See: Cutting Files and Folders (p. 131)

Folders, Deselecting

See: Selecting Files & Folders (p. 388)

Folders, Moving

See: Moving Files & Folders (p. 279)

Folders, Renaming

See: Renaming Files & Folders (p. 367)

Folders, Selecting

See: Selecting Files & Folders (p. 388)

Fonts

..QuicKeys..

Install

Click **🏁 Start**, <u>S</u>ettings, <u>C</u>ontrol Panel,

Double-click 📁 ,
Fonts

click <u>F</u>ile on the menu bar, Install New Font

Delete

Click **🏁 Start**, <u>S</u>ettings, <u>C</u>ontrol Panel,

double-click 📁 , select *font*,
Fonts

click <u>F</u>ile on the menu bar, <u>D</u>elete

or

Click **🏁 Start**, <u>S</u>ettings, <u>C</u>ontrol Panel,

double-click 📁 , select *font*,
Fonts

right-click *font*, <u>D</u>elete

or

Click **🏁 Start**, <u>S</u>ettings, <u>C</u>ontrol Panel,

double-click 📁 , select *font*, *Delete*
Fonts

General Information

See: System (p. 98)

Go To

See: Windows Explorer|Tools|Go To (p. 504)

Hard Disks, Partitioning

See: Fdisk (MS-DOS) (p. 206)

Hardware Profiles

See: System (p. 98)

Help

..QuicKeys..

Open

F1

or

Win+F1 (Microsoft Natural Keyboard)

or

Click **Start**, Help

or

Click Help on the menu bar

or

Ctrl+Esc, H

Open in a Dialog Box

Click **?**, then click *section* of dialog box

..QuicKeys..

Channels

Click on the toolbar.

or

Click <u>F</u>avorites on the menu bar, Channels.

Cycle Forward through Form Elements

Click [Forward →] on the toolbar.

or

Alt+right arrow

or

Ctrl+Tab

Cycle Backward through Form Elements

Click [← Back] on the toolbar.

or

Alt+left arrow.

or

Ctrl+Shift+Tab.

Edit Page

Click [Edit] on the toolbar.

or

Click <u>E</u>dit on the menu bar, Page.

Favorites

Click on the toolbar.

or

Click F<u>a</u>vorites on the menu bar.

Favorites, Add Current Page

Click <u>F</u>avorites on the menu bar,
<u>A</u>dd to Favorites.

or

Ctrl+D

Find Text in Current Page

Ctrl+F

or

Click <u>E</u>dit on the menu bar, <u>F</u>ind (on this page).

Full Screen

Click [Fullscreen] on the toolbar.

or

F11

or

Click <u>V</u>iew on the menu bar, <u>F</u>ull Screen.

History

Click [History] on the toolbar.

Home Page

Click [Home] on the toolbar.

or

Click <u>G</u>o on the menu bar, <u>H</u>ome Page.

Mail

Click [Mail] on the toolbar

or

Click <u>G</u>o on the menu bar, <u>M</u>ail

New Browser Window

Ctrl+N

or

Click <u>F</u>ile on the menu bar, <u>N</u>ew, <u>W</u>indow

Open a Different Page

Ctrl+O

or

Click File on the menu bar, Open

Print

Click on the toolbar

or

Ctrl+P

or

Click File on the menu bar, Print

Refresh

Click on the toolbar

or

F5

or

Click View on the menu bar, Refresh

Save Current Page

Ctrl+S

or

Click File on the menu bar, Save

Search

Click on the toolbar

or

Click Go on the menu bar, Search the Web

Stop Search

Click on the toolbar

or

Esc

or

Click View on the menu bar, Stop

Kernel Toys is a set of productivity tools that was developed by the Microsoft Windows Kernel Development Team. The tools are enhancements to the Windows 95 operating system and are not part of any shipping product. Kernel Toys are available, at no cost, from the Microsoft web site but they're not supported through official support channels.

Kernel Toys can be downloaded as a compressed file from the following Microsoft web site location:

http://www.microsoft.com/windows95/
downloads/contents/wutoys/ w95kerneltoy/

CAUTION: *Kernel Toys are for Windows 95 only. Do not attempt to use them with Windows 98.*

Here's what's in Kernel Toys:

MS-DOS Mode Configuration Wizard Customization Tool	Configure the Windows system without writing CONFIG.SYS and AUTOEXEC.BAT files.
Keyboard Remap	Reassigns functions to keys on your keyboard.
Logo Key Control	Suppresses the Windows logo when running games in MS-DOS.
Conventional Memory Tracker	Tracks memory used by the VMM32 program.
Windows Process Watcher	Monitor the CPU resources used by individual programs.

Shortcut Target	Displays the properties for a shortcut
Time Zone Editor	Create and edit time zone entries for the Date/Time icon in the Control Panel.

Installing Kernel Toys

1. Create a folder for Kernel Toys called Kernel.

2. Using Microsoft Internet Explorer connect to the following web page: http://www.microsoft.com/windows95/downloads/contents/wutoys/w95kerneltoy/

3. Click the link on the page to download W95KrnlToys.exe.

4. Save the file in your new Kernel folder.

5. Open the Kernel folder and double-click the W95KrnlToys.exe file.

   This will decompress the file adding several new files to the folder. Be sure to review the readme.txt file for more information.

6. Right-click on the Install.inf file, then click Install.

 Install Selected Files Only: If you want to selectively install the programs right-click on the .inf file that bears the name of the program, then click Install. Only that program will be installed.

Uninstalling Kernel Toys

The Kernel Toys can be individually uninstalled using Add/Remove programs in the Control Panel. See: "Add/Remove Programs" (p. 42) for more information.

See Also: Power Toys

Keyboard

Keyboard

Several characteristics of the keyboard can be changed using the *Keyboard* Control Panel tool, including character delay and repeat rate, cursor blink rate, language and keyboard type.

Quick Access

Click ![Start] , Settings, Control Panel,

then double-click
Keyboard

or

Right-click the language indicator on the taskbar, then click Properties

The Keyboard Properties are displayed with three available tabs, Speed, Language and General.

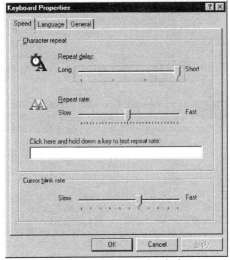

The Keyboard properties Speed tab

Speed

The character delay and repeat rate, and cursor blink rate can be adjusted on the Speed tab.

Character Repeat

When you hold down a key rather than press and release it, it will begin to repeat itself. This is convenient, for example, when you are drawing a line using the underscore.

Repeat Delay

The *Repeat Delay* controls the time between when you press a key down and the when the repetitive action begins to take place. To make the delay longer drag the slider to the left; to shorten the delay drag it to the right.

Repeat Rate

The Repeat Rate controls the speed at which the repetitive action proceeds. To slow the rate down drag the slider to the left; to increase the rate drag the slider bar to the right.

 Test Repeat Control Rates: You can test the delay and the repeat rate by moving the insertion point to the text box below the Repeat Delay and Repeat Rate controls, then hold down a key and watch the results.

Cursor Blink Rate

The *Cursor Blink Rate* or the speed at which the cursor or insertion point blinks is controlled with the this slider. Drag the slider to the left for Slow and to the right for Fast. You can see an example of the cursor to the left of the slider bar which will dynamically change to reflect the speed you have set.

Language

Installed keyboard languages and layouts

This list box displays the language(s) and keyboard layout(s) that Windows will load into the computer when it starts up. The available languages range from Afrikaans to Ukrainian, including the more common languages such as English, French, German, Italian and Spanish.

Note: If you don't see the language you need, it may be included in the Multilanguage Support. See "Multilanguage Support" for instructions on installing other languages.

Add

To add another language click Add, select a language from the drop-down list box, then click OK.

Properties

Each language has a default keyboard layout; however, some languages have alternate layouts you can choose use. To change the keyboard layout select a language, click Properties, select a layout from the drop-down list box, then click OK.

Remove

To remove an existing language, select the language in the list, then click Remove.

Default Language

The default language is the language that will load as the language of choice every time you start your computer. You can change the default by selecting the language in the list box above, then clicking Set as Default. The new default language will be displayed.

Switch Languages

Switching between different languages can be necessary when creating multilingual documents. You can switch between languages using one of two different key combinations Left Alt+Shift or Ctrl+Shift. Select the combination that will work best for you or turn off the option by selecting None. You can also switch by using the indicator as described below.

Enable indicator on taskbar

Selecting this option enables an indicator, En, on the taskbar that allows you to switch between different languages that you have loaded. To change from one language to another just click on the indicator, then select the language you want from the list of languages displayed. The indicator will display an appropriate abbreviation for the language currently loaded, so that you know what language you're working with at a glance.

The indicator can also be used to access the Keyboard Properties. Right-click the indicator, then Properties to open the Keyboard Properties sheet.

Note: To change the way Windows displays and sorts dates, times, currency and numbers use the Regional Settings tool in the Control Panel.

HOt Tip **Another Proofing Tool:** For more extensive proofing tools, contact Alki Software. They publish Proofing Tools for many different languages. These tools contain charts showing the location of the Window characters, keyboard layouts, a spelling checker, thesaurus and a hyphenation utility.

You can reach them at:
Alki Software Corporation
300 Queen Anne Ave. N., Ste.410
Seattle, WA 98109
Phone: 206-286-2600
Fax: 206-286-2785

General

Keyboard Type

The keyboard displayed for *Keyboard Type* is the keyboard currently in use. If this is not the correct keyboard or you want to change to a different type of keyboard you can do so by clicking the Change button. A dialog box is displayed that allows you to choose from other compatible keyboards. If the keyboard you are intending to use is not on the list, you can install the manufacturer's device driver for that keyboard from a disk by clicking the Have Disk button.

Hot Tip **Non-Standard Characters:** Many word processing applications can create some of the non-standard characters, for example, à, é, û, ö, ¿, ¡, and ç, that can be useful for foreign words. Use the Help for the application you're using to find out what key combinations can be used to create these special characters.

Hot Tip **Character Map**: If you want to use a character or symbol not displayed on your keyboard, but don't want to switch to a different keyboard or language, try using the Character Map. You may find other handy symbols there you'll want to use that don't exist in any language.

Default Location: \Control Panel\Keyboard

See Also: Accessibility Options; Character Map; Multilanguage Support; Regional Settings

Language Preferences

See: Keyboard|Language (p. 258); Multilanguage Support (p. 286); Regional Settings (p. 349)

98 Link Check Wizard

Checklinks

The *Link Check Wizard* (Checklinks) is a tool available in the Windows 98 Resource Kit. It scans your hard drive for desktop shortcuts and Start menu items that are no longer linked to a file and provides for their deletion.

Quick Access

On your hard drive (if the Windows 98 Resource Kit was installed):

> Click **Start**, Run, type
>
> **"c:\Program Files\Win98RK\Checklinks.exe"** then click OK. You must include the quotation marks.

or

> On the Windows 98 compact disc:
>
> Click **Start**, Run, type
>
> **d:\Tools\Reskit\Desktop\Chklnks**, then click OK. (Where *d:* is your CD-ROM Drive)

Note: The actual file name lives under two file names. If you install the Windows 98 Resource Kit tools to your drive it's named Checklinks.exe if you view it on the Windows 98 compact disc it's named Chklnks.exe.

The Link Check Wizard is included in the full Windows 98 Resource Kit and the Windows 98 Resource Kit Sampler. See: "Windows 98 Resource Kit" on for more information on installation and additional tools that are available.

When the Link Check Wizard scans your files and does not find the application or document to which a particular link was attached, the Link Check Wizard will list the link file as a dead link. You can then get more information on each file such as its location (path), the file it was linked to, and its error status, by right-clicking the file name. If you choose to delete the file, you can do so by selecting the check box next to the file name.

Default Location:
\Program Files\Win98RK\Checklnks.exe

See Also: Documents Menu; Shortcuts; Start Menu

Local Reboot

See: Close Program (p. 117)

Logview

Logview is a Windows 95 utility that can be used to view and edit log files that Windows creates during its various operations. There are seven log files that Windows maintains for the system operations. Following are their descriptions:

Bootlog.txt

If your previous boot was not successful, when you restart your system Windows automatically creates the Bootlog.txt. This log records the progress of the startup process. Viewing the log may provide insight as to why your system is failing during startup. Bootlog.txt can also be created on demand from the Windows startup menu.

Detlog.txt

If Windows does not recognize a new device that you've added to your system it logs information about the process in Detlog.txt. Viewing this log may provide information that could help you with the installation of the new device.

Netlog.txt

When you install Windows, Netlog.txt is used to record the network component detection and installation. If you are having problems with network connections, Netlog.txt may provide some clues.

Setuplog.txt

When you install Windows, Setuplog.txt is used to record the installation procedure. If you have problems during the installation process, check this log to see what's happened. Windows uses this log to determine what has been installed, and upon attempting to reinstall starts the installation process right where it left off.

Scandisk.log

If you use Scandisk to analyze and repair your disks, Scandisk.log is created when there are problems that prevent it from completing its operation. The information in this log can be used to clear up any obstacles that keep Scandisk from running its full course.

Modemdet.txt

When you install a new modem, Modemdet.txt is used to record any errors that are encountered during the detection and installation phase. If you are having problems installing a modem, Modemdet.txt may be helpful.

Ndislog.txt

During the loading of real-mode network components and the validation of the bindings, errors are recorded in the Ndislog.txt. Look here if you are having problems with network connections.

Installing Logview

Logview.exe is located on the Windows CD. If you'll be using it often, copy it to your local hard disk, create a shortcut to it, and execute it from there.

Note: Logview can also be downloaded from Microsoft's web site. The site is http//support.microsoft.com/support/ downloads/ DP1705.ASP. The file (Logvu.exe) that you download is a self-extracting compressed file. It will expand into three files: Logview.exe, License.txt, and Readme.txt when you double-click it.

Using Logview

When you start Logview, it will open a separate window for each of the log files and cascade them for easy access. To view a specific file, just click on the appropriate window. You can only view or print the files, no modification is allowed.

Default Location: \Other\Misc\Logview.exe (Windows 95 CD)

See Also: Bootlog.txt; Detlog.txt; Scandisk; Scandisk.log; Starting Windows; Startup Menu

Long File Name Backup (LFNBK)

There are many utility and backup programs that work with Windows 9x; however, if they have not been updated, they may not support long file names. It's always best to use programs that are compatible and support long file names, but if you have to use one that doesn't support long file names, be sure to back up your long file names before you use it.

Long File Name Backup (LFNBK) can be used to temporarily remove and store all of the long file names for a hard disk partition. It stores the names in a file named Lfnbk.dat in the root of the drive you are using. Once the long file names are backed up, you can run the program you need to run, then restore the long file names once you're finished.

To run LFNBK:

1. If you haven't used LFNBK before, you will probably need to copy it from the Windows CD to your Windows folder. It's located in the \Admin\Apptools\Lfnback folder on the Windows 95 CD and in the \Tools\Reskit\File\Lfnback folder on the Windows 98 CD.

2. Disable long name preservation by clicking **Start** Settings, Control Panel, then double-click System.

3. Next, click the Performance tab, the File System button, then the Troubleshooting tab.

4. Select the option Disable long name preservation for old programs.

5. Close all applications. LFNBK cannot re-name open files.

6. At the MS-DOS command prompt, type **lfnbk /b** [*drive:*] to back up and remove long file names for the specified drive.

7. Restart the computer and then run the utility you want to run.

To enable long name preservation, repeat the steps above.

To restore your long file names, type **lfnbk /r** [*drive:*] at the MS-DOS command prompt.

Command

Lfnbk [/V] [/B | /R | /PE] [/NT] [/Force] [/P] [*drive:*]

Options:

/V	Reports activity on the screen.
/B	Backs up and removes long file names for drive you are working with.
/R	Restores previously backed up long file names.
/PE	Extracts errors from backup database.
/NT	Does not restore backup dates and times.
/Force	Forces Lfnbk to run, even in unsafe conditions.

/P ....Reports the long file names but does not create the 8.3 aliases. Displays the long filenames, dates created, dates last accessed and dates last modified.

Drive: ....Specifies the drive(s) you want to back up.

Notes:

1. LFNBK will not repair long file name problems.

2. **LFNBK will not restore long file names that were renamed or moved.**

3. LFNBK may not always restore the exact alias for long file names.

4. When you restart Windows after running LFNBK the default Start menu will display. After you run lfnbk /r to restore, your custom Start menu will be displayed.

5. If your utility program changes the directory structure by removing subdirectories LFNBK will not be able to restore the long file names.

Default Location 98:
\Tools\Reskit\File\Lfnback\Lfnbk.exe

Default Location 95:
\Admin\Apptools\Lfnback\Lfnbk.exe

See Also: Naming Files & Folders

Map Network Drive

To make it easier to access network disk drives and folders, Windows 9x provides the *Map Network Drive* function. Using Map Network Drive, a letter can be assigned to a network disk drive, or more specifically to a folder on a drive. Once mapped, the user can use the drive letter rather than the full network path to reach a destination on the drive. When you need to map a drive letter to a network drive, you can do so using the Map Network Drive function. This function is available in Windows Explorer, My Computer or Network Neighborhood.

Quick Access

Select *drive* icon, then click on the toolbar

or

Right-click *drive* icon, then click <u>M</u>ap Network Drive

or

Click <u>T</u>ools on the menu bar, then <u>M</u>ap Network Drive (Windows Explorer)

or

Alt+T, then *M* (Windows Explorer)

or

Click <u>F</u>ile on the menu bar, then <u>M</u>ap Network Drive (Network Neighborhood)

Or

Alt+F, then *M* (Network Neighborhood)

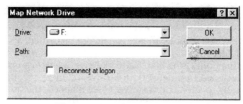

The Map Network Drive dialog box

To map a drive:

1. Select a letter from the Drive drop-down list box.

2. Next, click in the Path drop-down combo box, then type the full path to the network drive and or folder you want to map to.

   Remember to include the server name preceded by two backslashes, for example: \\servername\office\forms

3. If you want the mapping to establish itself every time you start your computer, select the Reconnect at logon check box.

4. Click OK to save your mapping.

Once mapped the drive will appear in Windows Explorer or My Computer just like a local drive.

See Also: Disconnect Network Drive; My Computer; Network Neighborhood; Windows Explorer

Media Player

..QuicKeys..

Open

98

Click , <u>P</u>rograms,

Accessories, Entertainment, Media Player.

or

95

Click , Programs,

Accessories, Multi-media, Media Player.

Move Cursor Backward
Right Arrow

Move Cursor Forward
Left Arrow

Play Marked Selection
Ctrl+Q

Play/Pause
Ctrl+P

Stop
Ctrl+S

Memory

..QuicKeys..

Display Memory Usage

Click , Programs, Accessories,

System Tools, System Information

or

Click **Start**, Settings, Control Panel,

, Performance
System

or

Click **Start**, Run, type **mem**, then click
OK

Modemlog.txt

The *Modemlog.txt* file records your modem activity
whenever a TAPI-enabled communications program establishes a communication session with
the modem. The log is created only if requested in
the modem's properties. Reviewing this log file
can sometimes help you when you're trying to
troubleshoot a modem connection problem.

If, at any time, you feel you are having problems with your modem connection, you can choose to create a modem log using the following method:

1. Click **🏛 Start**, Settings, Control Panel, then double-click Modems.

2. Select the appropriate modem from the list of installed modems, then click the Properties button.

3. Click on the Connection tab, then click the Advanced button.

4. Select the Record a log checkbox in Windows 95, or the Append to log in Windows 98, then click OK.

5. To close the dialog boxes click OK, then Close.

Viewing the Modem Log

To view the modem log, use Notepad to open the file named modemlog.txt. The file is located in your Windows folder.

HOt Tip **What does the log mean?** To find out how to decipher the contents of the log file you can reference a Microsoft article called "How to create and use the Modemlog.txt file" (q142730), which you'll find on Microsoft's support web site, http://support.microsoft.com/support. Use the Search function to search for the reference code listed above.

Default Location: \Windows\Modemlog.txt

See Also: Logview|Modemdet.txt

Modems

Modems is a Control Panel tool that is used to install new modems and configure modems that already exist in your computer.

Quick Access

Click **Start**, Settings, Control Panel,

then double-click
Modems

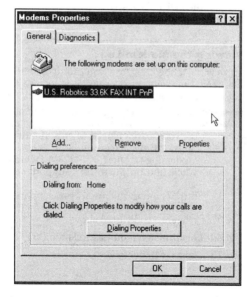

General

On the General tab you can add new modems, remove modems, and modify the properties of existing modems.

Add

In most cases Windows will automatically detect your modem when it starts up; however, you may still find a need to install or reinstall a modem once your system is up and running. To install a modem select Add; you are then led through the process step by step.

Remove

To remove an existing modem, select the modem from the modem list, then click Remove.

CAUTION: *The modem is removed immediately; there is no verification.*

Properties

To view or change the properties of a modem, select the modem from the modem list, then click Properties.

 Control Modem Noise: If your modem is too loud you can control the speaker's volume in the modem's Properties.

Dialing Properties

Dialing Properties lets you change the way your modem dials calls. You can create different Dial From locations, dial a number to get an outside line, include credit card numbers for long distance, and disable call waiting.

Disable Call Waiting: If you want to disable call waiting you can do so in Dialing Properties. Just select the option, then select the code that disables it.

Note: If you are unable to use 56K in your hotel room, don't be surprised. Many hotel PBX systems do not support 56K.

Diagnostics

On the *Diagnostics* tab, Windows displays the operating communication ports and the hardware that is using them.

Driver

Identifies the drive used for the communications port selected in the list.

More Info

Provides more information on the port selected such as the interrupt, address, and UART.

Help

Help launches a troubleshooting dialog that may help you resolve problems you might be encountering.

See Also: Add New Hardware; Dial-Up Networking

Mouse

Mouse

Mouse is a Control Panel tool that is used to control the operation, visual representation, and the type of mouse installed in your system.

Quick Access

Click [🏁 Start], Settings, Control Panel,

double-click

Mouse

Buttons

On the *Buttons* tab you can specify whether the mouse will be used with the right hand, which is the default, or the left hand. The double-click speed can also be adjusted so that it matches your personal reaction time. By moving the slider back and forth to adjust the time between clicks and testing your double-click in the test area you can make the double-click more comfortable for you.

Pointers

The *Pointers* tab provides a way to select a scheme, which determines what your pointer will look like. The list below the Scheme drop-down list box shows the available pointers that can be used for that scheme. To select a new pointer, double-click the pointer, double-click the icon that represents the pointer, then click OK.

HOt Tip **Pointers for Presentations:** If you give presentations using Microsoft PowerPoint, select the Windows Standard (extra large) scheme. It makes your pointer easier to see for both you and your audience.

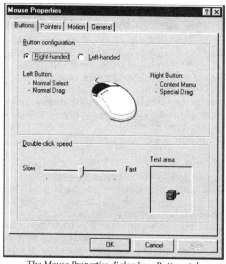

The Mouse Properties dialog box, Buttons tab

Note: Windows supplies additional mouse pointer schemes, but you may have to install them if they haven't already been installed. You can do this using **Add/Remove Programs** in the **Control Panel**. Select the **Windows Setup** tab, then **Accessories**. There you'll find **Mouse Pointers**. See "Add/Remove Programs" (p. 42)for more information.

Motion

On the *Motion* tab you can adjust how fast the pointer moves across the screen and indicate whether or not you want the pointer to leave trails. Trails leave an image showing where the pointer has come from, which makes it easier to see. Using the slider you can adjust how long the trails will be.

 General

The *General* tab allows you to change from one mouse to another. If you decide to use a different type of mouse permanently or temporarily, you will need to tell Windows what mouse you are using. Click the Change button and a list of manufacturers and their mice will be listed. Select the combination that meets your needs, then click OK. If your mouse isn't listed, click Have Disk; you'll then need to provide a disk with the appropriate mouse drivers on it.

See Also: Accessibility Options

Moving Files & Folders

Files and folders can be moved to other areas of the same drive or to different drives. When a file or folder is moved, the original is deleted and a copy or duplicate is created at a new location. During the moving process the data is temporarily stored in the Clipboard. Following are several methods that can be used in My Computer or Windows Explorer to move files and folders:

Drag and Drop

Shift+drag *file* or *folder* to the *destination* on a different drive

or

Drag *file* or *folder* to the *destination* on the same drive

or

Right-click *file* or *folder* and drag to the *destination*, then click Move Here

or

Ctrl+Shift, click *file* or *folder* and drag to the *destination*, then click Move Here

Hot Tip **Move, Copy or Shortcut?** When you use the drag and drop method to *move* a file or folder, there is no special symbol displayed with the pointer as it is placed over the destination.

If an arrow is displayed, you are creating a *shortcut* to the file or folder rather than moving it.

If a plus sign (+) is displayed with the pointer, you are *copying* the file or folder.

Hot Tip **Cancel Drag and Drop**: If you're in the middle of using the drag and drop method and want to cancel your action, just press Esc before you drop.

Hot Tip **Right-Click and Drag**: When working with folders, right-click and drag the folder—you will be given a choice between moving and copying.

Cut and Paste

Right-click *file* or *folder*, click Cut, right-click the destination, then click <u>P</u>aste

or

98

Select *file* or *folder*, click

on the toolbar, move to the destination, then click

or

Select the *file* or *folder*, click

on the toolbar, move to the destination,
then click [paste icon]

or

Select the *file* or *folder*, press *Ctrl+X*, move to
the destination, then press *Ctrl+V*

or

Select the *file* or *folder*, click <u>E</u>dit on the menu
bar, Cu<u>t</u>, move to the destination, click <u>E</u>dit,
then <u>P</u>aste

Hot Tip **Mix and Match Commands**: You can
combine the Cut or Paste commands
from the menu, toolbar or shortcut
menus. For example, you could use the
Cut command from the shortcut menu,
and then use the Paste command from
the toolbar.

Note: When copying a folder, its entire contents including all files and folders are
moved. If you drag a folder to another
folder of the same name, the folder is
moved *into* the destination folder, it
does not replace it. To replace a folder of
the same name, drag the folder to the
parent folder or drive.

See Also: Copying Files & Folders; Cutting Files
and Folders; Selecting Files & Folders; Undo

Moving Windows

See: Arranging Windows (p. 63)

MS-DOS

 MS-DOS is still available and can be used for many different functions. If you need to run programs in MS-DOS mode you'll find they run more smoothly and trouble free than ever before. Of course there are still some things that only MD-DOS can do, which makes having access to it a nice benefit.

If you need run any of the MS-DOS commands you should have no trouble executing them from the command line—Windows provides a path to their location. All the commands are located in \Windows\Command folder.

Quick Access

Click , Programs, then MS-DOS Prompt

HOt Tip Create a Shortcut to MS-DOS: If you use MS-DOS frequently, create a shortcut on your desktop that will open an MS-DOS window. When you create the shortcut use the following command for the Command Line:
C:\Windows\Command.com
Don't forget to designate a shortcut key combination, such as *Ctrl+Alt+D,* so that you can open an MS-DOS window at any time.

Long File Names

When working with long file names at the MS-DOS prompt you have two choices:

> Use the 8.3 alias, for example **Purcha~1.doc**.

or

> Use the long file name in quotes, for example "Purchase Order.doc." If nothing follows the file name, you can use just one quote, for example cd "\My Documents.

..QuicKeys..

Close or Exit

Click ☒ on the title bar
or
> Double-click *program* icon on title bar

or
> Click *program* icon on title bar, <u>C</u>lose

or
> Right-click *program* button on taskbar, <u>C</u>lose

or
> Type **exit**, then press *Enter*

Copy Selected Text

> Click 📋 on the toolbar

Fonts

> Click **A** on the toolbar

or
> Right-click *program* icon, P<u>r</u>operties, <u>F</u>ont

Full Screen On/Off

> *Alt+Enter*

or

Click  on the toolbar

Open

> Click **Start**, <u>P</u>rograms, MS-DOS Prompt

or

> *Ctrl+Esc*, *P*, MS-DOS Prompt

Paste Copied Text

> Click on the toolbar

Properties

> Click on the toolbar

or

> Right-click *program* icon, P<u>r</u>operties

Run DOS Command

> Click **Start**, <u>R</u>un, type **command**, OK

or

> *Ctrl+Esc*, *R*, type **command**, *Enter.*

Run DOS Program in Background

> Click on the toolbar.

Select Text

> Click on the toolbar, then drag

rectangle around *text.*

Default Location: \Windows\Command

See Also: Dir (MS-DOS); Naming Files & Folders; Renaming Files & Folders

Microsoft Natural Keyboard

..QuicKeys..

Cycle Through Taskbar Program Buttons
Win+Tab

Explorer
Win+E

Find
Win+F

Find Computer
Ctrl+Win+F

Help (Windows)
Win+F1

Run dialog
Win+R

System Properties
Win+Pause

Windows, Minimize All
Win+M

Windows, Undo Minimize All
Shift+Win+M

Multilanguage Support

Windows 9x installs support for many different languages during the initial setup. There are several, however, that must be installed separately if they're needed. The following selections are available under *Multilanguage Support*:

    Baltic Language Support
    Central European Language Support
    Cyrillic Language Support
    Greek Language Support
    Turkish Language Support

Support for these languages can be installed through the Control Panel. Here's how:

1. Click **Start**, Settings, Control Panel, then double-click the Add/Remove Programs icon.
2. Click the Windows Setup tab, then scroll through the Components list box until you find Multilanguage Support.
3. Select Multilanguage Support, then click Details.
4. Select the support you need, click OK.
5. Click OK again.
   If you originally installed Windows using a CD-ROM or floppy disks, you may be prompted to insert one of the disks into your computer.
6. Reboot your computer to have the changes take effect.

The languages are now installed and can be added to the list of available languages in Keyboard Properties.

See Also: Keyboard|Language; Regional Settings

My Briefcase

My Briefcase

My Briefcase provides a convenient way to synchronize files that you edit on more than one computer. It works similarly to a real briefcase. You put files in it to take home, work on the files at home, then bring the briefcase back to work and work on them at work.

For example, let's say you took a word processing file home from the office on your portable computer. You made some changes to the file and the next morning, back at the office, you needed to update the original file on the network. My Briefcase would be the perfect tool for the job, and could handle the whole process in just a few clicks.

One of the benefits of using My Briefcase is that you don't have to think about or visually compare files when it's time to synchronize them. My Briefcase takes care of the details.

Quick Access

Double-click on the desktop

My Briefcase

CAUTION: *My Briefcase uses the date and time stamp on each file to determine which file is the latest version. When using My Briefcase to synchronize files, make sure the system clock and calendar in both computers are in synch; otherwise, My Briefcase may not update the correct file.*

My Briefcase, Windows 98

Uses For My Briefcase

There are several ways you can use My Briefcase to transport files. The following are a few examples:

Floppy Disk Transport

If you need to copy files from one computer to another, and the computers are not connected to one another, you can use a floppy disk to transport My Briefcase, and keep the files synchronized. Following are the instructions for using My Briefcase when using a floppy disk to transport files:

1. Copy the file(s) or folder(s) you want to work with to My Briefcase, using one of the methods listed below. See "Copying Files To My Briefcase" (p. 292).

2. Copy My Briefcase to a floppy disk using one of the following methods:

   Right-click the My Briefcase icon, select Send To, then 3½ Floppy (A), or whatever is appropriate for your computer.

   or

   Double-click My Computer, then drag My Briefcase from the desktop to the 3½

Floppy (A:) icon, or whatever is appropriate for your computer, in the My Computer window.

or

Right-click 🏠 Start, select Explore, scroll up the left pane until you see the 3½ Floppy (A:) icon, or whatever is appropriate for your computer. Drag My Briefcase from the desktop to the 3½ Floppy (A:) icon. You may have to use the Restore button on the Explorer window to reduce its size so you can see the desktop.

Note: The My Briefcase icon disappears from the desktop once it's been copied to the floppy drive. When you copy My Briefcase back to your desktop, it reappears.

CAUTION: *If you exceed the capacity of the floppy disk when copying My Briefcase to a floppy drive, it will not automatically span to a second disk.*

Hot Tip **Need more space on your floppy disks**? Use DriveSpace to nearly double their capacity. See "DriveSpace" for more information.

Hot Tip **Another alternative to floppy disks** is a Zip or Jazz drive, which can store 100MB to 600MB of data. Of course, you will have to have one on each computer to facilitate the transfers.

Hot Tip **You can create additional briefcases** if you need to divide files up into groups, so that they will fit onto one floppy disk. Remember to leave enough room on each disk for the file(s) to grow. See "Creating A New Briefcase."

3. On your other computer you can use the file(s) directly from the floppy disk or you can copy My Briefcase to your hard drive.

If you already have a folder for My Briefcase on your desktop, make a new folder and copy My Briefcase into the folder. You cannot have two My Briefcases on your desktop at the same time.

To copy My Briefcase from the floppy drive, double-click My Computer, then double-click 3½ Floppy (A:), drag My Briefcase from the floppy drive to your desktop.

4. Now you can work on your file(s) directly from My Briefcase. There are two ways to open a file:

Double-click on the My Briefcase icon, then double-click the *file* you want to open.

or

If you already have the application open, you can use the Open dialog box to locate your file. On the menu bar select File, Open, then click the **Look in** list box. Locate My Briefcase, double-click the *folder*, then double-click the *file* you want to open.

5. After you are finished working on your file, save the file to My Briefcase.

6. When you return to the office, insert the floppy disk that contains My Briefcase into the drive on your computer.

7. Synchronize the file(s) using one of the methods listed below. See "Synchronizing Files and Folders."

Portable Computer Connected To A Network

If you have a portable computer connected to a network and work on files out on the network, but also take them home to work on, My Briefcase provides a convenient method for keeping them synchronized. Following are the instructions for using My Briefcase when connected to a network:

1. Copy the file(s) or folder(s) you want to work with from a network server to My Briefcase using one of the methods listed below. See "Copying Files To My Briefcase."

2. Shut down, then disconnect your computer from the network.

3. Take your computer home, work on the files out of My Briefcase. Do not remove the files from My Briefcase. If you do, the sync will be broken and when you return to the office, you won't be able to update the files on the network using My Briefcase.

4. When you return to the office, connect your computer to the network. Make sure you are connected to the same server that stores your original files.

5. Synchronize the file(s) using one of the methods listed below. See "Synchronizing Files and Folders."

Desktop Computer Connected To A Network

If you have a desktop computer connected to a network, but prefer to work on your files on your local hard drive, which provides faster access and saves, My Briefcase provides an easy-to-use method for synchronizing the files.

1. Copy the file(s) or folder(s) you want to work with from a network server to My Brief-

case, using one of the methods listed below. See "Copying Files To My Briefcase."

2. Work on the files out of My Briefcase. Do not remove the files from My Briefcase. If you do, the sync will be broken and you won't be able to update the files on the network using My Briefcase.

3. Synchronize the file(s) using one of the methods listed below. See "Synchronizing Files and Folders."

Computer Connected To Another Computer Using A Direct Cable Connection

The same methods used for a "Portable Computer Connected To A Network" can be used for two computers connected with a direct cable connection.

Copying Files To My Briefcase

Copy the files or folders to My Briefcase using one of the following methods:

Right-click the *files* or *folders*, select Send To, then My Briefcase.

or

Click the *files* or *folders* and drag them onto the My Briefcase icon.

or

Right-click the *files* or *folders* and drag them on to the My Briefcase icon, then select Make Sync Copy.

or

Right-click the *files* or *folders* and drag them on to the My Briefcase icon, then select Make Sync Copy of Type. From the list box, select the specific file type(s) that should be copied.

Only those file types specified are copied to My Briefcase.

Note: All methods above provide identical results — a synchronized copy in My Briefcase. Each copy contains the data, version and location of the original file.

Split From Original

When you no longer want two files connected you can split them apart using the following menu command:

Select the file, click <u>B</u>riefcase on the menu bar, then click <u>S</u>plit From Original.

Synchronizing Files And Folders

When you copy file(s) or folder(s) to My Briefcase, each copy contains the data, version and location of the original file. After you have worked on your file(s) in your briefcase you need to periodically update the originals. Before you update the originals make sure you are connected to the computer or server storing the originals.

Note: If the My Briefcase icon is not on your desktop, right-click the Desktop, select New, then Briefcase. If there is no Briefcase option on the menu and My Briefcase is not in the default location, it probably has not been installed. See "Default Location" and "Installation" below.

Note: The first time you open My Briefcase you'll see a welcome window. Read it, then click Finish. The welcome window will not be displayed the next time you open My Briefcase.

Updating The Originals

The files or folders in My Briefcase need to be updated whenever, the briefcase version or the original, are modified.

If no modifications have been made to either version, the Status in My Briefcase will display Up-to-date. If a modification has been made to either version, the Status will display Needs updating.

Note: If My Briefcase is open and you make changes to a file the window may not display the most recent Status. Click View on the menu bar, then Refresh to make sure your view is the most current.

If My Briefcase shows files or folders that need updating, you can update the items using either *Update All* or *Update Selection*.

The Update My Briefcase dialog box.

Update All

 Update All selects and updates all files that need updating.

Update Selection

 Update Selection only updates files that you have selected from the list.

Update Actions

Whether you use Update All or Update Selection a new window opens which lists the files that need updating. The file in My Briefcase is listed on the left and the file in the remote location is listed on the right. In between the two is the Update Action. The Update Action determines which file is used to update the other; however, two other actions, Skip and Delete, are also available.

To change the Update Action, right-click anywhere on the file's entry, then click the appropriate selection.

⇒
Replace   Uses the file on the left to update the file on the right.

⇐
Replace   Uses the file on the right to update the file on the left.

↘
Skip   Skips the update procedure for that file.

When you are finished, click Update at the bottom of the window to start the update procedure.

Installation

To install My Briefcase select **🏁 Start** , Settings, Control Panel, double-click Add/Remove Programs, select Windows Setup tab. In the Components list box, select My Briefcase, then click OK.

Default Location:
\Windows\Desktop\My Briefcase

See Also: Copying Files & Folders

My Computer

My Computer

My Computer is a file management tool that is used to browse through drives, folders, files and other resources. Using My Computer you can perform many commands that help you with folder and file management, starting programs, opening documents and printing documents. You can copy, move, rename, create and delete files and folders using the tools contained in My Computer. My Computer is represented by an icon on the desktop which looks like a desktop computer.

Quick Access

Double-click ![icon] My Computer on your desktop

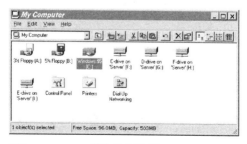

My Computer Window

The My Computer window displays icons for all the floppy drives, hard drives, CD-ROM drives, network drives, Control Panel, Printers and Dial-Up Networking. The window and the objects in the window can be controlled using the commands located in the menus on the menu bar.

Windows 98, Web View

..QuicKeys..

There are many ways to accomplish different tasks in My Computer. Following are the most common actions and their commands.

Activate Menu Bar

Alt

or

F10

Close

    Click ![X] on the title bar

or

    Double-click *program* icon

or

    Alt+F4

or

    Alt+F, then *C*

or

    Alt+Spacebar, then *C*

Close Window and All Parent Folders

    Shift+the Close button ![X]

Details

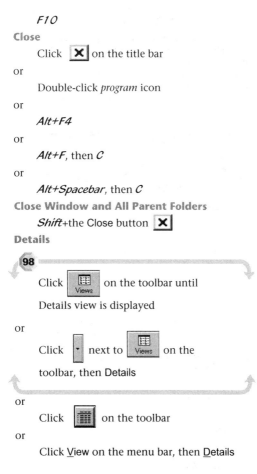

98

    Click ![Views] on the toolbar until

    Details view is displayed

or

    Click ![·] next to ![Views] on the

    toolbar, then Details

or

    Click ![details icon] on the toolbar

or

    Click <u>V</u>iew on the menu bar, then <u>D</u>etails

or

> Right-click background, click <u>V</u>iew,
> then <u>D</u>etails

or

> *Alt+V*, then *D*

Display Combo Box

> Click

or

> *F4*

or

> *Alt+Down Arrow*

Find

> *F3*

or

> *Win+F* (Microsoft Natural Keyboard)

or

> Click <u>F</u>ile on the menu bar, then Find

or

> *Alt+F*, then *F*

Find Computer

> *Ctrl+Win+F*, then *C*
> (Microsoft Natural Keyboard)

Go To First Object

> *Ctrl+End*

Go To Folder

> *Ctrl+G*

Go To Last Object

> *Ctrl+Home*

Large Icons

Click on the toolbar until
Large Icons view is displayed

or

Click next to on the toolbar,
Large Icons

or

Click on the toolbar

or

Click <u>V</u>iew on the menu bar, then Large
Icons

or

Right-click background, click <u>V</u>iew, then
Large Icons

or

Alt+V, then *G*

Line Up Icons

Right-click background,
click Arrange Icons, then *sort method*

or

Right-click background, then click Lin<u>e</u> up
Icons

or

Click <u>V</u>iew on the menu bar, then Lin<u>e</u> up
Icons

or

Alt+V, then *E*

List View

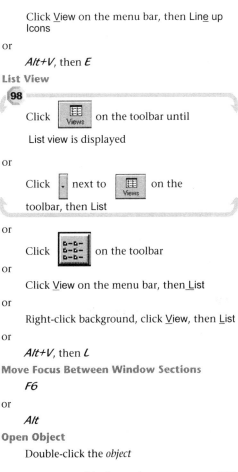

Click [Views] on the toolbar until

List view is displayed

or

Click [▾] next to [Views] on the

toolbar, then List

or

Click [☷] on the toolbar

or

Click <u>V</u>iew on the menu bar, then <u>L</u>ist

or

Right-click background, click <u>V</u>iew, then <u>L</u>ist

or

Alt+V, then *L*

Move Focus Between Window Sections

F6

or

Alt

Open Object

Double-click the *object*

or

>   Right-click the *object*, then click <u>O</u>pen

Open Object and Close Current Window

>   *Ctrl*+double-click the *object*

or

>   *Ctrl*+right-click *object*, then click <u>O</u>pen

Refresh View

>   *F5*

or

>   Click <u>V</u>iew on the menu bar, then <u>R</u>efresh

or

>   *Alt+V*, then *R*

Select the First Object

>   *Home*

Select the Last Object

>   *End*

Small Icons

>   Click 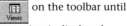 on the toolbar until

>   Small Icons view is displayed

or

>   Click next to on the

>   toolbar, then S<u>m</u>all Icons

or

>   Click on the toolbar

or

Click <u>V</u>iew on the menu bar,
then S<u>m</u>all Icons

or

Right-click background, click <u>V</u>iew, then
S<u>m</u>all Icons

or

Alt+V, then *M*

System Menu, Open

Double-click *program* icon

or

Alt+Spacebar

View Parent Folder

98

Click on the toolbar

or

Click 🔼 on the toolbar

or

Backspace

For more information about copying, deleting,
moving and renaming files and folders, see the
following sections: "Copying Files & Folders,"
"Deleting Files & Folders," "Moving Files &
Folders," or "Renaming Files & Folders."

View

One of the nice features of My Computer is that
you can change the way you view your folders and
files. You can change the views from the View
menu. If the toolbar is displayed you can also
make changes using the buttons on the toolbar.
The following options are available from the View
menu:

Toolbar

Status Bar

As Web Page (Windows 98)

Large Icons

Small Icons

List

Details

Customize this Folder

Arrange Icons

Line Up Icons

Refresh

Options (Windows 95)

Folder Options (Windows 98)

For more information on these options, see "View," p. 453.

 Alternative Access: Some of the options on the View menu can also be accessed by right-clicking the background of the right pane of the window.

 To open two instances of My Computer at the same time, you need to have the folder option in Options|Folder (Windows 95) or Folder Options|General|Custom (Windows 98) set to Browse folders using a separate window for each folder. Next, open the two windows you want to work with and close all other windows. Right-click the taskbar then select either the Tile Vertically or Tile Horizontally option. You can now copy and move files from one window to another.

Go

The options on the Go menu provide functions to move backwards, forwards, and up one level in the hierarchy as well as direct access to various other destinations within Windows. Selecting an option from the menu will move you to the target destination without further interaction.

Favorites

The options on the Favorites menu are similar to the options on the Go menu in that they provide a method to move directly to a destination. Favorites; however, takes the concept a big step forward by providing a method to add and organize your own destinations, whether they be on your local drives, network drives, or on the Internet.

For more information see "Favorites," (p. 203).

Opening Folders or Objects

The folders or objects displayed in the My Computer window can be expanded or opened two different ways.

 View Object Description: When you select As Web Page from the View menu, you can display a description of the object or its statistics before you open it. Select the object and the information will display on the left side of the window under My Computer.

Using the Windows Explorer View

You may prefer to open My Computer and folders within My Computer with the dual-pane Windows Explorer view. You can do this any time by right-clicking the icon or folder and then selecting Explore.

If you would like to make the Windows Explorer view the default view for My Computer, follow these steps:

1. Double-click My Computer.

2. Click View, then Options from the menu bar.

3. Click the File Types tab.

4. In the Registered File Types list box, select Folder.

5. Click the Edit button.

6. In the Actions list box, select Explore, then click the Set Default button. Explore should now be in bold.

7. Click the Close button twice.
   Now, whenever you use My Computer, it will automatically open using the Windows Explorer view.

HOt Tip **To change from My Computer to the Windows Explorer view on-the-fly**, right-click on the folder you want to open, then select Explore. The folder will open using Windows Explorer.

Note: By default, My Computer opens a new window every time you open a folder or object. If you want to change the default so that the current window is closed as you open a new one automatically, you can do so using the View menu, Options, then Folder.

HÒt Tip **How to tell what's happening when you drag and drop:** Look at the lower right corner just before you drop the file. If the file is being copied, there will be a plus sign, an arrow if a shortcut is being created and nothing if the file is being moved. If the result is not what you want, drag the file back to where it came from before you release the button and it will cancel the operation.

Note: When you view the icon for a CD-ROM drive, notice that the icon name dynamically changes to reflect the name of the CD that is in the drive.

HÒt Tip **Change the My Computer Icon**: If you want to change the name of the My Computer icon, remove it or change the default icon you can do so in the Registry.

CAUTION: *The following instructions involve changing settings in the Registry. If the changes are not made properly, serious problems may result. Be sure to backup your Registry before continuing. See: "Registry" for more information about backing up and editing the Registry.*

Using Regedit, open the Registry and move to HKEY_CLASSES_ROOT\CLSID subtree. Open the folder whose name is 20D04FE0-3AEA-1069-A2D8-08002B3030 9D. To change the name double-click the default icon in the right pane to edit the data. Type the name you want to use.

To change the icon, expand the folder 20D04FE0-3AEA-1069-A2D8-08002B3030 9D, then open the DefaultIcon folder. Double-click the appropriate entry in the right pane to edit the data. Replace the path and icon name with whatever you want.

HOt Tip **To quickly move through a list of folders and files by name**, click in the window pane you want to work in (if it's the right pane, also click the column header for Name to put the objects in alphabetical order), then press the first letter of the folder or file name you are looking for. The focus will move to the first folder or file that starts with the letter you typed. If you type the same letter again the focus will move to the next one that starts with the letter you typed.

See Also: Clipboard; Copying Files & Folders; Deleting Files & Folders; Dir (MS-DOS); Favorites; Section 4 - File Types; Find; Moving Files & Folders; Quick View; Selecting Files & Folders; Shortcut Menu; Undo; View; Windows Explorer

Naming Disks

Each diskette or disk drive can be given an eleven character name called a volume label. Spaces are allowed; however, you cannot use + , = [ ] / \ ; * ? " : < > | . The displayed names for diskettes will default to the description and logical drive letter. The displayed names for disk drives will default to the logical drive letter. For example: 3½ Floppy (A:) or (C:)

If a name is given to a diskette, the name will not be displayed in My Computer or Windows Explorer. However, if a name is provided for a disk drive, the name will display with the drive letter, for example: My Drive (C:)

To name a diskette or disk drive:

1. Double-click .
   My Computer

2. Right-click the *diskette* or *disk drive* icon you want to name, then click Properties.

3. On the General tab at the Label field, type the *name*, then click OK.

Note: CD-ROM drives cannot be named. When you view the icon for a CD-ROM drive, notice that the icon name dynamically changes to reflect the name of the CD that it was given at the time of manufacture.

Naming Files & Folders

In Windows 9x you can use up to 255 characters to name files and folders. This makes naming files and folders much easier than the previous Windows and MS-DOS convention of 8.3 or 11 characters. Spaces are allowed, but you cannot use / \ ; * ? " : < > | .

The file extension can also be longer. Many applications, however, still use the three character convention for their default extension. Even though you can use file names up to 255 characters, you should limit the length of your names so that they can be easily typed, and so that when used in a path, the total length of the path does not exceed the limit of 260 characters.

CAUTION: *If you are accessing files across a network, you may not be able to use long file names. The server you are working with determines whether it or not it will recognize or preserve long file names.*

HOt Tip **Files and Folders are Listed in Alphabetical Order**: When you view the contents of a folder, the files and folders are listed in alphabetical order. Keep this in mind when you name files or folders so that they appear in a logical position.

Windows 3.x and MS-DOS Compatibility

Windows 9x creates a second name that complies with the previous Windows and MS-DOS convention of 8.3 so that the files and folders can remain backwards compatible.

Note: Long file and folder names cannot be viewed in DOS or by 16-bit applications.

HOt Tip **To see the 8.3 alias that Windows 9x creates** for a file or folder right-click the file or folder in My Computer or Windows Explorer, then select Properties. The alias is displayed under MS-DOS name.

Windows 9x uses the following rules to create an alias or MS-DOS 8.3 compatible file name:

• Remove the following characters + , ; = [ ] / \ * ? " < > | and any spaces or periods other than the last period.

• Use the first six characters of the long file name plus a numeric tail, ~*n* (where *n* is a number). If this name is not unique keep adding one to *n* until nine is reached. If the name is still not unique the system will use the first five characters plus *~nn* (where *nn* begins at 10 and ends at 99).

- Use the first three characters after the last period for the three character extension. For example: **A Very Long Name.New.Name** would generate an 8.3 compatible name of **AVERYL~1.NAM**

CAUTION: *Utilities designed to work with Windows 3.x and DOS generally are not aware of and do not know how to work with long file names. Using these older utilities to perform disk or file management activities may destroy your long file names.*

It's always best to use utilities that were designed for Windows 9x; however, if you need to run a utility that does not support long file names be sure to back up your long file names. See: "Long File Name Backup (LFNBK)" (pg.266)

CAUTION: *If you are installing a 16-bit application into a folder with a long file name and you don't use the 8.3 alias, the install procedure will fail. To find out what the 8.3 alias is, just view the file name in MS-DOS; you'll be able to see both the 8.3 alias and the long file name.*

Eliminating Numeric Tails from File Names

If you would prefer to have the system use characters instead of the numeric tails (*~n*), when creating MS-DOS 8.3 compatible file names, you can modify the Registry to do so. Here's how:

CAUTION: *The following instructions involve changing settings in the Registry. If the changes are not made properly, serious problems may result. Be sure to backup your Registry before continuing. See: "Registry" (p. 351) for more information about backing up and editing the Registry.*

1. Click **Start**, Run, type **regedit**, then press *Enter*.
2. Move through the tree structure as follows: HKEY_LOCAL_MACHINE\System\ CurrentControlSet\Control\FileSystem
3. Select FileSystem in the left pane.
4. Click Edit on the menu bar, New, Binary Value, type **NameNumericTail** then press *Enter*.
5. Double-click NameNumericTail. The Edit Binary Value window is displayed.
6. Type a **0** (zero), then click OK. The value in the Data column should be 00. (Should you decide to restore the original naming convention, use 1 instead of zero.)
7. Click Registry on the menu bar, then Exit.

Note: When numeric tails are turned off and the first eight characters of two file names are the same, Windows will create a numeric tail for the second file even though numeric tails are turned off.

Using Long File Names in MS-DOS

When you are working from the MS-DOS command line you can use either the long file name or the 8.3 file name. If you use the DIR command, both file name formats are displayed.

You can use either format at the MS-DOS command line, but if a long file name contains spaces, you will need to enclose the entire path in quotes. For example:

"\My Documents\Forms\New Quote.doc"

The default command line character limit is 127 characters, which might prove limiting when using long file names. To extend the character limit to 255, you must add or change a switch setting for the SHELL command in Config.sys. If you do not have a SHELL command in Config.sys, add the following line:

shell=c:\windows\command.com /u:255

If you already have this command in your Config.sys, just add or modify the switch setting so that it is set as /u:255.

See Also: Long File Name Backup; Registry; Renaming Files & Folders

Ndislog.txt

See: Logview|Ndislog.txt (p. 263)

Netlog.txt

See: Logview|Netlog.txt (p. 263)

Network

..QuicKeys..

Connect (Map) Network Drive

or

Click on the toolbar.

In Explorer, select *drive*, click <u>T</u>ools on the menu bar, <u>M</u>ap Network Drive or, select *drive*, *Alt+T*, *M*

or

In Network Neighborhood, right-click *drive*, <u>M</u>ap Network Drive.

or

In Network Neighborhood, select *drive*, click <u>F</u>ile on the menu bar, <u>M</u>ap Network Drive

or

Select *drive*, *Alt+F*, *M*

Disconnect Network Drive

or

Click on the toolbar

Right-click *drive*, <u>D</u>isconnect

or

In Explorer, select *drive*, click <u>T</u>ools on the menu bar, <u>D</u>isconnect Network Drive

or

Select *drive*, *Alt+T*, *D* (Explorer)

or

In Network Neighborhood, select *drive*, click <u>F</u>ile on the menu bar, <u>D</u>isconnect

or

Alt+F, *D* (Network Neighborhood)

Properties

Alt+double-click   Network Neighborhood

or

Right-click Network Neighborhood, then click Properties

or

Click **Start**, Settings, Control Panel,

then double-click Network

Search for Computer

Click **Start**, Find, Computer...

or

Ctrl+Win+F, Computer (Microsoft Natural Keyboard)

or

Ctrl, Esc, F, C

Network Neighborhood

Network Neighborhood is similar to My Computer and Windows Explorer, but it takes a little different approach. Like My Computer and Windows Explorer, it is a file management tool that allows you to browse through servers, resources, folders, and files. The difference is that it takes a network approach, displaying all the servers on your network rather than local and mapped drives. As you double-click a server, its resources including drives and printers are displayed. Once you reach a resource, such as one for a drive, you can browse it just as you would a mapped drive.

Quick Access

Double-click

Using Network Neighborhood

There are many ways to accomplish different tasks in Network Neighborhood. Most of the actions and commands used are the same as those used in My Computer and Windows Explorer. See "My Computer" and "Windows Explorer" for more information on these actions and commands.

Following are a few that are more specific to Network Neighborhood.

Find Computer

> Right-click Network Neighborhood, then click **Find Computer**

or

> Click , **Find**, then **Computer**

or

> *Ctrl+Win+F*
> *(Microsoft Natural Keyboard)*

or

> *Ctrl, Esc, F*, then *C*

> **HOt Tip** **Use the UNC with the Run Command**: If you know the Universal Naming Convention (UNC) for the server you want to access, you can use it in the Run command to access its resources. The UNC for a server always starts with a "\\", for example, \\servername. Click Start, Run, type the UNC, then click OK. A window with the server's resources is displayed.

Map Network Drive

> Click **File** on the menu bar, then **Map Network Drive**

or

    Alt+F, then *M*

Properties

    Alt+double-click

or

    Right-click , then click P̲roperties

or

    Click **🏁Start** , S̲ettings, C̲ontrol Panel,

    then double-click

For more information about copying, deleting, moving and renaming files and folders see the following sections: "Copying Files & Folders," "Deleting Files & Folders," "Moving Files & Folders," or "Renaming Files & Folders."

H0t Tip **Hide Shared Drives**: If you want to hide shared drives, folders and printers on peer-to-peer network you can do so by making the last character of the shared name a "$". The resource will then be invisible to users, but they could still access the resource if they know the name.

H0t Tip **Use Network Neighborhood to Install a Printer**: You can install a printer directly from Network Neighborhood. Locate the printer resource on the appropriate server, right-click the resource, then click Install. For more information see "Printers" (p. 326).

 **Use Registry to Change Network Neighborhood Icon:** If you want to change the name of the Network Neighborhood icon, remove it or change the default icon you can do so in the Registry.

CAUTION: *The following instructions involve changing settings in the Registry. If the changes are not made properly, serious problems may result. Be sure to backup your Registry before continuing. See: "Registry" for more information about backing up and editing the Registry.*

Using Regedit open the Registry and move to HKEY_CLASSES_ROOT\CLSID subtree. Open the folder whose name is 208D2C60-3AEA-1069-A2D7-08002B30 309D. To change the name double-click the default icon in the right pane to edit the data. Type the name you want to use.

To change the icon, expand the folder 208D2C60-3AEA-1069-A2D7-08002B30 309D, then open the DefaultIcon folder. Double-click the appropriate entry in the right pane to edit the data. Replace the path and icon name with whatever you want.

See Also: Clipboard; Copying Files & Folders; Deleting Files & Folders; Dir (MS-DOS); Favorites; Section 4—File Types; Find—Computer; Find—Files or Folders; Moving Files & Folders; My Computer; Printers; Quick View; Selecting Files & Folders; Shortcut Menu; Undo; View; Windows Explorer

Number Format

See: Regional Settings (p. 349)

Partitioning Hard Disks

See: Fdisk (MS-DOS) (p. 206)

Passwords

Passwords

Passwords is a Control Panel tool that lets you set up and change passwords for your local computer and for networks you may be connected to. Security on a local level is limited. Anyone who has physical access to the computer can easily use a floppy disk to start the computer and bypass the password security. Password protection will, however, keep most people from accessing your machine.

Quick Access

Click **Start**, Settings, Control Panel,

double-click
Passwords

Change Passwords

The Change Passwords tab lets you change your Windows password as well as other network passwords.

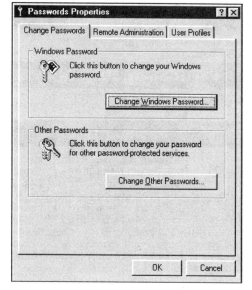

Change Windows Password

The Windows password restricts access to your local computer. It is not a sophisticated security device; in fact, it can be bypassed rather easily. However, it will keep most people from accessing your machine. When enabled, you will be prompted to enter your password shortly after your computer starts up.

To change your password:

1. Click the Change Passwords tab.
2. Click the Change Windows Password button.

3. Type the Old Password you were using, then press *Tab*.
   The password you type appears as asterisks.
4. Type the New Password, then press *Tab*.
5. Type the New Password again to confirm, then click OK.

 Eliminate Password Prompt: If you are the only one using your computer and you do not have User Profiles enabled, you can remove the password prompt so you don't have to enter it every time you start up. To do so simply use the Change Windows Password tool, type your Old Password, then click OK. Do not type in a New Password. The next time you start your computer you won't be asked for a Windows password.

Change Other Passwords

Change Other Passwords lets you change passwords other than the Windows password, such as a password associated with a network computer.

 Remote Administration

Remote Administration lets you specify whether or not a network administrator has the rights to set up and monitor shared resources on your computer. Here you establish passwords the remote administrator must use to access your computer, so that they can create, change, or monitor the shared resources.

User Profiles

Windows accommodates multiple users of the same computer by letting you set up a profile for each user. This allows each user to configure the desktop to match their own working style. This could include desktop colors, icons on the desktop, screen savers, history logs, and program groups.

Windows, by default, is set up for only one user. If you want to establish different user profiles, select the appropriate option on the User Profiles tab. Select the User Profile Settings you want to include, then click OK. If you do not select these options, you will share the setting with the other users. Your computer will need to be restarted for the changes to take effect.

The next time you start your computer you will be required to enter a user name and password. If it is a new user to the system a new profile will be established. Once you have signed in, you can modify the system to suit your needs. These settings will be saved for future sessions.

See Also: Applications; Arranging Icons; Arranging Windows; Desktop; Display

Pop-Up Menu

See: Shortcut Menu (p. 397)

Power Toys is a set of productivity tools that was developed by the Microsoft Windows Shell Development Team. The tools are enhancements to the Windows 95 operating system and are not part of any shipping product. Power Toys are available, at no cost, from the Microsoft web site but they're not supported through official support channels.

Power Toys can be downloaded as a compressed file from the following Microsoft web site location:
http://www.microsoft.com/windows95/downloads/contents/wutoys/w95pwrtoysset/

> **CAUTION:** *Power Toys are for Windows 95 only. Do not attempt to use them with Windows 98.*

Here's what's in Power Toys:

CabView · · · · · · · · View CAB files just like you would view an ordinary folder.

CDAutoPlay · · · · · · Makes autoplay work on any nonaudio CD.

Command · · · · · · · Right-click a folder and start an MS-DOS prompt at that location.

Contents Menu · · · · Right-click a folder or container and get a cascade menu displaying the contents of the folder one level deep.

Desktop Menu · · · · · Adds a desktop menu to your taskbar.

Explore From Here · Right-click a folder or container and use Explorer with the folder as it's root.

FindX · · · · · · · · · · Lets you add custom commands to the Find menu. Includes Find On The Internet, Find In the Knowledge Base, Find Address, Find E-mail Message.

FlexiCD · · · · · · · · · A taskbar notification that allows you to control audio CDs. FlexiCD provides control for starting, stopping, ejecting and moving between tracks.

Quick Res · · · · · · · · Changes the screen resolution without having to restart your computer.

Round Clock · · · · · · Creates a round analog clock without a square window.

Send To X · · · · · · · · Adds the following commands to the Send To menu: Sent To Any Folder, Sent To Clipboard as Contents, Sent To Clipboard as Name, Sent To Command Line.

Shortcut Target · · · · · Displays the properties for a Menu shortcut's target by right-clicking the shortcut. Adds the complete shortcut menu of the target to the shortcut's shortcut menu.

Telephony Location Selector	Mobile users can change their dialing location from the taskbar.
Tweak UI	A tool that helps you to change menu speed, mouse sensitivity, window animation and sound, shortcut appearance and default names, icons that appear on your desktop, boot parameters and more.
Xmouse	Makes the focus follow the mouse without clicking, like X Windows.

Installing Power Toys

1. Create a folder for Power Toys called Power.

2. Using Microsoft Internet Explorer connect to the following web page: http://www.microsoft.com/windows95/downloads/contents/wutoys/w95pwrtoysset/

3. Click the link on the page to download W95PowerToy.exe.

4. Save the file in your new Power folder.

5. Open the Power folder and double-click the W95PowerToy.exe file.

   This will decompress the file adding several new files to the folder. Be sure to review the readme.txt file for more information.

5. Right-click on the Install.inf file, then click Install.

Hot Tip **Install Selected Programs**: If you want to selectively install the programs, right-click on the .inf file that bears the name of the program, then click Install. Only that program will be installed.

Uninstalling Power Toys

The Power Toys can be individually uninstalled using Add/Remove Programs in the Control Panel. See: "Add/Remove Programs" (p. 42) for more information.

See Also: Add/Remove Programs; Kernel Toys

Print Screen or Window

To print a captured screen, copy the screen to the Clipboard using one of the following commands, paste it into a Paint or WordPad document, then use the Print command to print the screen.

..QuicKeys..

Capture Screen

Print Screen

Capture Active Window

Alt+Print Screen

or

Shift+Print Screen

Printers

Printers

Printers is a Control Panel tool that allows you to install and modify printer drivers. You can also monitor their activities through the use of the print queues. The Printers tool is also available from the Start Menu's Settings option.

..QuicKeys..

Add Printer

Click **Start**, Settings, Printers,

double-click Add Printer

Change Printer Settings

Click **Start**, Settings, Printers,

right-click , Properties

Open Printers Folder

Click **Start**, Settings, Printers,

or

Click **Start**, Settings, Control Panel,

double-click Printers

or

Ctrl+Esc, S, P

Pause Printing

Double-click on the taskbar, click

Printer on the menu bar, Pause Printing

or

Right-click on the taskbar, select

printer, Pause Printing

or

Right-click in the Printers folder, Pause Printing

Print a File

Drag file to

or

Right-click file, Print

or

Select file, click File on the menu bar, Print

Printer Ports, Change

Click **Start**, Settings, Printers,

right-click , Properties, Details,

Print to the following port

Remove Printer

Click **Start**, Settings, Printers,

right-click , Delete

Set As Default

Click **Start**, Settings, Printers,

right-click , Set As Default

View Print Queue

Double-click 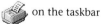 on the taskbar

or

Right-click 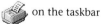 on the taskbar, select printer

or

Right-click in the Printers folder, Open

Add Printers

To add a printer to your system, you must set up a driver in the Printers folder.

1. Click , Settings, then Printers to open the Printers folder.
2. Double-click the Add Printer icon.
   A Wizard will begin to guide you through the process.
3. Click Next at the first prompt.
4. Select Local Printer or Network Printer depending on your needs.
5. If you selected Network Printer, type in the network path to the printer or queue on your network's server, or use the Browse button to find it. Select Yes if you intend to print from MS-DOS applications, then click Next.
6. Select the Manufacturer from the left list box, then select the Printer model from the right list box.
   or
   If the printer is not listed, insert the disk that came with the printer, which has the printer driver on it. Click Have Disk, select the appropriate drive, then click OK.
7. Select the port that the printer will be connected to, then click OK.
8. Type in a name for your printer, then indicate whether this printer will be the default printer for Windows. There can be only one default printer selected at any one time.

9. If you want to print a test page select the option, then click <u>F</u>inish.

Your printer is now installed and ready to use.

HOt Tip **Create Additional Printers Folder**: You can create an additional Printers folder by giving the folder a specific name. To do this, right-click your Desktop, select <u>N</u>ew and then Folder. Type the following name for the folder: **Printers.{2227A280-3AEA-1069-A2DE-08002B30309D}**. When you press *Enter* to save the name, only "Printers" will be displayed for the name, the rest will be hidden. You can now drag this new folder to your Start button, Office toolbar or anywhere you would like.

95

HOt Tip **Enhanced Printer Troubleshooter**: If you are having problems with your printer, you can get additional help from the Enhanced Printer Troubleshooter (Epts.exe) which is located in the \Other\Misc\Epts folder on the Windows 95 CD. Double-click the Epts.exe file and follow the instructions.

Default Location: \Control Panel\Printers
See Also: Control Panel

Printing

..QuicKeys..

Add Printer

Click **Start**, Settings, Printers,

double-click Add Printer

Change Printer Settings

Click **Start**, Settings, Printers,

right-click , Properties

Open Printers Folder

Click **Start**, Settings, Printers

or

Click **Start**, Settings, Printers,

double-click Printers

or

Ctrl+Esc, S, P

Pause Printing

Double-click on the taskbar,

click Printer on the menu bar, Pause Printing

or

Right-click on the taskbar,

select *printer*, Pause Printing

or

Right-click in the Printers folder,

Pause Printing

Print a File

Drag *file* to

or

In Explorer or My Computer, right-click *file*, Print

or

Select *file*, click File on the menu bar, Print

or

ALT+F, P

Printer Ports, Change

Click **Start**, Settings, Printers,

right-click , Properties, Details,

Print to the following port:

Remove Printer

Click **Start**, Settings, Printers,

right-click , Delete

Set As Default

Click **Start**, Settings, Printers,

right-click , Set As Default

View Print Queue

Double-click 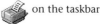 on the taskbar

or

Right-click on the taskbar, select *printer*

or

Right-click in the Printers folder, <u>O</u>pen

Programs

See: Applications (p. 51)

Program Manager

Progman

The Windows 3.x *Program Manager* still exists in Windows 98 and Windows 95; however, you will probably find that the new tools have more to offer.

The Desktop, Start menu and the Programs menu have replaced the functionality of the Program Manager.

To open Program Manager, go to Windows Explorer, and double-click Progman.exe. If you plan to use Program Manager on a regular basis, create a shortcut to it.

Default Location: \Windows\Progman.exe

See Also: Desktop; Shortcuts; Start Menu; Start Menu|Programs

Quick-Fix Engineering

Qfecheck

Quick-Fix Engineering is a tool you can use to find out which versions of system files that have been updated are installed on your computer. This tool can also be used to check whether the versions installed match the versions listed in your computer's registry.

Quick Access

Click , Run, type **qfecheck.exe**,

then click OK.

Registered Updates

When a system update is installed it is recorded in your Registry. *Registered Updates* displays a list of those system file updates. To see the file name and version number expand the entry by double-clicking an update icon or click the "+" next to the entry.

If a file or component on your computer does not match the version listed in your computer's registry, it is marked as Invalid. If it is designated as Not Found, either the file is not installed on your computer, or the Update Information tool cannot find the file on your computer.

HOt Tip **Problems with Programs Associated with Update**: If you are having problems with programs that are associated with an update, reinstall the update. This will often resolve problems with files marked Invalid and Not Found.

Updated Files Found

Some system update files may not be in the Registry. To find files that have not been registered, click the Search Files button on the Updated Files Found tab, and then specify the path you want to search.

When the search is complete you may have files listed that do not appear on the Registered Updates list. In most cases it's probably because you installed an update without using the installation program, or you installed one of the early update releases.

Note: The list of files on the Registered Updates tab is not affected when you search for files on the Updated Files Found tab.

Default Location: \Windows\Qfecheck.exe

See Also: Updating Windows 95; Version, Windows Update

Quick View

Quikview

Quick View is a program that lets you preview many types of files without having to open their original application. Quick View is particularly helpful when you want to delete a file and would like to see what's in the file before you delete it. Since you don't have to open the application you have virtually instantaneous access to the files.

Quick Access

Right-click the *file*, then Quick View

or

Select the *file*, click File on the menu bar, then Quick View

or

Drag a *file* to an open Quick View window

Note: If Quick View is not available on the shortcut menu, it either hasn't been installed or there is no viewer available for the file type you are trying to view. See: "Installing" below.

H0t Tip **If Quick View does not show up for files that do not have a standard registered file type**, you can do one of three things:

1. Enable the Quick View option for the file type (you may have to add the file type if it's something unique).

2. Create a shortcut for Quick View in the Send To folder.

3. Create a shortcut for Quick View on your desktop, then you can drag and drop files onto it.

Editing Files from Quick View

Quick View is strictly a viewer. No editing or modifications can be made directly to the files while in the Quick View window. If you need to edit the file, however, you can open the file's original application from the Quick View menu bar using File, Open, Open File for Editing or click on the toolbar.

Changing Views

There are several options you can use to change the look and feel of the Quick View window and the file displayed. These options are all located on the View menu.

Toolbar

The *toolbar* is on by default. It provides quick access to several options including Open File for Editing, Increase Font Size, Decrease Font Size and Replace Window. These options can also be accessed through the menus.

Status Bar

The *Status Bar* is on by default and displays a description of the toolbar buttons or menu options on the bottom of the window.

Page View

Page View switches between document view and page view.

Replace Window

By default, Quick View opens a separate window for each new view.
If *Replace Window* is selected, each new view will be displayed in the current window. This option is also available on the toolbar .

Landscape

Landscape is used to switch from portrait to landscape view.

Rotate

Depending on the file type, *Rotate* can be used to rotate the image 90 degrees for each time it is executed.

Font

The style and size of the font used in the Quick View window can be changed using the Font option. The default is Arial 10 pt. The font size can also be increased or decreased using the two buttons on the toolbar: .

Additional Viewers: Microsoft supplies viewers for many of the common file formats. If you are looking for additional viewers, you can contact the company that wrote the Quick View program for Microsoft, Inso Corportation. Their software product, Quick View Plus 4.5, extends the viewing capabilities of Windows to over 200 file formats. A trial version containing 30 fully functional viewers is available on their web site, (http://www.inso.com). You can also contact them at:

Inso Corporation
401 N. Wabash, Suite 600
Chicago, IL 60611
800-333-1395
312-329-0700

Installing

Quick View is not installed by default when you choose the Typical Installation during setup. If it does not appear on the shortcut menu, you will have to install it. To install Quick View:

1. Click **Start**, Settings, then the Add/Remove Programs icon in Control Panel.

2. Click on the Windows Setup tab.

3. Select the Accessories option from the Components list, then click the Details button.

4. Scroll down, find Quick View, then select it.

5. If you don't have your CAB files available on your hard disk, you will need to have your Windows 9x CD or diskettes available.

6. Click OK.

Quick View is now available on your shortcut menu.

Default Location:
\Windows\System\Viewers\Quikview.exe

See Also: File Types; Explorer|Options|File Types; CAB Files

Recycle Bin

Recycle Bin

The *Recycle Bin* is a temporary storage area for files that have been deleted from the hard disk drive(s). When a file is deleted, it is moved to the Recycle Bin and then at a later time, depending on the actions you take or the properties you have set, the files will be permanently removed from the drive(s). If you inadvertently delete a file, you can restore it from the Recycle Bin as long as the Recycle Bin has not been emptied.

Note: If the Recycle Bin has files in it, the trash can icon on the desktop shows paper coming out of the top. If there are no files in the Recycle Bin, the trash can appears empty.

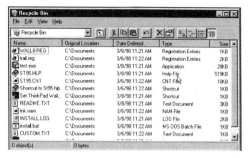

Quick Access

Double-click on the desktop.

Recycle Bin

CAUTION: *Files deleted from the MS-DOS prompt, a floppy diskette or a network server's hard drive are not moved to the Recycle Bin - they are permanently deleted.*

HÔt Tip **To view or edit one of the files in the Recycle Bin**, drag and drop it onto its application's executable file and it will be opened in the application. When you are finished, just close the file or save it under a new name. There's no need to delete it, since it was never restored.

Emptying the Recycle Bin

If you want to delete files permanently from your disk drive and recover the disk space they occupy, delete them from the Recycle Bin. The Recycle Bin may periodically empty itself (see "Maximum Size of Recycle Bin" below). However, you may find you want to empty it completely or selectively at other times.

To empty the Recycle Bin from the desktop:

Right-click on the desktop, then

Recycle Bin

click Empty Recycle Bin

To empty the Recycle Bin from within the Recycle Bin:

Click File on the menu bar, then Empty Recycle Bin

To selectively empty the Recycle Bin:

Select the *files* or *folders*, click File on the menu bar, then Delete

Restoring Files and Folders

The purpose of the Recycle Bin is to allow you to recover (restore) files or folders you have deleted. It provides you with a second chance, in case you've made a mistake or changed your mind.

When files or folders are moved to the Recycle Bin, their name and path are stored with them. This is very convenient since you don't have to remember where the file came from when it comes time to restore it. If the original folder does not exist, you will be prompted for permission to recreate it. You can, however, restore a file to a folder other than its original folder, if necessary.

To restore files or folders:

Select the *files* or *folders*, click File on the menu bar, then Restore

or

Right-click the *files* or *folders*, then click Restore

Select the *files* or *folders*, then click

or

Select the *files* or *folders*, click <u>E</u>dit on the menu bar, then <u>U</u>ndo delete

or

Right-click the *files* or *folders*, then click <u>U</u>ndo delete.

Note: To restore a file or folder to a folder other than its original folder, just move it from the Recycle Bin to its new folder, rather than using the Restore command.

H&t Tip **Find a File in Recycle Bin**: There is no *Find* command available within the Recycle Bin window; however, you can use the column headings to sort the files and folders. By default, the files and folders are sorted by name. Changing the sorted order (by clicking the column heading) to Original Location, Date Deleted, Type or Size may help you find a file or folder you are looking for. For example, use Original Location to group files by folder, or use Date Deleted to list from oldest to newest or newest to oldest. Note: *If you don't see any column headings, switch the View to Details.*

H&t Tip **Undo a Deletion**: If you delete a file or folder and realize you made a mistake, you can immediately use the <u>U</u>ndo command to reverse the process, rather than having to restore from the Recycle Bin.

Undeleting Files

When files are emptied from the Recycle Bin they can no longer be recovered using tools within Windows. However, if you have a previous version of MS-DOS 6.x you can use its Undelete.exe program to try to recover your files. Here's how:

1. Copy the Undelete.exe file to your \Windows\Command folder.

2. Restart your computer in MS-DOS mode (Undelete must be run from DOS).

3. At the DOS prompt, type **lock**, then Enter.

4. Type **undelete**, then *Enter*.
   Follow the prompts to undelete files.

5. When you are finished undeleting, type **unlock**, then *Enter*.

6. To start Windows, type **exit**, then *Enter*.

Note: When a file has been deleted, the file remains on the disk drive. However, the first character of the file name is changed, which prohibits the system from displaying it. The Undelete command allows you to change that first character back to what it was. If the file has been written over with another file, even Undelete cannot help you recover the file.

Properties

The Recycle Bin has properties that can be set which determine how deleted files are processed and how the Recycle Bin works.

To view and configure the properties:

> Right-click on the desktop, then click P̲roperties
>
or
>
> Double-click on the desktop, click F̲ile on the menu bar, then P̲roperties

Configure drives independently

> Select this property if you want to configure each disk drive separately. When selected, each drive will have its own properties tab in which you can make adjustments.

Use one setting for all drives

> Select this property if you want to set up all your drives using the same settings. Each drive will still maintain its own Recycle Bin, but they will all use the same settings.

Do not move files to Recycle Bin

> When this property is selected, files that are deleted do not go into the Recycle Bin, but are permanently deleted. Selecting this property effectively disables the Recycle Bin.

HOt Tip **To delete an individual file or folder permanently**, hold down the *SHIFT* key while deleting them. The file or folder will not go to the Recycle Bin but will be permanently removed from the disk drive at the time of deletion.

Maximum size of Recycle Bin

> The Recycle Bin periodically empties itself, permanently deleting the oldest files first. The maximum storage area allowed on the hard disk for deleted files is controlled by this

setting. It's based on a percentage of your hard disk space. If you have the setting set at 10%, which is the default, the Recycle Bin will reserve 10% of the total hard drive space for deleted files. Once this area is filled it will begin to permanently delete the oldest files first from the Recycle Bin.

Hot Tip **To determine the proper size for your Recycle Bin**, open the Recycle Bin, then click the Date Deleted column heading twice, sorting the items in reverse chronological order. Scroll down the list and permanently delete all items that are over one month old. Now, select all items by pressing *CTRL+A,* then look at the amount of space displayed in the status bar of the Recycle Bin window. Convert this number to a percentage of your total drive space and set the maximum size of the Recycle Bin appropriately.

Display delete confirmation dialog

When this property is selected, a confirmation dialog box is displayed every time you attempt to delete a file or folder.

CAUTION: *If this property is not selected, files will be deleted immediately and no warning will be displayed.*

Recycle Bin Icon: To change the name of the Recycle Bin icon, remove the icon, or change the default icon you can do so in the Registry.

Using **Regedit**, open the Registry and move to HKEY_CLASSES_ROOT\CLSID subtree. Open the folder whose name is 645FF040-5081-101B-9F08-00AA002F9 54E. To change the name, double-click the default icon in the right pane to edit the data. Replace "Recycle Bin" with whatever you want.

To change the icon, expand the folder 645FF040-5081-101B-9F08-00AA002F9 54E, then open the DefaultIcon folder. Double-click the appropriate entry in the right pane to edit the data. Replace the path and icon name with whatever you want.

..QuicKeys..

Adjust Size of Recycle Bin

Right-click Recycle Bin, P<u>r</u>operties, move slider to adjust size

or

Select Recycle Bin, *Alt+Enter*, move slider to adjust size

Delete All Files and Folders

Right-click Recycle Bin, Empty Recycle <u>B</u>in

Delete Selected Files or Folders

Right-click *file* or *folder*, <u>D</u>elete

or

Click <u>F</u>ile on the menu bar, <u>D</u>elete

or

Alt+F, D

Open

Double-click Recycle Bin

Restore All Files and Folders

Select all *files* and *folders*, right-click a *file* or *folder*, <u>R</u>estore

or

Select all *files* and *folders*, click <u>F</u>ile on the menu bar, <u>R</u>estore

Restore File or Folder

Right-click *file* or *folder*, <u>R</u>estore

or

Select *file* or *folder*, click <u>F</u>ile on the menu bar, <u>R</u>estore

or

Select *file* or *folder*, *Alt+F, E*

Default Location: \Desktop\Recycle Bin

See Also: Copying Files & Folders; Deleting Files & Folders; Section 4 —File Types; Moving Files & Folders; Selecting Files & Folders; Undo; View

RegClean

RegClean is a utility used to scan the Registry and clean up unnecessary entries for Windows, Internet Explorer 3.0 and 4.x, all versions of Microsoft Office and Visual Basic. RegClean analyzes the Registry for erroneous values in the keys, records them in an undo file, then removes them from the Registry.

Installing RegClean

To use RegClean you first need to download a copy of the program from Microsoft's Support web site:

> http://support.microsoft.com/support/
> downloads/DP3049.ASP.

CAUTION: *The most current version of RegClean fixes several problems that existed in previous versions. Be sure to use at least version 4.1a build 7364.*

Using RegClean

To use RegClean:

1. Double-click the RegClean icon.
   A progress dialog box is displayed.

Caution: RegClean may take up to 30 minutes to analyze your Registry. At times it may have appeared to have stopped working when checking remote or removable drives. Have patience and let it finish.

Once RegClean has finished and the progress meters have disappeared, you are prompted to either exit RegClean or allow RegClean to fix the errors that it found.

2. If RegClean did not find any errors, or if you don't want to fix errors it found, click Cancel.

or

   If RegClean found errors and you want to fix them, click Fix Errors.

3. When the progress meter disappears, RegClean has finished. Click Exit to close the window.

Undoing RegClean

When RegClean fixes the Registry, it creates an undo file named Undo *computer yyyymmddhhmmss*.reg. To undo, or put back what RegClean removed from the Registry, just double-click the file.

See Also: Registry; Registry Editor

Regedit.exe

See: Registry Editor (p. 361)

Regional Settings

Regional Settings

Regional Settings is a Control Panel tool that you can use to set the default formats for numbers, currency, time and date. These formats can be set up by country, which will apply the proper formatting for all of the items to meet that country's needs. This is usually sufficient, but you can customize each of the items to meet specific requirements.

Quick Access

Click , Settings, Control Panel,

Regional Settings

You can change the Regional Settings to any of the available languages and/or countries using the drop-down list. When you select a particular language and/or country, the settings under all the other tabs will change to the appropriate format.

It's usually best to set up the initial settings using the Regional Settings, then go into each tab to customize the individual settings.

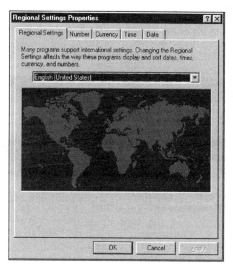

Note: Changing the Regional Settings to a different country does not change the language support or keyboard layout. To change these settings, use the Keyboard tool in the Control Panel.

Microsoft and other application developers make specific-language versions of their products. Contact the specific publisher for more information.

Each of the items under the Number, Currency, Time and Date tabs is fairly self explanatory. Select the tab you want to work in and use the drop-down lists to make any changes you feel necessary. Click OK to save your changes.

Note: The settings in Regional Settings, whether customized or not, are defaults. If a particular application chooses to override these settings or not use them, it can. If you seem to be having conflicts with an application, consult with the publisher to resolve the problem.

Default Location:
\Control Panel\Regional Settings

See Also: Accessibility Options; Character Map; Keyboard; Multilanguage Support

Registry

The *Registry* is a database that stores configuration settings for both the operating system and the applications that run on it. It replaces the .ini files from Windows 3.x, and the Autoexec.bat and Config.sys files of MS-DOS.

It is composed of two files, *User.dat* and *System.dat*. The User.dat file contains user-specific information such as user profiles, desktop settings, personal printers and network settings. System.dat contains information about hardware, software and computer specific settings. By default, both files are stored in the Windows folder; however, under certain circumstances they could be stored in other locations.

CAUTION: *Since the Registry contains important configuration information, changes to it could create problems with the operating system or applications. Be careful. These problems can be as serious as the computer not being able to boot up, or applications not running and functioning properly.*

Editing the Registry

To make changes to the Registry, use the Registry Editor. For more information on the Registry Editor see the section "Registry Editor (p. 361)."

Backing Up and Restoring the Registry

If you plan on making changes to the Registry, it's always a good idea to make a backup copy before you begin. Windows automatically backs up your Registry every time you start your computer; however, in Windows 95 it overwrites the previous backup. In many cases, without knowing it, you can overwrite a perfectly good Registry backup with a bad one. Windows 98, by default, stores five backups and that number can be increased to 99. For more information, see "ScanReg."

There are several methods that can be used to back up your Registry on demand rather than depend on the backups created when you start up.

Using the Registry Checker

Windows 98 provides the *Registry Checker*, an MS-DOS based utility, for scanning, backing up, and restoring the Registry. See the section "Registry Checker"(p. 357) for more information.

Copy Registry Files

One method that is easy to do is to copy the Registry files and place them in a designated backup folder. Here's how:

1. Create a folder in your Windows folder called RegBackup.

2. Restart your computer choosing Safe Mode Command Prompt Only. For more information see "Startup Menu." (pg. 432)

3. At the MD-DOS command prompt, type **attrib –h –s –r system.dat**, then press *Enter.*

4. Now at the MD-DOS command prompt type **attrib –h –s –r user.dat**, then press *Enter*.

These two commands set the attributes of the files so that you can copy them to another location.

5. Type **copy system.dat \Windows\RegBackup**, then press *Enter.*

6. Now type **copy user.dat \Windows\RegBackup**, then press *Enter.*

7. Reset the file attributes by typing type **attrib +h +s +r system.dat**, then press *Enter.*

8. Do the same for user.dat. Type **attrib +h +s +r user.dat**, then press *Enter*.

You now have copies stored in a safe place.

To restore your Registry, start your computer in Safe Mode Command Prompt Only, then copy the backup files back to their original location.

 Create a Batch File: Include the commands above in a batch file for easy execution.

Hot Tip **Secure Your Backup**: Make sure that the folder that you store your backups in, whether you're using this backup method or another method, is included in your standard backup selection. You want to have a secured copy stored away from your computer.

95 Using the Configuration Backup Utility

Windows 95 comes with a utility called CfgBack, which you can use to backup the Registry. CfgBack can make up to nine different backups. You can use any one of those backups when it's time to restore.

> **CAUTION**: *CfgBack only runs in Windows, so if your computer isn't operating properly you won't be able to use CfgBack to restore your Registry.*

To install the backup utility, follow the next few steps:

1. Create a folder on your hard drive called Registry Backup.
2. Load the Windows 95 CD and copy all the files in the \Other\Misc\Cfgback folder, then paste them into to the Registry Backup folder.
3. Create a shortcut to the Cfgback.exe for quick access.

To Back Up your Registry Using CfgBack:

1. Double-click the CfgBack shortcut or the Cfgback.exe file.
2. Type a unique name for your backup in the Selected Name Backup text box.
3. Click the Backup button.

4. You'll be asked if you want to continue with the backup. Click Yes.

5. When the backup process has finished, you'll receive confirmation that it was successful. Click OK.

The name you typed in at the beginning of the process will now appear in the List of Previous Backups box.

To Restore your Registry Using CfgBack:

> **CAUTION:** *Don't attempt to use your computer for any other purpose while using CfgBack to restore your registry. CfgBack may terminate prematurely which may prohibit you from restarting Windows.*

1. Double-click the CfgBack shortcut or the Cfgback.exe file.

2. Select the backup you want to restore from the List of Previous Backups list box.

3. Click Restore.

4. You'll be warned that you are about to replace your current Registry with a backup copy. If you're sure you want to do that, click Yes to continue.

Exporting the Registry

You can export and import the Registry using the Registry Editor or its command line equivalent Regedit.exe. Both create a text file (.reg) which can then be imported to restore the Registry. See the section "Registry Editor" (pg. 361) for more information.

Recreating the Registry

If you have some sort of corruption in your Registry you may receive a Windows Protection Fault error during the boot-up process. The following steps show you how to recreate the Registry:

1. Restart your computer in MS-DOS mode by pressing *Shift+F5* when you see Starting Windows 9x or use your Windows Startup disk to boot your system.

2. At the C:\ prompt type **regedit /e reg.reg** and press *Enter*.

3. Type **cd Windows** and press *Enter*.

4. Type **attrib -h -s -r system.dat** and press *Enter*.

5. Type **attrib -h -s -r user.dat** and press *Enter*.

6. Type **ren system.dat system.bup** and press *Enter*.

7. Type **ren user.dat user.bup** and press *Enter*. The .bup files can be deleted later, after you're sure Windows is working properly.

8. Type **cd **, then *Enter*.

9. At the C:\ prompt type **regedit /c reg.reg** and press *Enter*.

10. Reboot your computer.

Default Location: \Windows\User.dat and System.dat

See Also: Backup; Emergency Recovery Utility; Registry Editor; RegClean; ScanReg

The *Registry Checker* is a Windows 98 utility for scanning, backing up, and restoring the Registry. It finds and fixes registry problems and routinely backs up the Registry every time Windows starts up. If the Registry Checker finds a serious problem with the Registry, it tries to restore the most recent backup copy. If there is no backup copy, it tries to repair the Registry. This can also be accomplished manually by executing ScanReg /fix at the MS-DOS command prompt.

The Registry Checker also compacts the Registry if it finds unused space. This reduces the size of the Registry, which improves performance.

The Registry Checker maintains five compressed backups by default. Each new backup replaces the oldest file. These files are stored in the \Windows\Sysbackup folder, which is a hidden folder. The file name used is Rb*xxx*.cab, where *xxx* is a unique number automatically assigned when it is created. The backup file contains copies of the entire Registry including, User.dat, System.dat, Win.ini, and System.ini.

The Registry Checker can be run manually in protected mode using ScanRegW.exe or in real mode using ScanReg.exe.

Running the Registry Checker and Backing Up the Registry

To run the Registry Checker manually:

In Windows:

1. Click **Start**, then <u>R</u>un.
2. Type **scanregw**, then click OK

3. If the Registry does not have any problems click Yes; otherwise, click No.

4. When the backup is complete, click OK.

In MS-DOS:

1. Restart your computer choosing Command Prompt Only. For more information see "Startup Menu."

2. At the MS-DOS command prompt type **scanreg**, then press *Enter*.

3. Select Start, then press *Enter*.

4. Select Create Backups, then press *Enter*.

5. When the backup is complete, press *Enter*.

6. Restart your computer.

CAUTION: *Before running ScanReg in MS-DOS, be sure that Himem.sys is available. You may have to add one of the following commands to your Config.sys so that the system can find Himem.sys.*

  Device=a:\Himem.sys

or

  Device=c:\Windows\Himem.sys

To Restore Your Registry

1. Restart your computer choosing Command Prompt Only. For more information see "Startup Menu" (p. 432).

2. At the MS-DOS command prompt, type **scanreg /restore**, then press *Enter*.

3. Select the backup file you want to restore from, select Restore, then press *Enter*.

4. When the Registry Checker is finished restoring the Registry, press *Enter* to restart your computer.

Command

Scanregw (Windows)

Scanreg (MS-DOS)

Options for both:

/Backup ....Creates a backup of the Registry without prompting the user.

"/comment=" ....Specifies that a comment is attached to the backup which can be displayed with the /restore option.

Options for Scanregw only:

/Autoscan ....Scans the Registry every time it is run but only creates a backup once per day.

/Scanonly ....Scans the Registry every time it is run returning an error level but does not create a backup.

Options for Scanreg only:

/Restore ....Lists all backup files available sorted by date and time.

/Fix ....Repairs the Registry.

Changing Configuration Settings for ScanReg

The Registry Checker's default settings can be modified by editing the ScanReg.ini file. ScanReg.ini is located in the \Windows folder and can be edited using Notepad. Following are the settings and their descriptions:

Backup= ....Enables and disables the Registry Checker backups. Backup= 0 disables Backup= 1 enables

MaxBackupCopies= .....Maximum number of backups to store. Values can be from 0 to 99. The default is five.

BackupDirectory= ....Specifies the location of the backup folder where the CAB files are stored. The default is: \Windows\Sysbckup.

Files=[dir code,]............Adds system files to be
file1,file2,file3   backed up. The dir code can be:
10: windir (ex. C:\windows)
11: system dir (ex. C:\windows\system)
30: boot dir (ex.c:\)
31: boot host dir (ex. c:\)

Optimize= ....Enables and disables automatic Registry optimization. Optimize=0 disables Optimize=1 enables

Default Locations: \Windows\ScanRegW.exe \Windows\Command\ScanReg.exe \Windows\ScanReg.ini

See Also: RegClean; Registry; Registry Editor

Registry Editor

Regedit

Microsoft provides a tool called the *Registry Editor* that is used to make changes in the Windows Registry. The editor displays the contents of the Registry in six keys. Each of these keys contains subkeys, which are reached through a hierarchical structure similar to the one used in Windows Explorer.

> **CAUTION:** *The following instructions involve changing settings in the Registry. If the changes are not made properly, serious problems may result. Be sure to backup your Registry before continuing. See: "Registry" for more information about backing up the Registry.*

Editing the Registry

To make changes to the Registry:

1. Click **🔳 Start** , then <u>R</u>un

2. In the Open text box, type **regedit**, then click OK.
   The Registry Editor window opens.

 If you plan to use the Registry Editor regularly, **create a shortcut for regedit.exe** and copy it to your desktop or another appropriate location.

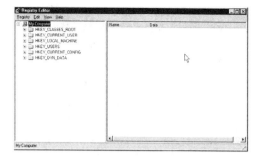

The Registry is organized into keys and subkeys. You can navigate through the keys just like you would in Windows Explorer. For more information on navigating in Windows Explorer, see the section "Windows Explorer" (p. 488).

Searching the Registry

If you need to find an entry in a key or subkey, but you don't know where it's located, you can search for it using a word or phrase that you know is contained in the key or subkey. To search for a word or phrase:

1. Open the Registry Editor.
2. Click Edit on the menu bar, then Find.

or

Press *Ctrl+F*
The Find dialog box is displayed.

3. Type in the word or phrase you want to find, then click Find Next.
You may want to further refine your search using the Look at or Match whole string only options.

4. Find will select the first key or subkey that contains what you searched for. If it's not what you're looking for:
Click <u>E</u>dit on the menu bar then <u>F</u>ind Next.

or

Press *F3*
Find will move to the next match.

Editing a Subkey

Once you find the subkey you want to edit, you can make changes to it as follows:

1. Select the subkey in the right pane of the Registry Editor.
2. Click <u>E</u>dit on the menu bar, then Modify.
   or
   Right-click the subkey, then click Modify.
   The Edit String dialog box is opened.
3. Make the changes to the text string in the Value Data text box, then click OK to save your changes.

Deleting a Subkey

To delete a subkey:

1. Select the subkey in the right pane of the Registry Editor.
2. Click Edit on the menu bar, then Delete.
   or
   Right-click the subkey, then click Delete.
   The subkey is deleted.

Activating Registry Changes

To assure that any changes you have made to the Registry are in effect, you can do one of two things:

Shut down Windows, then restart Windows

or

> Shut down Explorer (the Windows administrator, not Windows Explorer), then restart Explorer

Shutting down Windows takes quite a bit of time; however, shutting down Explorer takes significantly less time. Here's how to shutdown Explorer:

1. Press *Ctrl+Alt+Del*.

2. Select Explorer in the Close Program dialog box.

3. Click the End Task button.

4. When the Shut Down Windows dialog box is displayed, click No (Cancel in Internet Explorer 4.x).

5. In a few seconds an information box will be displayed. Click End Task.
   Windows can only be active if a copy of Explorer is running. Since you've just removed it, Windows will try to load it again. When it loads, Explorer reads the settings from the Registry, incorporating any changes that have been made to it.

Importing and Exporting

The Registry can be imported, exported or recreated using the commands listed on the Registry menu in the Registry Editor. When the Registry is exported, whether it be the whole registry or just a specific branch, a .reg file is created. When you need to restore the Registry you import these .reg files.

When the Registry is so badly corrupted that you can't start Windows, you can use the command line version of Regedit to accomplish the same tasks. On the startup disk you'll find Regedit.exe which you can use with the following command syntax and options.

Command

Regedit [/**L**:*system*] [/**R**:*user*] *file1.reg, file1a.reg...*

Regedit [/**L**:*system*] [/**R**:*user*] /**E** *file3.reg* [*regkey*]

Regedit [/**L**:*system*] [/**R**:*user*] /**C** *file2.reg*

Options:

/**L**:*system* ....Specifies the location of System.dat.

/**R**:*user* ....Specifies the location of User.dat.

file1.reg ....Specifies one or more .reg files to import into the Registry.

/**E** *file3.reg*......................Specifies the filename to which the Registry should be exported.

Regkey ....Regkey is optional. It specifies the starting point (Registry key) from which an export will take place. If no regkey is specified, the command regedit /e exports the entire Registry.

/**C** *file2.reg* ....Specifies the .reg file to use to replace the entire contents of the Registry.

Default Locations: \Windows\Regedit.exe and on the Windows startup disk

See Also: RegClean; Registry

Removing Hardware Device Drivers

See: System|Device Manager|Remove (p. 438)

Renaming Disks

Each diskette or disk drive can be renamed with an eleven character name called a volume label. Spaces are allowed; however, you cannot use + , = [ ] / \ ; * ? " : < > | . The displayed names for diskettes will default to the description and logical drive letter. The displayed names for disk drives will default to the logical drive letter. For example: 3½ Floppy (A:) or (C:)

If a name is given to a diskette, the name will not be displayed in My Computer or Windows Explorer; however, if a name is provided for a disk drive, the name will display with the drive letter; for example: My Drive (C:).

Quick Access

Double-click [My Computer] , right-click the

disk *drive* icon you want to rename, click Properties, on the General tab at the Label field, type the new *name*, then click OK.

Note: CD-ROM drives cannot be renamed. When you view the icon for a CD-ROM drive, notice that the icon name dynamically changes to reflect the name of the CD it was given at the time of manufacture.

See Also: Formatting Disks; Naming Disks

Renaming Files & Folders

In Windows 9x you can use up to 255 characters to rename files and folders. This makes renaming files and folders much easier than in the previous Windows and MS-DOS convention of 8.3 or 11 characters. Spaces are allowed, but you cannot use / \ ; * ? " : < > | .

Even though you can use long file names up to 255 characters, you should limit the length of your names so that they can be easily typed, and so that when used in a path, the total length of the path does not exceed the limit of 260 characters.

Quick Access

Click the *file* or *folder* name, pause, click it a second time. The name should appear selected. Type the new **name**, replacing the existing name, then press **Enter.**

or

Right-click the *file* or *folder* name, click Rename, type the new **name**, replacing the existing name, then press **Enter.**

or

Select the *file* or *folder*, press **F2**, type the new **name**, replacing the existing name, then press **Enter.**

Note: If you make a mistake while renaming a file or folder, press **Esc** to cancel the process and return to the original name. If you've already saved the change, use the Undo command to reverse the process.

CAUTION: *If the extensions for registered files are not displayed when you see them in My Computer or Windows Explorer, do not type the extension when renaming the files. Do so will add the extension on to the already existing (but hidden) extension. For example, if the existing file is named Old File.doc and the new file name you type is New File.doc, the resulting file name would be New File.doc.doc.*

CAUTION: *If you are accessing files across a network, you may not be able to use long file names. The server you are working with determines whether or not it will recognize or preserve long file names.*

Hot Tip **Use Rename Command for Multiple Files:** If you need to rename more than one file at a time using wildcards, you can still do so using the Rename command at the MS-DOS command line prompt.

See Also: Naming Files & Folders; Rename; Undo

Resource Kit

See: Windows 95 Resource Kit (p. 487); Windows 98 Resource Kit (p. 487).

Resource Meter

Rsrcmtr

The *Resource Meter* is used to monitor the amount of memory that Windows, applications and other resources are currently using. If you are running out of memory while running multiple applications at the same time, you can determine which applications are using the most memory by working with the Resource Meter.

The three resources that are monitored are:

- **System Resources** - used by system objects, for example, windows, dialog boxes and icons.

- **User Resources** - used by interface-related objects, for example, windows and dialog boxes.

- **GDI** (Graphical Device Interface) **Resources** - used by graphical objects such as icons and other system graphical objects.

Quick Access

Click **Start**, Programs, Accessories, System Tools, Resource Meter

Note: If the Resource Meter is not available under System Tools, it most likely hasn't been installed. To install it, use Add/Remove Programs, Windows Setup in the Control Panel. The Resource Meter is listed as "System Resource Meter" under Accessories.

Displaying Memory Usage

To display the memory usage:

> Double-click the Resource Meter icon, ▓
> in the status area of the taskbar. The follow-
> ing window will be displayed:

or

> Right-click the Resource Meter icon ▓ ,
> then Details

or

> Hold the mouse pointer over the Resource
> Meter icon ▓

> and wait for the following display to
> appear:

CAUTION: *The Resource Meter uses memory while it's running, but when you close the Resource Meter you will gain back that memory.*

Determining Memory Usage

To find out which applications are using the most memory follow the next few steps:

1. Record the memory usage with all applications running.

2. Close the suspect application and then take a look at the Resource Meter again. The difference is the amount of memory the application was using.

3. Follow the same procedure with each application to determine which ones are using the most of memory.

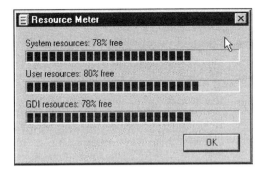

Exiting the Resource Meter

To exit the Resource Meter and reclaim the memory it is using, right-click the Resource Meter icon 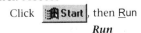, then click Exit.

Default Location: \Windows\Rsrcmtr.exe

See Also: System|Performance;
System Information

Restoring Files & Folders

See: Recycle Bin|Restoring Files & Folders (p. 347)

Run

Run allows you to execute programs, open documents or open folders using a command line approach.

Quick Access

Click **Start**, then Run

or

Ctrl+Esc, then *R*

or

Win+R (Microsoft Natural Keyboard)

Using Run

To use Run, follow these steps:

1. Once the Run dialog box is open, type the program filename or the path to the folder you want to open in the Open text box. You can enter the name by typing, selecting from the drop-down list box, or using the browse function.
   To connect to a shared computer, be sure to type its full network path in the Open text box.

2. Click OK to start the program or open a folder.

HOt Tip **Avoid Typing!** You can drag programs, documents or folders into Run's Open text box and Windows will type out the full path for you including file extensions. You can modify the text and then execute the command.

HOt Tip **Control Contents of List Box**: If you feel the selections in the drop-down list box are getting unmanageable you can delete or edit the items in the Registry.

CAUTION: *The following instructions involve changing settings in the Registry. If the changes are not made properly, serious problems may result. Be sure to backup your Registry before continuing.*

Using Regedit, navigate through the Registry to:
\HKEY_CURRENT_USER\Software\ Microsoft\Windows\CurrentVersion\ Explorer\RunMRU.
In the right pane all the items will be listed. You can edit an item by double clicking it or you can delete an item by selecting it, then pressing *Delete*. Do not, however, delete the MRUList.

See Also: Applications; Registry

Safe Mode

Safe Mode is an alternative startup option that is used to help in a diagnostic process. When you start Windows in Safe Mode it uses basic default settings with minimum functionality. Generic rather than device specific drivers are used, and the use of printers, modems, CD-ROMs, and other external devices is not allowed. You can, however, choose to start in Safe Mode with network functionality, which is useful in certain situations.

Quick Access

Use the following keystrokes during the startup process when re-booting your computer. Press the keys just before the Windows graphic screen appears.

Windows in Safe Mode

> *F5*

or

> *Shift*

or

> *F8, 3*

Windows in Safe Mode with Network

> *F6*

or

> *F8, 4*

Note: If Windows is has a problem starting up, it may start in Safe Mode without your intervention. If this happens, first try using Shutdown to shut down your computer, then restart your computer normally. If it starts up normally you're ready to go; if not you'll have to dig deeper to find the problem.

See Also: Starting Windows; Startup Menu; System Configuration Utility

ScanDisk

Scandskw

ScanDisk is a utility that analyzes your hard drives and diskettes and repairs any errors that it finds. It works on both standard physical drives and compressed drives.

ScanDisk can correct problems with the drive surface, corrupt files and directories, the File Allocation Table (FAT) and compressed volume files (CVF).

Note: ScanDisk does not work on network drives, CD-ROM drives or drives created using the DOS commands such as SUBST, ASSIGN, JOIN or INTERLINK.

CAUTION: *Do not run previous versions of ScanDisk with Windows 9x. Earlier versions of ScanDisk cannot handle long file names, and will break the links between short file names and long file names.*

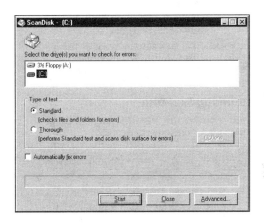

Quick Access

Click , Programs, Accessories, System Tools, ScanDisk.

or

Right-click a *drive* icon, Properties, Tools, then Check Now.

or

Click , Run, type **scandisk**, then click OK.

or

At a DOS prompt, type **scandisk**, then press *Enter*

HOt Tip **When to Run ScanDisk**: Run ScanDisk whenever your system or applications lock up, crash or end abnormally. A General Protection Fault (GPF) is always a cue to run ScanDisk. As a general maintenance procedure, run it at least once a week.

ScanDisk will run automatically if it detects that Windows was shut down improperly or if it detects a hard disk error. *Note: The original release of Windows 95, 4.00.950, does not have this feature.*

Running ScanDisk

After starting the ScanDisk program using one of the Quick Access methods above, you are ready to configure ScanDisk to perform the tests you desire.

1. Click the *drive* you want to test to select it.

2. Select the *type* of test.

3. Select Automatically fix errors (recommended).

4. Click Options (see below), if running a thorough test, to change any of the default settings.

5. Click Advanced (see below) to change any of the default settings.

6. Click Start to start the testing process.

Drive Selection

The first choice you need to make is which drive to test. ScanDisk defaults to drive C, but you can test any other drive by clicking the appropriate drive in the list box to select it. To test more than one drive, hold down the *Ctrl* key, then click any additional *drives* you want to test.

Type of Test

Select the type of test you want to run.

Standard

Standard tests files and folders for logical errors such as cross-linked files, lost file fragments, invalid file names and invalid dates. If the option *Automatically fix errors* is selected, ScanDisk will try to correct any problems it finds.

Thorough

Thorough performs the same tests that Standard does, but additionally tests the surface of the drive for defects. If any physical defects are found, the data is moved to another location and the sectors are marked bad. These marked bad sectors can no longer be used for storage.

Automatically fix errors

Selecting *Automatically fix errors* tells ScanDisk that it should fix any errors found, without any notice to the user. If you don't select this option ScanDisk will display an error message every time it finds an error and request that you determine how to fix it.

Advanced

The *Advanced* button is available for both types of tests. The Advanced settings control the operation, logging of errors, and disposition of damaged files and fragments.

Display Summary	
Always (Default)	A summary of information about your disk and the errors encountered is always displayed.
Never	A summary of information is never displayed.
Only if errors found	A summary of information about your disk and the errors encountered is displayed only if errors are detected.
Log File	
Replace log (Default)	ScanDisk will create a record of its activity in a log file called Scandisk.log and store it in the root of drive C. This option replaces any previous log with a new log of the same name.
Append to log	ScanDisk will append a record of its activity to a log file called Scandisk.log stored in the root of drive C.
No log	No information is saved to a log file.

Note: The log file Scandisk.log is a text file that can be viewed with Logview, Notepad or WordPad.

See the section "Scandisk.log" (p. 384) for more information.

Cross-Linked Files	
Delete	Deletes any cross-linked files when found. Frees disk space but no recovery of data is possible.
Make copies (Default)	Makes a copy of each cross-linked file. If there is a chance that information can be recovered from these files this option should be used.
Ignore	Does not correct any cross linked files. Cross-linked files can cause many types of problems; leaving them could be risky.
Lost File Fragments	
Free	Removes any lost file fragments, which frees up the disk space used by them.
Convert to files (Default)	Converts lost file fragments to files with names beginning with FILE and ending with sequential numbers (FILE0001). If there is a chance that information can be recovered from these files, this option should be used.

Check Files For	
Invalid file names (Default)	File names are checked to see if they are valid and usable. If a file name has been corrupted it may not be able to be opened.
Invalid dates and times	File dates and times are checked to see if they are valid and usable. If a date or time has been corrupted certain programs such as backup, setup, copy or briefcase may make incorrect assumptions while working with the file.
98	
Duplicate names	Finds files that share the same name and are broken.
Check host drive first (Default)	If your drives have been compressed using either DoubleSpace or DriveSpace, ScanDisk will check the host drive (the uncompressed drive on which the compressed drive is stored) for the compressed drives first. If the host drive contains errors, it can affect the compressed drives, so checking it first is the best approach.
98	
Report MS-DOS mode name length errors	Reports file names and folders whose length exceeds the 66 character limit for MS-DOS.

Options

The *Options* button is available only if Thorough has been selected for the Type of Test. The default settings provide the most thorough and complete testing of the media. Consequently, changing any of the options will result in a test that is less than complete. Following is an explanation of the options.

Areas of the Disk to Scan	
System and Data areas	The entire disk is scanned for physical damage.
System area only	Only the system area of the disk is scanned for physical damage. This area holds the programs that start and operate the computer.
Data area only	Only the data area of the disk is scanned for physical damage.
Do not perform write testing	The default setting performs a read and write test on every sector. Selecting this option prohibits ScanDisk from performing the write test.
Do not repair bad sectors in hidden and system files	If ScanDisk finds problems with sectors that store hidden or system files the data will not be moved, as some programs look for these files at specific locations and will not operate properly if the data is moved.

Hot Tip **Check Your Hard Disk with Every Start up:** Create a shortcut for ScanDisk and place it in your Startup folder (see p.431) so that your hard disk is checked every time you start your computer. The command you would put in your Shortcut to start ScanDisk, check your C drive, and close ScanDisk automatically would look like the following:

c:\Windows\Scandskw.exe c: /n

Hot Tip **Run Scandisk Automatically**: If you want to run ScanDisk automatically on a regular basis, consider purchasing Microsoft Plus! It has a scheduling agent called System Agent that allows you to set up a specific time to automatically run ScanDisk.

Command

Scandskw [*drive:*] [/**a**] [/**n**] [/**p**]

Scandisk *drive:***dblspace**.*nnn*

Scandisk *drive:***drvspace**.*nnn*

Options:

Drive: ....Specifies the drive(s) you want to check.

/**A** or /**All** ....Checks all your local, nonremovable hard disks.

/**N** or /**Noninteractive** .Starts and closes ScanDisk automatically.

/**O** ....Removes long file names and all extended file attributes from specified disk. (**Warning!** If no drive is specified, all fixed disks are processed.)

/P or **/Preview**..............Prevents ScanDisk from correcting any errors it finds.

Nnn ....File name extension for the hidden host file.

Notes:

1. ScanDisk appears to be fixing errors when running scandskw in Preview mode, but it doesn't. "Preview" will be displayed in the caption of the main ScanDisk window when running in Preview mode.

2. ScanDisk generates exit codes that can be used in batch file programming to determine if an action should be taken based upon the code. Following are the exit codes:

Exit Code	Description
0x00	Drive checked, no errors found
0x01	Errors found, all fixed
0xFA	Check could not start—cannot load or find Dskmaint.dll
0xFB	Check could not start—insufficient memory
0xFC	Errors found, but at least some were not fixed.
0xFD	At least one drive could not be checked.
0xFE	Check was cancelled.
0xFF	Check was terminated because of error.

Here's an example of how the exit code can be captured in a batch file:

start /w scandskw c: d: /n
if errorlevel *exitcode* goto *command*

The start /w command used in this example allows the batch file to stop and wait for

ScanDisk to finish running; otherwise, the batch file would try to continue as soon as ScanDisk was launched.

Default Location: \Windows\Scandskw.exe and \Windows\Command\Scandisk.exe

See Also: Disk Defragmenter; Scandisk.log; Shortcuts; Startup Folder

Scandisk.log

Scandisk.log is log file created by ScanDisk during the disk scanning process. It appends a record of its activity to this file, which is stored in the root of drive C:. If you want to know the results of your ScanDisk operations, such as when the tests were run, what tests were successful, and what problems were encountered, review this file.

Scandisk.log is a text file that can be viewed with Logview, Notepad, or WordPad.

Default Location: \Scandisk.log

See Also: Logview; ScanDisk

ScanReg

See: Registry Checker (p. 357)

Scraps

Scrap

Windows supports *scraps*, which are pieces of data taken from an OLE document and stored on your desktop or in a folder. These scraps can then be used in other documents by dragging them from their storage location into the document.

Quick Access

Select a portion of text, picture or other information from within an OLE document such as one created in WordPad, Microsoft Word or Microsoft Excel.

Click on the selected *object* and drag it to the desktop or folder.

or

Right-click on the *object* and drag it to the desktop or folder, then click Create Scrap Here (Move Scrap Here will delete your original object).

or

Select the *object*, Copy it to the clipboard, then Paste it to the desktop or folder.

A scrap is a new file created from the original application, represented by an icon that looks something like the one below.

WordPad
Document Scrap
'reach up to the ...'

Notice that the name of the scrap is composed of the name of the application and the first part of the text it contains. If it will be helpful to you, you can rename it like any other object.

Viewing

To see what's in the scrap, double-click the scrap icon. The contents will be displayed in the original application from which it was created.

Using

To use the scrap, drag the scrap icon from your desktop or folder to an open document. The contents of the scrap will be copied into the document. You can use scraps as many times as you want.

HOt Tip **Creating scraps from a spreadsheet** application is a little different than from a word processing document:

1. Select the data as you normally would in the spreadsheet.

2. Place your pointer on the border or frame of the selected data (it should look like an arrow), then drag the selected data to your desktop or folder.

3. When you open the scrap, you will see the whole spreadsheet with the selected data highlighted. When you use the scrap in another document, however, only the selected data is copied into your document.

HOt Tip **Insert Scrap into a Minimized Document:** If you are tight for space on your desktop, you can position the insertion point at the place in your destination document where you want your scrap inserted, then minimize the application. On the desktop, locate the scrap you want to use, then drag it to the minimized application button on the taskbar, but do not release the mouse button. The document will open, and you can then copy the scrap into it at the place you left the insertion point.

HOt Tip **Use Scrap as a Bookmark:** When you right-click and drag selected text to the desktop, you have an option to **Create Document Shortcut Here**. If this option is selected, a shortcut is created on the desktop that points to the selected text in the document. Some applications require you to save the original document after you create the shortcut. If you don't, you will receive an error message when you try to use the shortcut. When you use this shortcut it acts as a bookmark, returning you to the specific point in the document where you left off.

Hot Tip **Use Scraps as Notes to Yourself**. If you are reading an e-mail or a memo from one of your friends or associates and you want to create a reminder to yourself about its contents, copy only the part that interests you to the desktop as a scrap. You'll have just the information you need right at your fingertips.

Note: Some applications, such as Notepad, do not support scraps. More and more publishers, however, are adding this capability to their products. If you are not sure whether an application supports scraps, just try it. If dragging the object doesn't work, try using Copy and Paste.

See Also: Shortcuts

Screen Saver

..QuicKeys..

Change

Right-click background of desktop, Properties, Screen Saver tab

or

Click **Start**, Settings, Control Panel,

double-click , Screen Saver tab

Disable Temporarily

Click **Start** to display the Start menu.

The screen saver will not launch while the Start menu is displayed.

See Also: Display|Screen Saver

Selecting Files & Folders

When you want to Cut, Copy, Move, Delete, Restore, Send To or Print files, folders or objects, you need to select them before you can execute a command. Here are several different methods you can use to select files or folders.

Single File or Folder

Click the *file, folder* or *object.*

or

Right-click the *file, folder* or *object* (this will also display the shortcut menu).

or

Use the arrow keys to move to the *file, folder* or *object.*

or

Type the first letter of *file, folder* or *object* name.

Multiple Sequential Files or Folders

Click the first *file, folder* or *object* in the sequence, hold down the **Shift** key, then click the last *file, folder* or *object* in the sequence.

or

Click in the background just to the right of the first *file, folder* or *object* in the sequence, hold down the mouse button and drag a rectangle around the *files, folders* or *objects* you want to select, then release the mouse button.

or

Right-click in the background just to the right of the first *file, folder* or *object* in the sequence, hold down the mouse button and drag a rectangle around the *files, folders* or *objects* you want to select, then release the mouse button (this will also display the shortcut menu).

or

Click the first *file, folder* or *object* in the sequence, hold down the **Shift** key, then use the arrow keys to move to the last *file, folder* or *object* in the sequence.

or

Click *file, folder* or *object*, hold down the Shift key, then press **Ctrl+Home** to select all *files, folders* or *objects* to the beginning of the list.

or

Click *file, folder* or *object*, hold down the Shift key, then press **Ctrl+End** to select all *files, folders* or *objects* to the end of the list.

HOt Tip **Any of the procedures above can be done in reverse.** For example, click the last *file, folder* or *object* first, then the first *file, folder* or *object*.

HOt Tip **Drag from Upper Right to Lower Left**: Dragging a rectangle to select *files, folders* or *objects* can be difficult to control; especially when working against the left side of a window or pane. You can start in any blank area of the background but when you are working against the left side of a window or pane, drag starting at the upper right corner, then move to the lower left corner - it works every time.

Multiple Non-Sequential Files or Folders

Click on the first *file, folder* or *object*, hold down the *Ctrl* key, then click on each additional *file, folder* or *object* you want to select. The additional *files, folders* or *objects* can be selected in any order you choose.

or

Select the first *file, folder* or *object*, hold down the *Ctrl* key, then use the arrow keys to move to the next *file, folder* or *object* you want to select. Press the *Spacebar* to select the next *file, folder* or *object*. Continue this process until all the *files, folders* or *objects* are selected.

All Files or Folders in a Panel

Click anywhere in the pane that contains the *files, folders* or *objects* you want to select, or click a specific *folder* or *object* in the left pane in Explorer, then press *Ctrl+A* (selects everything within the folder you checked).

or

Click anywhere in the pane that contains the *files, folders* or *objects* you want to select or click a specific *folder* or *object* in the left pane in Explorer, click <u>E</u>dit on the menu bar, then Select <u>A</u>ll. (Selects everything within the folder you checked).

Inverting A Selection

After making a selection using any of the methods above, you can invert the selection. Inverting the selection reverses the selection, selecting all *files, folders* or *objects* that were not originally selected.

After making a selection, click <u>E</u>dit on the menu bar, then <u>I</u>nvert Selection.

Canceling A Selection

All Files & Folders

To cancel the selection for all files and folders, click in the background of the pane or window.

Single File or Folder

To cancel the selection for a single file or folder, hold down the *Ctrl* key, then click the specific *file, folder* or *object*.

To cancel the selection for a single file or folder, hold down the *Ctrl* key, use the arrow keys to move to the specific *file, folder* or object, then press the *Spacebar*.

See Also: Copying Files & Folders; Deleting Files & Folders; Moving Files & Folders; Restoring Files & Folders; Printers; Send To,

Send To

The *Send To* command, which is available on the Shortcut menu, is used to open, copy, move, print, fax or mail files, folders or objects to commonly used applications or destinations. The default destinations that appear in the Send To menu depend on what programs have been installed. The most common are 3½ Floppy (A), Fax Recipient, Mail Recipient and My Briefcase.

In Windows98, Desktop as Shortcut and My Documents have been added to the Send To menu as new default destinations.

Quick Access

Right-click a *file* or *folder* or *object* to call the Shortcut menu, click Se**n**d To, then select a *destination*.

or

In My Computer or the right pane of Explorer, select a *file* or *folder* or *object*, click <u>F</u>ile on the menu bar, click Se<u>n</u>d To, then select a *destination*.

The Send To command will only appear on the menu if a file or folder or object has been selected.

 Send To Default Settings: By default, if you use Send To to send a file to a folder on the same disk drive or volume, the file is moved. If you send it to another disk drive, it's copied. If you want to move a file or folder rather than copy it, hold down the **Shift** key when selecting the *destination*. If you want to copy a file or folder, hold down the **Ctrl** key.

Adding Items to the Send To Menu

You can add new destinations to the Send To menu by creating shortcuts in the \Windows\SendTo folder.

To create a shortcut in the Send To folder:

1. Right-click the *file* or *folder* or *object*, then drag and drop it to the \Windows\SendTo folder.
2. Select Create Shortcut(s) Here.
3. Open the Send To folder. The new shortcut is displayed.
4. Change the name of the shortcut if you so desire. The shortcuts should point to the destination you want to send to.

Note: If each user has a separate user profile on your computer, the SendTo folder will be located in \Windows\Profiles\User folder. See "Setting Up Individual Send To Folders" below.

Whenever you right-click on an object and select Send To, the new destination will appear in the menu.

Here are some suggested destinations you might want to add to your Send To menu:

- Applications (Notepad, WordPad, Quick View, Paint, etc.)
- Desktop
- Folders (common local and network filing areas, for example, My Documents)
- Quick Launch toolbar (Window 98 only)
- Jazz Drives
- Printers
- Recycle Bin
- Zip Drives

HOt Tip **Organize Your Send To Menu:** If your Send To menu is getting crowded, create folders in the SendTo folder and move your shortcuts into the new folders. Now cascading menus will display your choices in an organized fashion.

Note: When adding applications to the Send To menu, keep in mind that they have to be able to accept a file name as a parameter when executed. If you are able to drag and drop a file on the application's executable to open it, then the application should work fine from the Send To menu.

Note: When you create a shortcut for a printer or fax modem, you will need to create the shortcut on your Desktop first and then drag it into your SendTo folder.

HOt Tip **Use Power Toys to Add Commands:** If you want to add some additional commands to the Send To menu, such as Send To Any Folder, Send To Clipboard as Contents, Send To Clipboard as Name and Send To Command Line, download the Windows 95 Power Toys utility from Microsoft's Web site (http://www.microsoft.com/windows/software/powertoy.htm) and use it to add these options to your menu.

HOt Tip **Send to the SendTo Folder:** To make adding shortcuts to the SendTo folder easier, add a shortcut for the SendTo folder to the SendTo folder. Now, when you want to add a file or folder to the SendTo folder you can use the Send To command to do so. To accomplish this task, you'll have to create a shortcut for the SendTo folder on the desktop first, then copy it to the SendTo folder. Leave a copy of the shortcut on the desktop just in case you want to drag and drop a file or folder there.

Setting Up Individual Send To Folders

Each user will, by default, use the global Send To folder. To configure your computer so that each user can have a separate Send To folder, follow these steps:

CAUTION: *The following instructions involve changing settings in the Registry. If the changes are not made properly, serious problems may result.* **Be sure to backup your Registry before continuing**. *See: "Registry" for more information about backing up and editing the Registry.*

1. Create a Send To folder in the *user's* personal folder. The personal folders are located in the \Windows\Profiles folder.

2. Log on using the *user's* name you want to make changes for.

3. Use the Run command on the Start menu to launch the Registry Editor by typing **regedit.exe**, then press *Enter*.

4. Move through the tree structure as follows: HKEY_USERS*user name*\\Software\Microsoft\Windows\CurrentVersion\Explorer\Shell Folders

5. Locate the SendTo string, then edit it to reflect the path to the *user's* Send To folder. For example,C:\Windows\Profiles*user name*\SendTo.

6. Next, create a new string named SendTo in: HKEY_USERS*user name*\Software\Microsoft\Windows\CurrentVersion\Explorer\User Folders
Use the same path to the *user's* SendTo folder as you did above for the string value.

7. Create shortcuts in the Send To folder for the *user*.

8. Shut down, then restart the computer for the changes to take effect.

9. Repeat the above steps for each user for whom you want to create an individual Send To folder.

Default Location: \Windows\SendTo

See Also: Shortcuts; Printers; Power Toys; Quick View; Registry

Setuplog.txt

See: Logview|Setuplog.txt (p. 263)

Shortcut Menu

The *Shortcut* menu is the menu that you access by right-clicking an object. The menu contains options that pertain to the object selected. These options are usually available from a menu bar, but the convenience of right clicking makes the shortcut menus a preferred tool.

Quick Access

    Right-click *object*

or

    Select *object*, *Shift+F10*

Objects that have shortcut menus include Files, Folders, Icons, Title Bars, Toolbars, Taskbar, Buttons on the Taskbar, Window Backgrounds, the Desktop, and many other objects. Try right-clicking anything and see what you get - you may find an easier way to accomplish a task.

The commands that are listed on the shortcut menus can include Cut, Copy, Paste, Rename, Delete, Open, Open With, Send To, Create Shortcut, Properties, and many others that are specific to

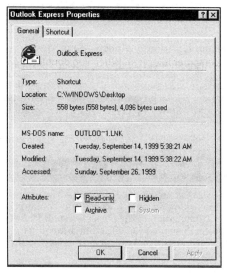

the object selected. For more information on these commands see the appropriate section for each command.

Note: Some applications will add themselves to your shortcut menus such as WinZip, McAfee virus scanner, and network commands.

See Also: Copying Files & Folders; Deleting Files & Folders; File & Folder Properties; Moving Files & Folders; Renaming Files & Folders; Selecting Files & Folders; Send To; Shortcuts

Shortcuts

A shortcut is an icon that stores information about where a program, disk, folder, file, printer or computer is located. When you double-click on a shortcut it performs the appropriate task for whatever it's connected to. For example, if the shortcut is for a program's executable file, the program will launch, or if it is connected to a folder, the folder will open.

You can identify a shortcut by the small arrow that appears in a square box in the lower left corner of the icon. The following shortcut to My Documents provides an example.

Shortcut to My
Documents

..QuicKeys..

Change Icon

Right-click *object*, Properties, Shortcut tab, Change Icon button

or

Shift+F10, R, Ctrl+Tab to Shortcut tab, *Alt+C*

Create in Shortcut in Same Folder

Right-click *object*, Create Shortcut

Create Shortcut in Another Folder

Right-click *object* and drag to *folder*, Create Shortcut(s) Here

or

> *Ctrl+Shift* and drag *object* to folder,
> Create Shortcut(s) Here

or

> Select *object*, click Edit on the menu bar,
> Copy, click on *folder*, click Edit on the menu
> bar, Paste Shortcut

or

> Select *object*, *Ctrl+C*, click on *folder*,
> *Alt+E, S*

Create Shortcut on Desktop

> In Explorer or My Computer, right-click
> *object* and drag to desktop,
> Create Shortcut(s) Here

or

> *Ctrl+Shift* and drag *object* to desktop,
> Create Shortcut(s) Here

or

> Right-click *object*, Copy, move to *destination*,
> right-click, Paste Shortcut

or

> Right-click Desktop, New, Shortcut, Browse
> to find file or folder, Next, Finish

Create Shortcut to DOS

> Right-click desktop, New, Shortcut, type
> c:\windows\command.com, click Next,
> Finish

Create Shortcut to Network Drive (Connected)

> Right-click network *drive* icon, Create
> Shortcut, Yes (creates on desktop)

or

> Right-click desktop, New, Shortcut, type full
> network *path* (\\server\volume\directory)

Rename

> Right-click *shortcut* icon, Rena<u>m</u>e

or

> Click *shortcut* name, pause, click again

or

> Click *shortcut* icon, then *shortcut* name

or

> Select *shortcut*, **F2**

Creating Shortcuts

There are several ways to create a shortcut. Each depends on where you want the shortcut to reside when you are finished. Use the methods listed above in the Quick Access section.

HÔt Tip **Change Default Naming Convention for Shortcuts:** Windows automatically adds 'Shortcut To' to the name of every shortcut it creates. If you want to change this default so that it doesn't do this you can do so using one of the Power Toys, Tweak UI. See "Power Toys" (p. 323) for more information.

HÔt Tip **Create a shortcut to a specific section of an OLE document** by first selecting some text, right-clicking it and dragging it to the desktop, then selecting Create Document Shortcut Here. This shortcut, when executed, will open the document at the place where the shortcut was created.

Note: When you create a shortcut on the desktop for a CD-ROM drive, the icon name dynamically changes to reflect the name of the CD that is in the drive.

Shortcut Properties

As with any object in Windows a shortcut has properties that describe it. To access a shortcut's properties:

>   Right-click *object*, then click Properties

General

The General tab primarily lists information that is common to every file such as Name, Type, Location, Size, MS-DOS Name, Created, Modified, and Accessed. Attributes can also be set on the General tab. For more information see "File & Folder Properties" (p. 211).

Shortcut

The Shortcut tab contains more specific information about the shortcut and how it works.

Name

Name displays the name of the shortcut.

Target Type

Target Type displays the type of item the shortcut points to.

Target Location

Target Location displays the path to the target.

Target

Target displays the item that the shortcut points to. The Target can be modified if necessary.

Start In

Start In specifies the location that the shortcut resides in or the location that contains supporting files. Some programs need supporting files to run, Start In lets you specify that location.

Shortcut Key

Shortcut keys provide quick access to the shortcut. Shortcut keys must be a combination of keys including either *Ctrl* or *Alt* and another key, for example, *Ctrl+K*.

The combination will only work if the program being launched is on the desktop or Start menu, and it can't conflict with a keystroke combination that is assigned to any other function.

Run

An application can be run with its window minimized, maximized or normal. The default is a normal window. You can change to minimized or maximized by selecting the appropriate item in the Run drop down list.

Find Target

Find Target opens the folder that contains the target.

Change Icon

Change Icon lets you change the default icon to something more suited to your needs. When you select Change Icon, a palette is displayed from which you can choose a variety of different icons.

See Also: File & Folder Properties

Shut Down

Shut Down is used to prepare the computer to be turned off, to save and recognize changes to the Registry settings, and to switch between user profiles and log ons.

CAUTION: *Always use Shut Down prior to turning off your computer. Be sure to properly close all applications before shutting down Windows. If you don't, you may lose data that hasn't been saved.*

Quick Access

Click **Start**, Shut Down, select a Shut Down *option*, then Yes or OK

or

Alt+F4, select a Shut Down option, then Yes or OK

or

Ctrl+Esc, U, Enter

When system has locked up or crashed try:

Press *Ctrl+Alt+Delete*, click Shutdown

or

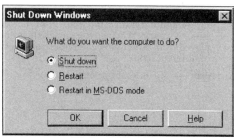

Windows 98 Shut Down

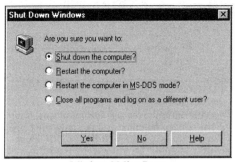

Windows 95 Shut Down

Press *Ctrl+Esc, U, Enter*

Shut Down Options

There are four Shut Down options you can choose
from. Each performs a different operation.

98 Shut down/ **95** Shut down the computer?

This option saves any system settings that
have been changed and prepares the computer to be turned off.

98 Restart/ **95** Restart the computer?

This option saves any system settings that
have been changed and prepares the computer to be restarted. It then warm boots
the computer, automatically restarting it.

Hot Tip **Restart Windows without Rebooting:** Holding down the *Shift* key when selecting Restart the computer? or Restart the computer in MS-DOS mode? bypasses the warm boot process and restarts Windows.

98 Restart in MS-DOS mode/ 95 Restart the computer in MS-DOS mode?

This option saves any system settings that have been changed and prepares the computer to be restarted. It then warm boots the computer, automatically restarting the computer in MS-DOS mode. To startup in Windows again, type **exit** or **win** at the MS-DOS prompt, then press Enter.

98 Log Off *user name*

Close all programs...has been replaced by **Log Off *user name*** which is located on the Start menu. Log Off displays the name of the user who is currently logged in, which may help to avoid any confusion concerning who the current user is.

95 Close all programs and log on as a different user?

This option only appears if you have installed a network, Direct Cable Connection, Dial-Up Networking or have set up different user profiles. It saves any system settings that have been changed and prepares the computer to be restarted. It then restarts the computer allowing the user to log on using a different name. This option does not exist in Windows 98.

CAUTION: *Do not power off your computer until the message "You can now safely turn off your computer" appears. To do so prematurely can lead to data corruption and orphaned temporary files.*

HOt Tip **Replace the Exit and Shut Down Screens:** The Exit and Shut Down screens that are displayed during the shut down process can be customized or replaced. The files are called Logow.sys and Logos.sys and are actually Windows Bitmap (.bmp) files, even though they have a .sys file name extension. The files are located in the \Windows folder. Use Microsoft Paint or any other image editor to manipulate or create images that suit your needs. Be sure to resize your bitmaps to 320x400, thenu use the same file names, Logow.sys and Logos.sys and they will be displayed during the shut down process.

HOt Tip **One Step Restart**: You can make restarting your computer a one-step process by creating an icon on your desktop that does it all.

1. Using Notepad, create a new file and in it type **@exit**.
2. Save the file in a convenient folder giving it a name that has a .bat extension.
3. Right-click the file, drag the file your desktop, then click Create Shortcut(s) Here.
4. Right-click the shortcut icon, click Properties, then the Program tab.
5. Select the Close on Exit box.

6. Next, click the Advanced button, select MS-DOS mode and clear Warn before entering MS-DOS mode.

7. Click OK, change the icon if you want to, then click OK to close the dialog box.

Shut Down Problems

If Windows does not shut down properly, you may find that your computer has quit responding and is hung up at the screen that says "Please wait while your computer shuts down," or "Windows 98 is shutting down." This problem can lead to data corruption and the orphaning of temporary files, both of which may adversely affect the applications you are running. It is highly recommended that you take the time to isolate the condition causing the problem and correct it.

Shutdown problems can be caused by any of the following conditions. Starting with the first condition, work through each one until you find the problem.

Incompatible programs loading from the Startup folder

To check and correct:

1. Move all the files in the Startup folder (Windows\Start Menu\Programs\Startup) to a temporary folder, then restart your computer.

2. Shut down your computer. If it works properly, one of the files that you have been loading at start up is probably the cause of your problems.

3. Copy the files back to the Startup folder one by one. After you copy each file back to

the folder, restart your computer, then immediately shut it down. When your computer fails to shut down properly, you'll know that the last file you put back is the one causing the problem.

4. This kind of problem usually is due to a corrupt file. You can choose to remove the file permanently from the Startup folder, or you can try reinstalling the application to try and replace the corrupt file.

Incompatible programs loading from the Win.ini file, specifically those listed in "Load=" and "Run="

To check and correct:

1. Click the 🏃Start button, then Run.

2. In the Open text box type **sysedit**, then click OK.

3. Click the Win.ini window.

4. Insert a semicolon in front of the Load= and Run= lines.

5. Save the file and exit.

6. Restart your computer and then immediately shut it down. If your computer shuts down properly, you'll know that one of the programs being loaded from the Load= or Run= lines is causing the problem.

7. Repeat the steps above, removing the semicolons one at a time. When your computer fails to shut down properly, you'll know which line is causing the problem.

8. Using Sysedit to edit the Win.ini file, insert a semicolon in front of the line causing the problem, then create a new line for the same command.

9 Add one of the programs from the original command line to this new command line.

10. Save the file and exit.

11. Restart your computer and then immediately shut it down. If your computer shuts down properly, repeat the process, adding another program to the command line. When your computer fails to shut down properly, you'll know that the last program you added is the one causing the problem.

12. Once you've identified the program causing the problem, contact the manufacturer of the program who may have additional information about a solution.

Commands loading from Autoexec.bat or Config.sys files

To check and correct:

1. Restart Windows.

2. Just before the Windows logo displays, press *F8*, then select Step-By-Step Confirmation from the Startup menu.

3. Press *Y* at each of the following prompts and *N* for any other prompts.
   Load Doublespace driver
   Process the system registry
   DEVICE=C:\WINDOWS\HIMEM.SYS
   DEVICE=C:\WINDOWS\IFSHLP.SYS
   Load the Windows graphical user interface
   Load all Windows drivers

4. Wait for Windows to finish loading, then shut it down. If Windows shuts down properly, one of the commands in Config.sys or Autoexec.bat is causing the problem.

5. To find the command line that is causing the problem, repeat the steps above, but press *Y* for one of the lines you pressed *N* for the first time. Press *N* for all other lines. Repeat this process until you identify the command line causing the problem.

6. Use Sysedit to edit the file containing the problem command line. Delete or remark out the line by inserting REM at the beginning of the line.

Memory conflicts that still exist when Emm386.exe is not loaded from Config.sys file

To check and correct:

1. Click **🎀 Start** , then <u>R</u>un.

2. In the <u>O</u>pen text box type **sysedit**, then click OK.

3. Click the Config.sys window.

4. In the Config.sys file, make sure the next two lines exist in the following order:
   device=c:\windows\himem.sys
   device=c:\windows\emm386.exe noems
   x=a000-f7ff

5. Save the file and exit.

6. Restart your computer and then immediately shut it down. If your computer shuts down properly, the problem may be caused by a memory conflict that still exists when Emm386.exe is not loaded from Config.sys.

7. To find out more information on resolving memory conflicts, see the article Q112816 "Locating and Excluding RAM/ROM Addresses in the UMA" in the Microsoft Knowledge Base.

Note: The Microsoft Knowledge Base can be accessed on the Internet. See the "Technical Support" section for information on using the Internet.

Virtual device driver being loaded from the System.ini file

To check and correct:

1. Click **Start**, then Run.
2. In the Open text box type **sysedit**, then click OK.
3. Click the System.ini window.
4. Insert a semicolon in front of every line that begins with device=, and ends with .386
5. Save the file and exit.
6. Restart your computer and then immediately shut it down. If your computer shuts down properly, you'll know that one of the virtual device drivers was causing the problem.
7. Repeat the steps above, removing the semicolons one at a time. When your computer fails to shut down properly, you'll know that the last device driver you enabled is the one causing the problem.
8. Usually this kind of problem is due to a corrupt or incompatible device driver. Contact the manufacturer of the driver who may have additional information about a solution for the problem.

Damaged Exit Windows sound file

To check and correct:

1. Double-click the Sounds tool in the Control Panel.

2. In the Events list box, select Exit Windows. Using the dropdown list box for Name, select (None).

3. Restart your computer and then immediately shut it down. If your computer shuts down properly, you'll know that the sound file was causing the problem.

4. Usually this kind of problem is due to a corrupt file. You can choose to use a different sound file or try replacing the bad sound file. If neither of these options works, you may have a bad device driver.

Advanced Power Management (APM) enabled

To check and correct:

1. Double-click the System tool in the Control Panel.

2. Select the Device Manager tab.

3. Double-click Advanced Power Management in the devices list box. If this device is not present, your computer does not have APM and you can ignore the rest of these steps.

4. Clear the Enable Power Management check box, then click OK.

5. Restart your computer and then immediately shut it down. If your computer fails to shut down properly, you'll know that the APM is causing the problem.

6. Usually this kind of problem is due to a incompatibility with your computer. Contact your PC's manufacturer, who may have additional information about a solution for the problem.

Conflict with one of the File System settings

To check and correct:

1. Double-click the System tool in the Control Panel.

2. Select the Performance tab, then click the File System button.

3. Select the Troubleshooting tab.

4. Select all the check boxes, click OK, then Close.

5. Restart your computer and then immediately shut it down. If it shuts down properly, you'll know that one of the file system settings is causing the problem.

6. Repeat the process above, clearing the file system setting checkboxes one at a time. After restarting your computer, see if it will shut down properly. When it doesn't, you'll know that the last setting cleared is the one causing the problem.

7. The performance of your system is dependent on these settings. Make sure that only the settings causing problems are selected.

Incompatible, damaged or conflicting device driver

To check and correct:

1. Double-click the System tool in the Control Panel, then Hardware Profiles.

2. Select the hardware profile that you are currently using (the default is Original Configuration), then click Copy.

3. Type a new name for the configuration (in this example *Test Configuration)*, then click OK. An alternative configuration has now been created.

4. Next, select the Device Manager tab. A list of installed device drivers is displayed.

5. Select a driver that you suspect is the problem, then click Remove.

6. In the Confirm Device Removal dialog box, select Remove from specific configuration.

7. Select Test Configuration from the Configuration drop-down list, then click OK.

8. Close the System tool window and restart your computer.

9. When prompted, select Test Configuration.

10. Shut down your computer and see if there is still a problem. If your computer shuts down properly, you have identified the bad driver. Try reinstalling the device driver to correct the problem. If you still have a problem, repeat the procedure above removing one device driver at a time until the shutdown is successful.

Review Bootlog.txt

Windows maintains an activity log called Bootlog.txt. This is a hidden text file located in the root of your C: drive. The entries made into this file can sometimes give you an indication of where a problem might be.

Use Notepad to view the file. Look for "Terminate=" entries at the end of the file. Each "Terminate=" entry should be followed by a "EndTerminate" entry. If Windows shuts down normally, the last line in the file should be "EndTerminate=KERNEL."

The following entries are the most common entries when there are problems:

Last Line	Possible Cause
Terminate=Query Drivers	Memory manager issue.
Terminate=UnloadNetwork	Conflict with real-mode network driver in Config.sys file.
Terminate=Reset Display	Disable video shadowing. Update your video driver.
Terminate=RIT	Timer-related problems with sound card or an old mouse driver.
Terminate=Win32	32-bit program blocking a thread, possibly Microsoft Visual C for Windows

Reset CMOS

If none of the methods above resolves the problem, you can try resetting the computer's CMOS back to its defaults. Consult the computer manufacturer's instructions on how to do this properly.

CAUTION: *Since there is no way to back up your CMOS settings, you will need to write them down so that you can recreate them if necessary.*

Note: Microsoft has two excellent articles regarding troubleshooting shut down problems on its "Personal Online Support" website.

For Windows 95, see article Q145926; for Windows 98, see article Q202633 at http://support.microsoft.com/support/kb/articles/

See Also: Bootlog.txt; Start Menu; System Configuration Editor

Start Button

See: Start Menu (below)

Start Menu

The *Start Menu* is the menu that appears when you click the Start button on the lower left of the screen. It provides a starting point for almost every program, function or command you may need to use on your computer. It lists several submenus and provides direct execution of several commands, which are described below.

Quick Access

Click **Start** on taskbar

or

Ctrl+Esc

or

Win (Microsoft Natural Keyboard)

or

Alt+S (no windows can be open, and no objects selected on Desktop)

The Windows 95 Start menu. *The Windows 98 Start menu*

Programs

The *Programs* option provides access to folders containing a group of programs and individual programs. When a program is selected from the Programs menu, the program is launched. A Program can be added to the menu by creating a shortcut to it in the \Windows\Start Menu\Programs folder or in a folder created within the Programs folder.

Hot Tip **Change Items in Start Menu:** To change items in your Start menu, right-click Start, then select Explore. Explorer will default to the Start Menu folder. You can then move into the Programs folder to make changes.

98 Favorites

Favorites lists files, folders and Internet sites that you frequently visit. When you select one of the items, it opens the file or folder, or connects you to the Internet site. For more information see the section "Favorites." (p. 203)

Channels

Channels provides access to the channels available on the Microsoft Network (MSN).

Links

Links lists hyperlinks to Internet sites that can be accessed directly, without having to first open Microsoft Internet Explorer. Initially Links lists only Microsoft Web sites that act as gateways to other sites on the World Wide Web (WWW).

Documents

The *Documents* menu stores the last 15 documents you opened, regardless of which application you used to open them and where they were located. This makes commonly-used documents easy to access since you can open both the application and the document at the same time.

To open the file and the application, just click on the file name.

Note: If you find Windows trying to access your floppy drive whenever you Open, Save or Rename a file, even though you are not executing a command that involves it, you're experiencing a side effect of the way the Documents menu works. Every time you execute one of these commands, Windows tries to update the Documents menu. If one of the shortcuts on the Documents menu references a file on a floppy drive, Windows will try to verify that the disk is in the drive, even if the drive is empty.

To temporarily stop Windows from spending time checking the floppy drives, you can do one of two things:

- If you know which document is causing the problem, clear it from your Documents menu by opening Explorer, navigate to Windows\Profiles\user name\Recent, click the document name, and delete it.

- If you do not know which document is causing the problem, clear the Documents menu. Windows will not have a reason to check the drive until another file is accessed on the drive. See "Clearing the Documents Menu" below.

Clearing the Documents Menu

If you want to clear all the shortcuts from your Documents menu follow the next few steps:

1. Right-click the taskbar, then click Properties.
2. Click the Start Menu Programs tab.
3. Click the Clear button in the Documents Menu section, the click OK.

Settings

Settings provides access to the Control Panel, Printers, and Taskbar, as well as Folder Options, Active Desktop and Windows Update in Windows 98.

Control Panel

The *Control Panel* is a folder that contains command, control and configuration programs that you can use to change the hardware, software and system settings for Windows. For more information see the section "Control Panel." (p. 119)

Printers

Printers is a Control Panel tool that allows you to create, modify, and monitor printers and their activities. For more information see the section "Printers." (p. 326)

Taskbar (& Start Menu)

The *Taskbar* (*Taskbar and Start Menu* in Windows 98) is a tool that provides access to programs you use regularly and to programs that are already open. For more information, see the section "Taskbar." (p. 444)

98

Folder Options

This option provides access to *Folder Options*, which allows you to change how you view files in folders and how Windows functions with certain file types. For more information see the section "View." (p. 453)

Active Desktop

Active Desktop provides options to change your Windows view and customize your desktop. For more information see the sections "Desktop"(p. 145 and "View." (p. 453)

Windows Update

Windows Update provides direct access to Microsoft's *Windows Update* web site. When you select this option Microsoft Internet Explorer is launched and you are taken directly to the site. At the site you can order updates or download updates depending on your needs. This service allows you to keeping your system in tiptop shape.

Find

Selecting *Find* displays a submenu containing several different Find options: Files or Folders, Computer, People and On the Internet. Each of these options launches a dialog box, which facilitates a specific search. To find out more about the different Find options, see the sections "Find–Files or Folders"(p. 229), "Find–Computer"(p. 226), or "Find–People" (p. 237)

Help

Help provides direct access to Windows online help.

There is a significant difference between Windows 95 and Window 98 Help. Windows 98 Help departs from the standard Help format to look more like a Web interface. This new interface allows you to seek help not only locally, but also through the Internet. Links are maintained with many of Microsoft's support areas.

Run

Selecting *Run* displays a dialog box from which you can open or execute (Run) a program. To find out more about the different uses of the Run dialog box, see the section "Run" (p. 371).

98 Log Off *user name*

To switch between users, select *Log Off*. This command replaces the Close all programs and log on as a different user command that was on the Shutdown dialog box in Windows 95.

To find out who is logged in to the computer you're using, just open the Start Menu, and Log Off will display the current user's name.

Suspend

Suspend may or may not be an option on your computer. It is primarily used to power down laptop computers and conserve power; however, it is sometimes available on desktop computers. The computer is ready to work at any time, prompted by user activity or an incoming phone call.

Eject

Eject may or may not be an option on your computer. It is used to release a laptop from a docking station when the docking station uses a motor to attach and detach the computer.

Shut Down

Shut Down provides access to the Shut Down dialog box, which lists several Shut Down options. For more information, see the section "Shut Down" (p. 404).

 Reorganize Start Menu: If your Start menu becomes too long or cluttered, you can reorganize it.

Create new folders within the \Windows\Start Menu\Programs folder and move your program shortcuts into the new folders, then delete any unneeded shortcuts. To move to the Programs folder quickly, right-click Start, select Open, then double-click Programs.

Adding Items

You can add items to the Start menu and the new items will appear on the top of the menu in alphabetical order. There are two methods you can use:

- Drag and drop to the Start button.
- Adding folders or files directly to the Start Menu folder.

Drag and Drop

Using the drag and drop method is quite easy. All you have to do is click on the file or folder you want to add to the menu and drag it to the Start button. It will automatically be added to the menu.

There is one disadvantage to adding folders this way; when you select the folder from the menu, it will simply open a folder and display the files or folders it contains.

Hot Tip **Create Cascading Menus:** If you copy the folder to the Start Menu folder, the files or folders will display as cascading menu items, a much more elegant method of display.

Adding to the Start Menu Folder

The second method of adding items to the Start Menu is to copy files or folders directly into the Start Menu folder. Using Windows Explorer or My Computer, copy the files or folders to \Windows\Start Menu.

One thing nice about adding items to the Start menu is that they are always available, even if your desktop is full.

Hot Tip **Change the Order of Start Menu Items:** If you want the items on your Start menu to display in an order other than alphabetical, or you would like to have a key to press quickly for each item, go to the Start Menu folder and rename the items adding a number in front of each name. For example, 1-Control Panel or 2-Games.

Hot Tip **Enable Changes Without Rebooting:** If you make a change in your Registry that affects the Start menu, you can enable the new changes without restarting Windows. Press *Ctrl+Alt+Delete* to display the Close Program dialog box, select Explorer, click End Task, then click No in the Shutdown Windows dialog box.

..QuicKeys..

Add Item

Drag *object* to **🅰 Start** on taskbar

Clear Documents Menu

Right-click blank area of taskbar, click Properties, Start Menu Programs tab, Clear

or

98

Click **🅰 Start** , Settings, Taskbar and Start Menu, Start Menu Programs tab, Clear.

or

95

Click **Start**, Settings, Taskbar,

Start Menu Programs tab, Clear.

Close

Click anywhere off of the Start menu

or

Esc

Open

Click **Start** on taskbar

or

Ctrl+Esc

or

Win (Microsoft Natural Keyboard)

or

Alt+S (no windows can be open and no objects selected on Desktop)

Remove Item

Right-click on blank area of taskbar, click Properties, Start Menu Programs tab, Remove, select *object*, Remove

or

98

Click **Start**, Settings, Taskbar and

Start Menu, Start Menu Programs tab,

Remove, select *object*, Remove, Close

or

95

Click **Start**, Settings, Taskbar,

(Taskbar and Start Menu in W98), Start Menu

Programs tab, <u>R</u>emove, select *object*,
<u>R</u>emove, Close

Default Location: \Windows\Start Menu

See Also: Control Panel; Favorites; Find–Files or Folders; Find–Computer; Find–People; Printers; Run; Shut Down; Taskbar

Starting Windows

Starting Windows is as simple as turning on the power switches for your computer, monitor, and peripherals. It starts itself with no other user intervention. There are a few start up variations, however, that you can use for troubleshooting, particularly when Windows doesn't start properly.

There are also options for booting to MS-DOS which can be useful when running certain utilities, like Scandisk. Another option allows you to start up in Safe Mode, which is quite useful for sorting out compatibility issues both during startup and while running your operations.

Startup Options

The following keys affect how Windows starts. To work properly they must be pressed before the Windows graphic or "splash screen" appears. If you're using Windows 95, press the keys when the message "Starting Windows 95" appears. Windows 98 does not have a starting message, so you'll have to experiment with the timing.

..QuickKeys..

Bypass Windows logo at startup
> *Esc*

Command Prompt Only (MS-DOS in Real Mode)
> *Shift+F5*

Command Prompt Only without Compressed Drives (MS-DOS in Real Mode)
> *Ctrl+F5*

Interactive Startup
> *Shift+F8*

Logged (\Bootlog.txt)
> *F8, 2*

Previous Version of MS-DOS
> *F4*

Startup Menu
> *F8*

Step-by-Step Confirmation
> *Shift+F8*

or

> *F8, 5*

Windows in Safe Mode
> *F5*

or

Shift

or

F8, 3

Windows in Safe Mode with Network

F6

or

F8, 4

Hot Tip **To see what's going on behind the Windows 9x screen** as you start up, press *Esc*. The Windows 9x screen will disappear and you'll be able to see some of the startup process.

Hot Tip **Remove Boot Delay:** Windows 95 provides a short delay when booting to allow the user to press *F8*, which boots the computer in MS-DOS mode. To remove the delay and allow the computer to boot faster, edit the Msdos.sys file. Add the following entry: BootDelay=0. Msdos.sys is a system file that has both the Read-only and Hidden attributes enabled. You need to turn off Read-only to edit the file.

Hot Tip **Replace Windows Startup Screen:** The Startup screen that is displayed during the startup process can be customized or replaced. The file is called Logo.sys and is actually a standard 256-color Windows Bitmap (.bmp) file, even though it has a .sys file name extension. Use Microsoft Paint or any other image editor to manipulate it or create a new image that suits your needs. If you are working with compressed drives, edit the logo.sys file on the uncompressed drive. Be sure to resize the image to 320 x 400. If the size is anything but 320 x 400, Windows will not display the screen. If your image appears stretched out, use the Stretch/Skew utility to adjust it. Use the same file name, Logo.sys, when saving and it will be displayed during the startup process. You will find an existing Logo.sys file only if you have installed Microsoft Plus!, but you can create a new file called Logo.sys and Windows will find and use it.

Beware — if you install Microsoft Plus! after you create a Logo.sys file, Microsoft Plus! will overwrite your file. Be sure to back up your custom Logo.sys file, so that you can replace it after the install.

You can slso change is the "It's now safe to turn off your computer" screen. Its file name is Logos.sys! Just follow the same procedures as for Logo.sys.

HOt Tip **Keep Windows Screen from Displaying:** If you want to keep the Windows logo from displaying on a regular basis, add the line Logo=0 to the [Options] section of the Msdos.sys file. Msdos.sys is a system file that has both the Read-only and Hidden attributes enabled. You need to turn off Read-only to edit the file.

Hot Tip **Boot to DOS Prompt Every Time:** To boot to a DOS prompt every time you start your computer, edit the Msdos.sys file and change the BootGUI=1 to Boot GUI=0. Msdos.sys is a system file that has both the Read-only and Hidden attributes enabled. You need to turn off Read-only to edit the file. Once your system is up you can type **win** at the command prompt to start Windows.

See Also: Bootlog.txt; Logview; Passwords; Safe Mode; Startup Menu

Startup Disk

See: Add/Remove Programs|Startup Disk (p. 42)

StartUp Folder

If you place a shortcut to a file or folder in the Startup Folder, it will be started automatically when you log on to your computer. Programs with shortcuts placed into the Programs folder are listed on your Start menu when you click **Start**, Programs. The Startup Folder resides within the Programs folder.

..QuicKeys..

Add Item to Program Menu

Right-click on blank area of taskbar, Properties, Start Menu Programs tab, Add, browse to select *file* (must be a FILE not a folder), Next, double-click Programs folder, Finish

Add Item to StartUp Folder

Right-click on blank area of taskbar, Properties, Start Menu Programs tab, Add, Browse to select *file*, Next, double-click StartUp folder, Finish

Remove

Right-click on blank area of taskbar, Properties, Start Menu Programs tab , Remove, double-click StartUp or Programs folder, select *object*, Remove

Start Windows Without Running Programs

Hold down *Shift* when Windows logo displays

Default Location: Windows/Start Menu/Programs/StartUp

See Also: Start Menu, Startup Menu

Startup Menu

The *Startup Menu* provides several options that can be used to start your system. Each method provides a different way in which your system will start or operate. These options are designed to help you troubleshoot problems associated with the start up process or problems you might be encountering during the operation of Windows.

Quick Access

Power on your computer. During the boot-up phase, but before the Windows screen displays, press *F8* or press and hold *Ctrl*.

Startup Menu Options

The following options are available from the Startup Menu.

- **Normal** - starts Windows as if it were started directly with no user intervention. It is the default option and is selected automatically if no other choices are made.

- **Logged** (\BOOTLOG.TXT) - starts normally but creates a special file called BOOTLOG.TXT as it loads. This file records the actions Windows takes as it starts up, including loading the device drivers and system components. It records the attempts to load and any actions that failed to load—this log file is a great place to look when troubleshooting a system.

- **Safe mode** - loads only the drivers that Windows needs to function. It bypasses the Registry, Autoexec.bat and Config.sys. It loads Ifshlp.sys and Himem.sys without the command line switches. If Windows loads properly in Safe Mode, you may have a problem with one of your drivers. Use the Step-by-step confirmation below to find the offending driver.

- **Safe mode with network support** - works the same as Safe Mode, but loads the drivers necessary to make your network connection.

- **Step-by-step confirmation** - allows you to start Windows and choose which lines in Wininit.exe, Config.sys, Autoexec.bat and Win.com you want to execute. If you skip a line and Windows loads properly, you've probably found the offending line. Removing or modifying the offending line may allow Windows to load properly.

- **Command prompt only** - Select this option if you need to start your system up in MS-DOS. You will be presented with the command line prompt for MS-DOS. To start Windows, type WIN and press Enter.

- **Safe mode command prompt only** - loads only the drivers that Windows needs to function. It bypasses the Registry, Autoexec.bat and Config.sys. It loads Ifshlp.sys and Himem.sys without the command line switches. If you are having startup problems, but Windows loads properly in Safe Mode, you may have a problem with one of your drivers.

- **Previous version of MS-DOS** - Choosing *Previous version of MS-DOS* is usually your last resort. When all else fails, you can try this option. You may be able to salvage your files and move them to another system when working from the previous version of MS-DOS.

Hot Tip **Use MS-DOS Edit Command to View Log Files:** When starting Windows in any of the MS-DOS modes, you will be able to use the MS-DOS Edit command to access the log files. This may be just the route you need to take to get things straightened out.

Note: Some options may not appear on your menu. It depends on how Windows was originally installed, and whether or not a previous version of MS-DOS or Windows was present during the installation.

..QuicKeys..

NOTE: The following keys affect how Windows starts. To work properly they must be pressed before the Windows graphic appears.

Bypass Windows logo at startup

Esc

Command Prompt Only
(MS-DOS in Real Mode)

Shift+F5
(Must reboot to return to Windows mode.)

Command Prompt Only without Compressed Drives (MS-DOS in Real Mode)

Ctrl+F5
(Must reboot to return to Windows mode.)

Interactive Startup

Shift+F8

Logged (\Bootlog.txt)

F8, Logged

Previous Version of MS-DOS

F4

Startup Menu

F8

Press and hold Ctrl

Step-by-Step Confirmation

Shift+F8

or

F8, Step-by-Step Confirmation

Windows in Safe Mode

F5

or

Press and hold *Shift*

or

F8, Safe Mode

Windows in Safe Mode with Network Support

F6

or

F8, Safe Mode with Network Support

See Also: Bootlog.txt; Logview; Passwords; Safe Mode; Starting Windows

Sysedit

See: System Configuration Editor (p. 441)

System

System

System is a Control Panel tool that allows you to make changes to the properties for the hardware devices that are installed in your system. You can also make adjustments for performance and troubleshoot problems you may be having with a hardware device.

..QuicKeys..

Right-click , Properties.

My Computer

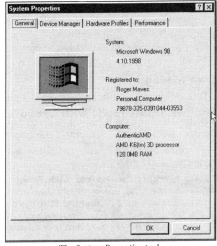

The System Properties tool.

or

Alt+double-click My Computer.

or

Click Start, Settings, Control Panel,

then double-click System.

or

Win+Break (Microsoft Natural Keyboard).

General

The General tab displays the version of Windows you have installed, who the software is registered to, and the computer manufacturer's support information.

Device Manager

The Device Manager tab lists all the hardware that is installed on your computer. The list is organized by hardware categories. Each category's detail can be viewed by clicking the "+" sign next to the category.

The Properties for each device can be viewed by double-clicking the device listing.

 Markers for Devices with Problems: If the icon for a device has an "X" through it, it is disabled. If it has a circled exclamation point through it, it has a problem. The problem is explained in the device's properties.

Properties

Properties displays the properties for the selected device.

Refresh

Refresh updates the hardware list. This may take a few minutes to complete.

Remove

Remove deletes the selected device.

 Delete Unneeded Devices: You may find devices listed in the Device Manager that do not physically exist or duplicate existing entries. In either case highlight the unneeded entry and use the Remove button to delete it.

Print displays a dialog box that has three options:

- System Summary
- Selected Class or Device
- All Devices and System Summary.

You also have the option of printing to a file, which can be helpful if you are trying to troubleshoot a problem and want to e-mail, transfer or fax the results to another party. Use Setup to select the Generic/Text Only printer driver.

CAUTION: *Be sure the Generic/Text Only printer driver is installed before you attempt to print. If it hasn't been installed, you can add it using the Printers tool in the Control Panel.*

Hardware Profiles

Hardware Profiles allows you to have multiple hardware setups so that you can choose between them at startup. For example, if you had hardware that was available from your laptop's docking station, but not when the computer was disconnected from the docking station, you might want to have different hardware configurations to accommodate the two.

Performance

On the Performance tab, Windows displays information on Memory, System Resources, File System, Virtual Memory, Disk Compression, and PC Cards.

File System Properties

In *File System Properties* you can adjust settings for Hard Disks and CD-ROMs. The default settings are usually the most appropriate; however, if you are having read or write problems with your devices, you may want to change these settings to see if it makes a difference in your system's operation.

Graphics Settings (Advanced)

If you are having graphics display problems, you may want to experiment with the setting in this dialog box. By default, the slider is set to full acceleration, the fastest setting; however, a slower setting may solve your problems.

Virtual Memory

Virtual memory is the memory Windows simulates on your hard drive. Normally, Windows manages this adequately on its own; however, if you want to manipulate the Virtual Memory settings you can do so using the dialog box associated with this button.

 Use Second Hard Drive for Swap File: If you have more than one physical hard drive in your computer and the second drive has more available space than your first, you can boost your performance by having Windows use the second drive for its swap file. For the best performance, remove all files from the drive, Defrag the drive (even if it claims it's not necessary), then set your virtual memory settings, both minimum and maximum, to 2-3 times the size of your RAM.

Improve Performance with Virtual Memory Settings: If you specify your own virtual memory settings, rather than let Windows continually readjust them, Windows will spend less time manipulating the swap file size, giving you more time for your programs. Your swap file should be 2-3 times the size of your RAM. Set both the minimum and maximum settings to this figure. This is also the amount of free disk space you should have if you decided to let Windows dynamically size the swap file.

Default Location: \Control Panel\System
See Also: Add New Hardware

System Configuration Editor

Sysedit

Sysedit is Windows 3.1x's System Configuration Editor. It was used to edit several files that controlled how MS-DOS and Windows worked. Windows 9x still uses some of these same files, so Sysedit can be used to modify these files as well. The files that are automatically opened with Sysedit are Autoexec.bat, Config.sys, Win.ini, System.ini, Protocol.ini and MSMail.ini.

Quick Access

Click **Start**, Run, type **sysedit**, then click OK.

Sysedit is a simple text editor that is similar to Notepad. Make any changes you feel necessary and save the files. You will most likely need to restart Windows for the changes to take effect.

Default Location: \Windows\System\Sysedit.exe

See Also: Notepad

98 System Configuration Utility

Msconfig

The *System Configuration Utility* is a tool that is can be used to troubleshoot Windows 98 configuration problems. It allows you to selectively change the system configuration settings. This provides for you, through a process of elimination, a method of including or excluding items in your system configuration without having to directly edit the configuration files.

The System Configuration Utility also provides tools to Backup and Restore your configuration files.

CAUTION: *Before making any changes to your configuration, use the Create Backup tool to back up your configuration files. This ensures that changes you make to your system can be reversed.*

Quick Access

Using My Computer or Windows Explorer, navigate to the \Windows\System folder, then double-click Msconfig.exe.

 Create a shortcut to Msconfig.exe on your desktop or in your Start menu (Programs|Accessories|System Tools menu) for easy access.

Troubleshooting

The first step in troubleshooting is to exclude the Autoexec.bat and Config.sys from your startup. You can do this by selecting Diagnostic Startup from the General tab. When your system restarts select Step-by-step confirmation and process all items but Autoexec.bat and Config.sys.

After your system restarts, see if the problem still exists. If it doesn't, you'll know your problem exists in one of the two files. If the problem still exists, you need to look further into other areas of the configuration.

Windows 98 provides a complete troubleshooting dialog, which leads you through the process. For more information on troubleshooting consult Help|Help Topics from within the System Configuration Utility.

Note: When you have too many applications loading up automatically at start up, your system may appear to stall or hang up. To correct this situation you can permanently or temporarily disable some of the programs that are loading. On the System Configuration Utility's Startup tab each program can be individually enabled or disabled using the check boxes next to each entry.

Default Location: \Windows\System\Msconfig.exe

See Also: Logview; Quick-Fix Engineering; RegClean; Registry; Safe Mode; Scandisk; Start Up Menu

Taskbar

The *Taskbar* is a tool that provides access to programs you use regularly and to programs that are already open. As you open programs they appear on the taskbar as buttons. To move to a new program all you have to do is click on the appropriate button.

Windows 98 adds a few icons to the taskbar that let you access programs directly, including Microsoft Internet Explorer and Microsoft Outlook Express. It also provides a quick way to minimize all windows and display your desktop by providing an icon called Show Desktop.

The Taskbar can be positioned on the top, bottom, left or right side of your desktop; however, the default position is at the bottom.

..QuicKeys..

Cycle through Taskbar Buttons

Win+Tab (Microsoft Natural Keyboard).

Hide, Auto

Right-click blank area of taskbar, Properties, Auto Hide.

Hide, Permanently

Right-click blank area of taskbar, Properties, clear Auto Hide if selected, then drag taskbar to edge of the desktop until it disappears.

Move

Click on blank area of taskbar, then drag to new position.

Move Focus to Taskbar

Ctrl+Esc, Esc

Properties

Right-click blank area of taskbar, Properties.

or

98

Click **Start**, Settings, Taskbar and StartMenu, Taskbar Options tab

or

95

Click **Start**, Settings, Taskbar.

or

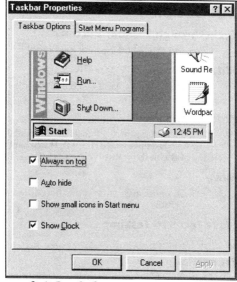

Ctrl+Esc, S, T

Resize

Place mouse pointer on border of taskbar. When double-headed arrow appears, click, then drag to new size.

Show Clock

Right-click blank area of taskbar, Properties, Show Clock checkbox.

Switch To Running Program

Alt+Tab

View Hidden Taskbar

> *Ctrl+Esc*

or

> Move mouse pointer to the edge of the desktop where you think the taskbar is docked.

or

> If Auto Hide is off, look for the edge of the taskbar, click on it and drag it out on to your desktop.

Properties

The taskbar properties address a few display options that you can use.

Taskbar Options

On the Taskbar Options tab you have four settings:

Always on top

> This makes sure that the taskbar is always visible, even when a program is being run full screen.

Auto hide

> Auto hide reduces the taskbar to a thin line at the selected location the top, bottom, or sides of the screen. To see and use the taskbar move the pointer to the edge of the screen–the taskbar appears. When you move the pointer off the taskbar it hides itself.

 Locate Hidden Task Bar: If you can't locate your taskbar, press *Ctrl+Esc.* The taskbar and the Start Menu will appear on top of any other open windows.

Show small icons in Start menu

If selected, the size of the icons in the Start menu is reduced, which in turn reduces the overall size of the Start menu.

Show clock

Specifies whether a digital clock is displayed on the taskbar. If you move the pointer onto the clock it will display the date. To change the time or date, double-click the clock. The time and date are read from the computer's internal clock.

HOt Tip **Show Volume Control on Task Bar**: If you would like the volume control to show up on your taskbar, double-click Multimedia in the Control Panel, select Show volume control on the taskbar, then click OK.

HOt Tip **Enable Registry Changes without Restarting Windows**: If you make a change in your Registry that affects the taskbar, you can enable the new changes without restarting Windows. Press *Ctrl+Alt+Delete* to display the Close Program dialog box, select Explorer, click <u>E</u>nd Task, then click No in the Shutdown Windows dialog box.

Start Menu Programs

The Start Menu tab lets you add and remove items from the Start menu.

Add

Add lets you add a program to the Start menu. To use this tool you need to know the program's command or be able to find it using the Browse function.

Remove

> *Remove* lists all the programs that currently reside in the Start menu. To remove a program select it, then click Remove.

Advanced

> *Advanced* launches Windows Explorer. You can then use it to copy or create shortcuts in the Start menu.

Clear

> *Clear* removes all files from the Documents menu contained in the Start menu.

See Also: Start Menu

Time

See: Regional Settings (p. 136)

Tips and Tour

See: Welcome to Windows 95 (p. 476)

Undo

You can reverse the most recent action you've just taken using the *Undo* command. It can be used with Copy, Move, Rename or Delete. For example, if you accidentally moved some files to another folder and realized it was the wrong folder, you could use the command Undo Move and recover from your mistake.

As actions are taken, each one is recorded and stacked one on top of the other. The **last ten ac-**

tions are kept in the stack. This allows you to undo actions one by one in reverse order.

HOt Tip **Use Undo Immediately:** It's best to use the Undo command immediately after taking an action in the same window or pane you are working in. If you continue to execute the stacked Undo commands, the Undos may be taking place in windows or panes you are not viewing. This can get quite confusing and may undo actions you don't want undone!

Quick Access

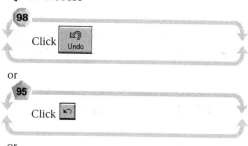

98

Click Undo

or

95

Click ↶

or

Click **E**dit on the menu bar, **U**ndo *action*

or

Right-click the background of a window, pane or the desktop, then select **U**ndo *action* from the shortcut menu

or

Ctrl+Z

CAUTION: *When you shutdown Windows, you lose the ability to undo your last 10 actions.*

Updates

See: Quick-Fix Engineering (p.334); Version - Windows (p. 451); Windows Update (p.507)

Version - File

See: File & Folder Properties|Version 211

Version - Windows

Periodically Microsoft releases a new version of Windows. These new versions may fix problems that existed in earlier releases and may even add new features to Windows. To stay up to date with your Windows installation, you'll want to make sure you have the latest version installed.

Each release or update of Windows is assigned a version number and description. To find out what version of Windows 9x you have:

Quick Access

Click **Start**, Settings, Control Panel,

double-click System, then click the General tab. The *version number* is located under the heading System.

or

Click **Start**, Run, type **qfecheck.exe**,

then click OK. The *version number* is located at the top of the Registered Updates tab.

or

At the MS-DOS prompt type **ver**, then press *Enter.*

Depending on which of the above methods of access you use, Windows displays different version numbers. Following are the versions currently available:

Description	Versions

Windows 95

Original Release	4.00.950
VER at DOS prompt	4.00.950
Service Pack 1	4.00.950a
VER at DOS prompt	4.00.950
OEM Service Release 2 (OSR2)	4.00.950b
VER at DOS prompt	4.00.1111
OEM Service Release 2.1 (OSR2.1)	4.00.950b*
VER at DOS prompt	4.00.1212
OEM Service Release 2.5 (OSR2.5)	4.00.950c
VER at DOS prompt	4.00.1111

Windows 98

Original Release	4.10.1998
VER at DOS prompt	4.10.1998
Second Edition	4.10.2222A
VER at DOS prompt	4.10.2222

*OEM Service Release 2.1 can be identified only by starting Add/Remove Programs in the Control Panel and checking for an installation option called "USB Supplement to OSR2" in the Windows Setup tab. If it exists, you are running OSR2.1; if not, OSR2.

Microsoft periodically provides updates, called *Service Packs/Releases*, to Windows. It's wise to install these Service Packs/Releases, as they fix known problems with the operating system and utilities.

HOt Tip | **What Updates Are on Your System?**
To find out exactly what updates have been installed on your system, run Quick-Fix Engineering. Click Start, Run, type **qfecheck.exe**, then click OK. A list of every update and patch is displayed.

Windows 98 makes it even easier with Windows Update. See the section "Windows Update" (p. 507) for more information.

See Also: Quick-Fix Engineering; Windows Update

View

One of the nice features that is available in Windows Explorer, My Computer, Network Neighborhood, Recycle Bin and any folder window, is that you can change the way you view your folders and files. These changes can be made using the options on the *View* menu. If the Toolbar is displayed, you can also make changes using the buttons on the Toolbar. The following options are available for you to use:

Toolbar(s)

Toolbar displays a toolbar near the top of the window just below the menu bar. Contained in the toolbar is a list box that enables you to change to a different folder quickly and easily.

The buttons on the toolbar duplicate the commands on the menus, but provide a single step approach. The *Up One Level* button does not have an equivalent menu command, but is quite useful. Upon execution it moves you up one level in the hierarchy from your current position.

Windows 98 offers more control over the toolbar, providing a way to add an Address Bar, Links, and Text Labels for the buttons.

Status Bar

Status Bar turns on the display of system information at the bottom of the window. When the Status Bar is on, the number of objects, disk space used for the selected object and free disk space are displayed dynamically as you navigate through the hierarchy.

98 Explorer Bar

In Windows 98 the *Explorer Bar* was introduced which adds an additional left windowpane to My Computer. However, instead of using it for an Explorer Tree as does Windows Explorer, it's used for other purposes such as Search, Favorites, History, and Channels. Only one option can occupy the windowpane at a time—to close the Explorer Bar, click the Close button.

As Web Page

As Web Page displays the objects in a window that looks very much like Microsoft Internet Explorer. The Toolbar, Address Bar, and overall design all reflect a "web" look. The intent is for you to have the same look and feel when managing your information whether you are using local drives, network drives, or web sites.

Large Icons

Large Icons displays the folders and files, left to right, as large icons with the name of the folder or file below it. No detail is displayed for the objects.

Letters   Winword.exe

Large icons view

 To see the details for a folder or file in Large Icon, Small Icon or List view, right-click the *object*, then select Properties or select the *object* and click the Properties button on the toolbar.

Small Icons

Small Icons displays the folders and files, left to right, as small icons with the name of the folder or file displayed to the right of it. No detail is displayed for the objects.

Small Icons view

List

List displays the folders and files, top to bottom, as small icons with the name of the folder or file displayed to the right of it. No detail is displayed for the objects.

Letters	Mscreate.dir	Winword.gid	Wrdbasic.hlp
Macros	Qwinword.fts	Winword.hlp	Wwintl32.dll
Startup	Qwinword.hlp	Winword7.reg	Wwpab.cnv

List view.
Note how the order of the objects differs from Small Icons
view.

Details

Details displays the folders and files, top to bottom, as small icons with the name of the folder or file, size, type, and date and time modified, displayed to the right of it.

Letters		File Folder	7/9/97 2:52 PM
Macros		File Folder	7/9/97 2:55 PM
Startup		File Folder	7/9/97 2:57 PM
Wordmail		File Folder	7/9/97 2:56 PM
Dialog.fon	48KB	Font file	3/20/96 12:00 AM
Email.dot	13KB	Microsoft Word Tem...	3/20/96 12:00 AM
Email1.dot	17KB	Microsoft Word Tem...	3/20/96 12:00 AM

Hot Tip **To reverse the sorted order of a column**, double-click the column heading.

Hot Tip **To change the column size**, drag the column heading separator left or right, or double-click the heading separator and the column will resize itself to the longest item in the column. To automatically adjust all the columns press *Ctrl* and the *Plus Sign (+)* on the numeric keypad.

Hot Tip **Save Your Explorer Settings:** If you make changes to the Windows Explorer windows settings, for example, changing the window size, pane size, sort order, toolbar status or display type, and the changes don't seem to be there the next time you open Windows Explorer, try this: arrange the Windows Explorer window the way you want. Then, while pressing *Ctrl+Alt+Shift*, click the Close button — your settings are saved. Another option is to use one of the Power Toys, Tweak UI. See "Power Toys"(p. 323), for more information.

98 Customize this Folder

This option only becomes available when a drive or folder is open. It allows you to make changes to the look and feel of the folder.

Create or edit an HTML document

If you want to manipulate the look and feel of the folder, you can select this option which creates and/or allows editing of an HTML page. An editor is opened in which you can modify the code. When you're finished with your changes, save the document with its given file name. The next time you view the folder, your changes will take effect.

Choose a background picture

This option allows you to select an existing picture file to be used as a background for your document window within the folder.

Remove customization

Select this option to restore the folder to its original state before customization.

Arrange Icons

Under the *Arrange Icons* menu there are five options you can use to arrange the order of the objects (folders and files) in the right pane of the Windows Explorer window: Name, Type, Size, Date, and Auto Arrange. When you select one of the options, all of the objects are reordered to comply with the selection. Auto Arrange is the default for the Large and Small Icon view, which puts the folders, then the files, in order by name.

Line Up Icons

Line Up Icons rearranges the objects according to an invisible grid, placing each object in line with its neighbor. This option is only available when using the Large or Small Icon view.

Refresh

If you've made changes to the folders or files that do not seem to appear in the window, select *Refresh* to obtain a new view. This is especially useful when working on a network server where others may have made changes without your knowledge. Refresh provides the latest view, reflecting the most recent changes.

 Set Up Automatic Refresh: If you would like Windows to perform a refresh automatically, you can modify the Registry to prompt it to do so.

CAUTION: *The following instructions involve changing settings in the Registry. If the changes are not made properly, serious problems may result. Be sure to backup your Registry before continuing. See: "Registry" for more information about backing up and editing the Registry.*

Using Regedit open the Registry and move to HKEY_LOCAL_MACHINE\ System\ CurrentControlSet\Control\ Update.

In the right window pane, right-click on UpdateMode, then select Modify. Change the 01 to 00, then click OK.

Restart your computer to use the new setting.

Options or Folder Options

The view and how it functions with certain file types can also be modified using *Options* (Windows 95) or *Folder Options* (Windows 98). Both can be selected from the View menu on the menu bar. There are two tabs for Windows 95 where you can make changes: *View* and *File Types*. Windows 98 has three tabs: *General*, *View* and *File Types*.

Folder Options - Windows 98 Tabs

General

The look and feel of the Windows desktop is specified in this tab.

Web style

Selecting this style makes your desktop and folders work like a Web page. The double-click is replaced by a single-click and selecting objects is accomplished by just pointing at them. It also lets you add information, change font styles, and use HTML pages as a background wallpaper.

Classic style

Selecting this style makes your desktop and folders work like they have in previous versions of Windows. Double-clicking executes, while a single-click selects an object.

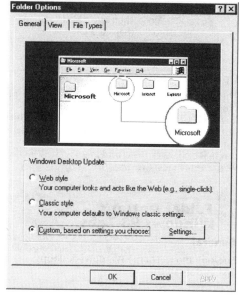

Custom

Selecting this style allows you to set up your desktop and folders to suit your own particular style.

To customize your settings, click Settings.

There are four settings you can control: Active Desktop, Browsing Folders, Viewing Web Content in Folders, and Clicking Items.

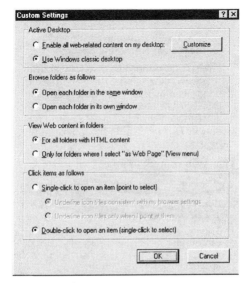

Active Desktop

Selecting the first option specifies that the Active Desktop be used. This means your desktop will look and work like a Web page. Active content can be added to it as any other Web page.

The second option activates the classic Windows desktop.

Browse folders as follows

The first option, Browse folders using a separate window, does not close the parent window when it opens a new window. If this option is selected, when you are browsing folders you can view the contents of a previous window by clicking on any part of the window that is showing, clicking 🔲 on the toolbar or pressing *Backspace*.

The second option, Browse folders using a single window, closes the parent window upon opening a new window. If this option is selected, when you are browsing folders you can view the contents of a previous window by clicking 🔲 on the toolbar or pressing *Backspace*.

View Web content in folders

Selecting the first option makes your folders work like a Web page. You can add information, change font styles, and use HTML pages as a background wallpaper.

The second option works similarly; however, each folder has to be specifically chosen to work as a Web page rather than the global approach in the first option.

Click items as follows

Selecting the first option specifies that to open items on the desktop and in folders requires only a single-click, just as a Web page would work.

The second option makes your desktop and folders work like they have in previous versions of Windows. Double-clicking executes, while a single-click selects an object.

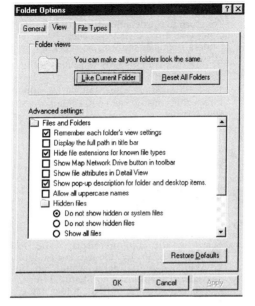

View

View controls how files and window pane descriptions are displayed. Windows 98 has additional controls that are not present in Windows 95.

Like Current Folder

> *Like Current Folder* changes all of your folder settings to reflect those on your View menu. Toolbar settings, however, are not affected.

Reset All Folders

To return to the default settings (those at the time you first installed), click Reset All Folders. Toolbar settings, however, are not affected.

Advanced Settings

The options under Advanced Settings allow for specific control over Files, Folders and Visual Settings.

Files and Folders

Remember each folder's view settings

If selected, each folder will save its current settings when closed. These settings will be used when the folder is reopened. If not selected, the folder will use its default settings from the installation.

Display the full path in the title bar

Selecting this option displays the full MS-DOS path in the title bar. For example, C:\Windows\Start Menu would be displayed instead of just Start Menu. If this option is not selected, only the folder name is displayed.

Hide file extensions for known file types

Selecting this option hides the file name extensions for certain registered file names. This provides a less cluttered screen display; however, it may not provide the detail you want to see.

Show Map Network Drive button in toolbar

If selected, two additional buttons will appear on the toolbar: Map Network Drive and Disconnect Network Drive.

Show file attributes in Detail View

Selecting this option displays the file attributes in an additional column in the Details view.

Show pop-up description for folder and desktop items

Selecting this option enables a pop-up description, which appears in a small window for folders and desktop objects that are selected within the window. This takes place when the view, As Web Page, is not selected; otherwise, it has no effect.

Allow all uppercase names

If selected file names will retain uppercase letters as they were originally named; otherwise, only the first letter of a file name will remain in uppercase.

Hidden Files

Only one of three options can be selected. Choosing to hide system or hidden files will reduce the clutter in your display and help to protect these important files from being changed or deleted.

CAUTION: *If you choose to show all files, you risk accidental damage or deletion of critical program files. If this occurs, Windows may not start up or work properly and may require reinstallation.*

Visual Settings

Hide icons when desktop is viewed as Web page

If selected all icons on the desktop will not be displayed, only the taskbar and HTML items will be visible.

Smooth edges of screen fonts

Selecting this option will smooth the jagged edges of fonts (especially large fonts) and graphic designs.

CAUTION: *Although the fonts and graphics will look better, your performance will be degraded.*

Show window contents while dragging

If selected the entire contents of a window will be visible while it is being dragged to a new location; otherwise, only the outline of the window will be visible.

Restore Defaults

This command will reset all the options in the dialog box back to their default state, as originally installed.

Options - Windows 95 Tabs

View

View controls how files and windowpane descriptions are displayed in Windows Explorer.

Hidden Files

These options control what files are hidden from view when working in Windows Explorer.

Show all files

Show all files displays all files regardless of what type of files they are.

Hide files of these types:

Hide files of these types hides only the types of files listed in the list box.

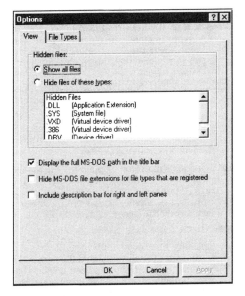

Hôt Tip **Locate Files by Type:** Windows Explorer does not have a sorting function by file name extension; however, clicking on the file type heading may get you close enough, or to make sure you are looking at a specific extension use the Find command located on the Tools menu. When using the Find command be sure to specify the folder you want to look in and use a wildcard with the extension, for example, *.txt.

Hot Tip **Save Windows Explorer's Window Size**. If you've resized your window and want to make sure it's in the same shape the next time you open Windows Explorer, click Vi̲ew on the menu bar, Options, then make any change on the View tab. Now, reverse the change you just made. this will make the Apply button active. Click Apply, then OK. When you open Windows Explorer the next time, it will retain these new settings.

Display the full MS-DOS path

Selecting this option displays the full MS-DOS path in the title bar, for example, C:\Windows\Start Menu would be displayed instead of just Start Menu. If this option is not selected only the folder name is displayed.

Hide MS-DOS file extensions

Selecting this option hides the file name extensions for certain registered file names. This provides a less cluttered screen display; however, it may not provide the detail you need to see.

Include description bar

To see a description above each windowpane select this option. The description above the right pane displays the full MS-DOS path name, which can be quite helpful. If you don't feel the information is valuable turn the option off and you'll have more room in your window.

Folder

The options on the *Folder* tab control the method in which folder windows are closed as you browse through your hierarchy.

The first option, Browse folders using a separate window, does not close the parent window when it opens a new window. If this option is selected, when you are browsing folders you can view the contents of a previous window by clicking on any part of the window that is showing, clicking 🔙 on the toolbar or pressing the *Backspace* key.

Note: The Folder tab is not available in Windows Explorer.

File Types

File Types is used to register specific file types with both Windows 98 and 95. When a file type is registered, a program can be associated with it that will be used to open that file type. For example, a text document with the file name extension of .txt could be associated with Notepad. Once associated, whenever a .txt file is double-clicked the file will be opened with Notepad.

There are many file types that are created as defaults when Windows is installed and others that are added by programs during their installation. Existing file types can be modified or removed, and new ones can be added.

Registered File Types

All the registered file types are listed in this list box. If you don't see the type you are looking for use the scroll bar to see more.

File Type Details

In the *File Type Details* panel the extension for the registered file and the program that will be used to open it are displayed. To see these details for a specific file type just select the file from the Registered File Types list box. The File Type Details will change to reflect your selection.

New Type

To create a new file type or association, click the New Type button, a dialog box will open in which you can add the new type and its properties.

Change Icon

Provides a method to change the icon that is associated with the file type.

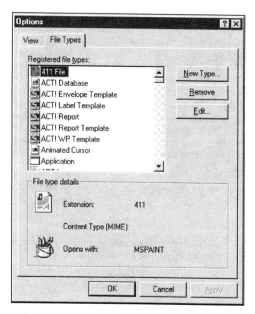

Description of type

This is the description of the file type—it's displayed when you use the Details view

Associated extension

Specifies the three-character file name extension for this file type.

Content Type (MIME)

MIME or Multipurpose Internet Mail Extensions is a protocol used to define file attachments for the Web. The type of file you are adding can be typed or selected from the drop-down list box.

Note: The Content Type (MIME) drop down list box is added to the Add New File Type dialog box during the installation of Microsoft's Internet Explorer; consequently, Windows installations where Microsoft Internet Explorer has not been installed will not have the this property.

Default Extension for Content Type

Use to specify the extension associated with this file type.

Actions

Lists the commands that are associated with this file type. These commands are displayed on the shortcut menu for this file type.

To add a new action, click the New button. You are asked to name the action and provide the command to execute it.

The Edit button is used to modify an existing action and Remove serves to remove an action from the list.

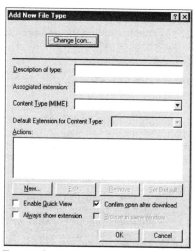

To specify that one of the actions should be the default action, select the action, then click Set Default. This default action will execute when a file of this type is double-clicked.

Enable Quick View

Indicates whether the file type is supported by Quick View. See "Quick View"(p. 335) for more information.

Always show extension

Specifies whether the file name extension should be displayed in a folder window.

Confirm open after download

Determines whether this file type should be opened immediately after being downloaded.

Browse in same window

Specifies that this file type will open in the existing window rather than creating a new window.

Create a File Type Association on the Fly: Whether you are in Windows Explorer or My Computer you can create an association to an existing file type on the fly by following the next steps. Select a file with the appropriate extension, press and hold down the Shift key while right-clicking the *file name,* then select Open With. Select the program you want to use to open this type of file, select the check box labeled Always use this program to open this type of file, then click OK. From now on, anytime you double-click this type of file, it will open with the associated program.

If you double-click a file that is not associated with an application program, the Open With dialog box will automatically appear. You can then create an association as described above.

To be able to open a file type with more than one application, you can create additional Actions that will appear on the shortcut menu when you right-click the file name. For example, if you have Notepad associated with .txt files but want to also have the choice of opening them with Microsoft Word, here's what to do. On the File Types tab, select the .txt file type from the list, then click the Edit button. Click the New button to create a new Action. Type **Open**

with Word in the Action text box. This text will later appear as a shortcut menu option. Next, type:

"c:\Program Files\Microsoft Office\ Office\winword.exe" /n

in the Application used to perform action text box, or use the browse function to find it. Click OK to save your changes, then close the remaining dialog boxes. Now, when you right-click a .txt file, the option Open with Word will display.

Note: If you find that your association doesn't seem to work when you double-click on a file whose name consists of more than one word, you need to make an addition to your command line. On the File Types tab, select the file type from the Registered file types list, then click Edit. Select open from Actions list, then click Edit. Add a space and "%1" (include the quotes) to the end of the command line in the Application used to perform action text box. The application will now work with file names of more than one word.

Note: If you notice that your associations have changed after you install a new application, you will need to remove the offending association and create a new one to reestablish the one you had before. Microsoft Internet Explorer is one of the big offenders. During its installation process it associates .gif and .jpeg files with Microsoft Internet Explorer even though they may already be associated with another application program. See "Remove" below.

Note: Do your file associations seem to change every time you restart your computer? If so, you may have an old win.ini file with file associations in it. Win.ini is not necessary for Windows 95 or Windows 98; however, it could still be on your computer from when you converted from Windows 3.1. Win.ini might be useful for compatibility purposes, so don't delete it. To correct the problem, edit the file with Notepad and remove any associations in the [Extensions] section that are causing you problems.

Remove

To remove an existing file type, select the file type in the Registered File Types list box, then click the Remove button.

Edit

To change the properties for an existing file type, select the file type in the Registered File Types list box, then click the Edit button. The Edit File Type dialog box will display allowing you to make changes.

See Also: Disconnect Network Drive; Section 4 —File Types; Map Network Drive; My Computer; Network Neighborhood; Recycle Bin; Windows Explorer

Virtual Memory

See: System|Virtual Memory (p. 440)

Volume Labels

See: Naming Disks (p. 308); Renaming Disks (366)

Welcome to Windows 95

The Welcome to Windows screen is displayed when you first start Windows. It offers several levels of help and instruction, which you can use initially to become accustomed to the Windows operating system.

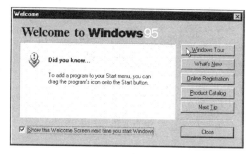

Tips

Welcome to Windows 95 provides 50 miscellaneous tips you can review. At the beginning of each work session a different tip is displayed. To see additional tips you can click the Next Tip button.

Windows Tour

Additional help is available by clicking the Windows Tour button. The tour will lead you through several basic Windows operating system functions such as:

- Starting a Program
- Exploring Your Disk
- Finding a File
- Switching Windows
- Using Help

Note: If the Windows Tour button is not displayed you will need to install it. Be sure to have the CD available before you start. Double-click Add/Remove Programs in the Control Panel, then click Windows Setup. Select Accessories, Details, then Windows 95 Tour. Click OK twice.

What's New

If you are curious about the differences between Windows 3.x and Windows 95 you can click the What's New button. A Windows Help dialog box is displayed that lists the following frequently asked questions:

- How do I start programs?
- What happened to my program groups?
- What happened to File Manager?
- What happened to Control Panel?
- More questions and answers

Selecting the last item displays several more questions.

Online Registration

You can use Online Registration to register your copy of Windows using a modem. If you select this option, Windows will dial up Microsoft and submit your registration. If you don't have your modem installed yet you will be given the opportunity to do so at this time.

If you choose not to register using your modem be sure to mail in your registration as soon as possible.

Disable/Enable Welcome to Windows 95

If you want to keep this screen from showing up again, clear the check box at the bottom of the screen labeled "Show this Welcome Screen next time you start Windows."

If you've turned the Welcome to Windows screen off and want to turn it back on again:

> Double-click the Welcome.exe file in the Windows folder, select the check box at the bottom of the screen, then click Close.

or

> Click **Start**, Run, type **Welcome.exe**, click OK, select the check box at the bottom of the screen, then click Close.

Default Location: \Windows\Welcome.exe

See Also: Windows 95 Resource Kit

Welcome to Windows 98

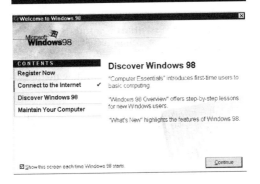

The Welcome to Windows screen is displayed when you first start Windows. It offers several levels of help and instruction, which you can use initially to become accustomed to the Windows operating system.

Register Now

Clicking Register Now starts the Registration Wizard so that you can register your Windows software online. Clicking the Begin button does the same thing.

Connect to the Internet

Connect to the Internet starts a Connection Wizard, which simplifies the process of connecting your computer to the internet.

Discover Windows 98

This selection contains four sections of information tailored to users of different experience levels.

Computer Essentials is a tutorial for those new to personal computers. It introduces the various pieces of computer hardware, use of the keyboard and mouse, basics of the Windows desktop, and basic window manipulation.

Windows 98 Overview is primarily for users upgrading from Windows 3.x or who need to familiarize themselves with the basic Windows interface. Main subject areas are:

- Starting a Program
- Exploring Files and Folders
- Finding Information
- Managing Open Windows
- Connecting to the Internet
- Exploring the Active Desktop

What's New gives a quick multimedia overview of the differences between Windows 95 and Windows 98.

More Windows 98 Resources contains information about other Windows training materials available from Microsoft.

Maintain your computer

Starts Maintenance Wizard, a method for scheduling Disk Defragmenter, ScanDisk and Disk Cleanup to run on a regular basis. Standardized settings are available, or you can create a customized schedule.

Disable/Enable Welcome to Windows 98

If you want to keep this screen from showing up again, clear the check box at the bottom of the screen labeled "Show this Welcome Screen next time you start Windows."

If you've turned the Welcome to Windows screen off, and want to turn it back on again:

> Double-click the Welcome.exe file in the Windows folder, select the check box at the bottom of the screen, then click <u>C</u>lose.

or

> Click **Start**, <u>R</u>un, type **Welcome.exe**, click OK, select the check box at the bottom of the screen, then click <u>C</u>lose.

or

> Click **Start**, <u>P</u>rograms, Accessories, System Tools, Welcome to Windows

Default Location: \Windows\Welcome.exe

See Also: Windows 98 Resource Kit

Window Menu

The Window Menu contains the most basic commands for controlling the size and location of the current window.

Open

> Click *program* icon on title bar

or

> *Alt+Spacebar*

Window

..QuicKeys..

Arrange Icons

Right-click background of *window*, Arrange Icons, then *sort method*

or

Click <u>V</u>iew on the menu bar, Arrange <u>I</u>cons, then *sort method*

or

Click a *column* heading (Details View)

Cascade

Right-click blank area of taskbar, <u>C</u>ascade (Windows)

Close

Click **X** on the title bar

or

Double-click *program* icon on title bar

or

Alt+F4

or

Alt+Spacebar, C

Cycle Through Windows

Alt+Tab

Make Active

Click anywhere in window.

Maximize

Click 🔲 on the title bar.

or

Double-click *title bar*

or

Right-click *program* or *document* icon on title bar, Ma<u>x</u>imize

or

Alt+Spacebar, X

Maximize All

Right-click blank area of taskbar, <u>U</u>ndo Minimize All

or

Shift+Win+M (Microsoft Natural Keyboard)

Minimize

Click ▬ on the title bar

or

Right-click *program* or *document* icon on menu bar, Mi<u>n</u>imize

or

Alt+Spacebar, N

Minimize All

Right-click blank area of taskbar, <u>M</u>inimize All Windows

or

Win+M (Microsoft Natural Keyboard)

or

Ctrl+Esc, then *Alt+M*

Move

Click on title bar then drag to new position

or

Alt+Space Bar, M, use the arrow key to move (*Esc* to cancel), then *Enter* to save

Open A Minimized Window

Click *button* on taskbar

Resize

Place mouse pointer on border of window until double-headed arrow appears, click, then drag to new size.

or

Alt+Space Bar, S, use the arrow key to resize (*Esc* to cancel), then *Enter* to save.

Resize Proportionally

Place mouse pointer on corner of window. When double-headed arrow appears, click, then drag to new position.

Restore

Click [image] on the title bar.

or

Double-click *title bar.*

or

Right-click *program* or *document* icon on title bar, Restore.

or

Alt+Spacebar, R

Restore MS-DOS Full Screen

Alt+Enter
(Toggles between full and restored screen)

Show All

Right-click blank area of taskbar, Tile or Cascade.

Show DOS Path and Filename in Title Bar

Click <u>V</u>iew on menu bar, Options, <u>V</u>iew, click the Display the full MS-DOS path in the title bar checkbox.

or

Alt+V, O, <u>V</u>iew, click the Display the full MS-DOS path in the title bar checkbox.

Show Toolbar

Click <u>V</u>iew, Toolbars, Select Options (Standard buttons, Address Bar, Links, Text Labels)

or

Click <u>V</u>iew on menu bar, <u>T</u>oolbar

or

Alt+V, T

Single Window Browse

In My Computer, click <u>V</u>iew on menu bar, Folder Options, General tab, Settings, Open each folder in the same window. The single window will change as you open each folder.

or

In My Computer, click <u>V</u>iew on menu bar, <u>O</u>ptions, Folder tab, check the Browse folders using single window option. The single window will change as you open each folder.

or

Alt+V, O, Alt+N

Sort Folders and Files

Right-click background of *window*, Arrange Icons, then *sort method*

or

Click View on the menu bar, Arrange Icons, then *sort method*

or

Click a *column* heading (Details View)

Switch Between Documents

Click Window on menu bar, then select *document*

or

Ctrl+F6

Switch Between Panes

In Explorer, click in *pane*

or

In Explorer, *F6*

Switch Between Windows Applications

Click taskbar *button*

or

Alt+Tab

Switch to Taskbar's Next Open Window

Alt+Esc

Tile Horizontally

Right-click blank area of taskbar, Tile Horizontally

Tile Vertically

Right-click blank area of taskbar, Tile Vertically

Undo Minimize All

Right-click blank area of taskbar, Undo Minimize All

or

Shift+Win+M (Microsoft Natural Keyboard)

Windows 95 Resource Kit

The Windows 95 Resource Kit is a technical guide to planning for, installing, configuring and supporting Windows 95.

The Windows 95 Resource Kit can be purchased as a book, or you can get the same information directly off your installation CD. The file you are looking for is Win95rk.hlp, which is located in the \Admin\Reskit\Helpfile folder. Copy it to your hard drive so that you can have quick access to its valuable information.

If you purchase the Windows 95 Resource Kit as a book, you will also receive with it a selection of utility programs for Windows 95.

If you are an MSDN subscriber, you can download the Windows 95 Resource Kit and the utility programs from Microsoft's web site. Information about subscribing is available on Microsoft's site.

Default Location:
\Admins\Reskit\Helpfile\Win95rk.hlp on Windows 95 CD-ROM

See Also: Window 98 Resource Kit

Windows 98 Resource Kit

The Windows 98 Resource Kit is a technical guide to planning for, installing, configuring and supporting Windows 98.

A free Resource Kit sampler comes on the Windows 98 CD-ROM. Its location on the CD-ROM is \Tools\Reskit. To install it, run setup.exe from the \Tools\Reskit folder.

It will be installed in \Windows\Start Menu\Programs\Windows 98 Resource Kit , and will appear as a listing on the Start Menu. This is not the full version of the Windows 98 Resource Kit.

If you purchase the Windows 98 Resource Kit as a book, you will also receive with it a selection of utility programs for Windows 98.

If you are an MSDN subscriber, you can download the Windows 98 Resource Kit and the utility programs from Microsoft's web site. Information about subscribing is available on Microsoft's site.

Default Installation Location: \Tools\Reskit (Windows 98 CD-ROM)

Default Location: \Windows\Start Menu\Programs\Windows 98 Resource Kit

See Also: Windows 95 Resource Kit

Windows Explorer

 Windows Explorer is a file management tool you can use to view the hierarchy of the files and folders on your disk drives. Windows Explorer makes it easy to organize your files and folders. You can copy, move, rename, create, and delete files and folders using the tools contained in Windows Explorer.

Windows Explorer uses a two-pane window, as opposed to My Computer, which uses only one pane to display the information. This allows you to view the folder hierarchy in the left pane (the Explorer Tree) while viewing the folder contents in the right pane.

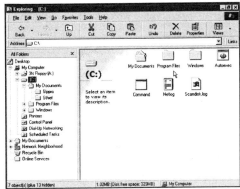

Windoww 98 3xplorer

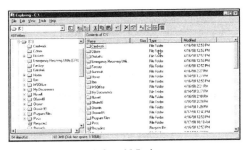

Windows 95 Explorer

Opening Windows Explorer

The Windows Explorer window can be opened in several different ways. The view that is displayed, and your hierarchical position in the folders, will be different depending on which method you choose.

Quick Access

Shift+double-click .

The My Computer resource under the Desktop icon will be your current hierarchical position.

or

Right-click **Start** , then click Explore.
The Start Menu folder under the Windows folder will be your active folder.

or

Right-click , then click Explore.

The My Computer resource under the Desktop icon will be your current position. If you are in the single pane view of My Computer, you use the same technique for any object if it can be explored.

or

If you are in the single pane view of My Computer, you can press *Shift*, then double-click the *object* you want to explore (this will work only if the object can be used with the Explore command).or

Click **Start** , Programs,

then choose Windows Explorer. The C-Drive resource under Desktop which is under My Computer will be your current hierarchical position.

or

Win+E (Microsoft Natural Keyboard)

Open More Than One Explorer Window: If you need more than one Windows Explorer window open, just repeat any of the actions above. To see them displayed side by side, minimize all other open windows, right-click a blank area of the taskbar, then select Tile <u>V</u>ertically or Tile <u>H</u>orizontally.

Shortcuts

A shortcut can be used to have Windows Explorer open in a specific hierarchical position. The command that is executed by the shortcut can specify a specific folder to be used as the current folder.

Example of command used in shortcut:

c:\Windows\Explorer.exe /n,/e,/root,c:

This command will open the Windows Explorer window using C: drive as its root. When you create the shortcut, designate a shortcut key combination, such as *Ctrl+Alt+E*, so you can open Windows Explorer at any time.

 Use Windows Explorer Icon for Your Shortcut: You can have your shortcut use the Windows Explorer icon by entering **c:\windows\explorer.exe** for the file name through the **Change Icon** browse window. To use other available icons such as floppy or hard drives enter **c:\windows\system\shell.dll**.

To learn more about the Explorer.exe command and its options, see the "Command" section below.

..QuicKeys..

There are many ways to accomplish different tasks in Windows Explorer. Following are the most common actions and their commands.

Activate Menu Bar

Alt

or

F10

Close

Click **X** on the title bar

or

Double-click *program* icon

or

Alt+F4

or

Alt+F, C

or

Alt+Spacebar, C

Close All Folders On Drive

Double-click the *drive* icon to close the tree, then press *F5*

Columns, Optimize Size

Ctrl+Plus Sign (on the numeric keypad)

Details

98

Click on the toolbar until <u>D</u>etails view is displayed

or

Click  next to the toolbar,
<u>D</u>etails

or

Click on the toolbar

or

Click <u>V</u>iew on the menu bar, then <u>D</u>etails

or

Right-click background, click <u>V</u>iew, then
<u>D</u>etails

or

Alt+V, D

Display Combo Box

Click ▼

or

F4

or

Alt+Down Arrow

Find

Click 🏁 Start, <u>F</u>ind

or

Win+F (Microsoft Natural Keyboard)

or

Click <u>T</u>ools on the menu bar, then <u>F</u>ind

or

Alt+T, F

Find Computer

Ctrl+Win+F (Microsoft Natural Keyboard)

Find Files or Folders

F3

or

Click on a blank area of the taskbar, then press *F3*

or

Right-click a *folder*, then click <u>F</u>ind

Go To First Object

Ctrl+Home

Go To Folder

Ctrl+G

Go To Last Object

Ctrl+End

Large Icons

98

Click [⊞ Views] on the toolbar until Large Icons view is displayed

or

Click [▾] next to [⊞ Views] on the toolbar, then Large Icons

or

Click [▯▯] on the toolbar

or

> Click <u>V</u>iew on the menu bar, then Large
> Icons

or

> Right-click background, click <u>V</u>iew, then
> Large Icons

or

> *Alt+V, G*

Line Up Icons

> Right-click background, click Arrange Icons,
> then *sort method*

or

> Right-click background, then click Line up
> Icons

or

> Click <u>V</u>iew on the menu bar, then Line up
> Icons

or

> *Alt+V, U*

or

> *Alt+V, E*

List View

Click 🖳 on the toolbar until List view is
displayed

or

Click ▾ next to 🖳 on the toolbar, then
<u>L</u>ist

or

Click 🖳 on the toolbar

or

Click <u>V</u>iew on the menu bar, then <u>L</u>ist

or

Right-click background, click <u>V</u>iew, then <u>L</u>ist

or

Alt+V, L

Move Focus Between Window Sections

F6

or

Alt

Open All Folders On Drive

Select the *drive* icon, then press * on the
numeric keypad

Open Object

Double-click the *object*

or

Right-click the *object*, then click <u>O</u>pen

Refresh View

F5

or

Click <u>V</u>iew on the menu bar, then <u>R</u>efresh

or

Alt+V, then *R*

Select the First Object

Home

Select the Last Object

End

Small Icons

Click on the toolbar until
Small Icons view is displayed

or

Click ▼ next to on the toolbar,

then S̲mall Icons

or

Click on the toolbar

or

Click V̲iew on the menu bar, then
S̲mall Icons

or

Right-click background, click V̲iew, then
S̲mall Icons

or

Alt+V, M

Switch Between Window Panes

F6

System Menu, Open

Double-click *program* icon

or

Alt+Spacebar

View Parent Folder

Click on the toolbar

or

Click on the toolbar

or

Backspace

For more information about copying, deleting, moving and renaming files and folders see the following sections: "Copying Files & Folders," "Deleting Files & Folders," "Moving Files & Folders," or "Renaming Files & Folders."

Using the Explorer Tree

The unique feature of Windows Explorer is the *Explorer Tree*, or left pane of the window. The Explorer Tree lets you view and move through the folder hierarchy without changing the view in the right pane. This allows drag and drop copying and moving without having to open up several windows. You can navigate through the Explorer Tree using the following techniques:

Collapse the Folder

Click minus sign (-) next to *folder*

or

Left Arrow

or

Minus Sign (-) on the numeric keypad

Expand Everything under the selection

* on the numeric keypad (NumLock must be on). This is slow - be patient!

Expand the Selection

> Click Plus Sign (+) next to folder

or

> *Right Arrow*

or

> *Plus Sign* (+)on the numeric keypad (Num Lock must be on)

Scroll Without Changing Selection

> *Ctrl*+Scroll Arrow or Scroll Box

or

> *Ctrl+Arrow key*

View Parent Folder

98

> Click ⬆ Up on the toolbar

or

> Click ⬆ on the toolbar

or

> *Backspace*

View

One of the nice features of Explorer is that you can change the way you view your folders and files. You can change the views from the View menu. If the Toolbar is displayed, you can also make changes using the buttons on the Toolbar. The following options are available from the View menu.

- Toolbar
- Status Bar
- As Web Page (Windows 98)
- Large Icons
- Small Icons
- List

- Details
- Customize this Folder
- Arrange Icons
- Line Up Icons
- Refresh
- Options (Windows 95)
- Folder Options (Windows 98)

For more information on these options see "View," p. 453.

Hot Tip **Right-Click to Access Some View Options:** Some of the options on the View menu can also be accessed by right-clicking the background of the right pane of the window.

98

Hot Tip **Switch Explorer View to My Computer View:** There may be occasions when you would like to switch from the Windows Explorer view to the single pane My Computer view. You can do so by clicking the Close button in the All Folders pane. To reverse the action click View, Explorer Bar, then All Folders.

HOt Tip **Display List of Drives at Opening:** If you would like Windows Explorer to display a list of all your hard drives and network drives in the right pane when you start Windows Explorer (the same as right-clicking My Computer, then selecting Explorer) you can do so by modifying the Properties for the shortcut that starts Windows Explorer. On the Shortcut tab in Properties, add to the command line in the Target text box the /select option right after /e. For example: c:\Windows\Explorer.exe/n,/e,/select,c:\

HOt Tip **Set Windows Explorer View as Default:** If you like the Windows Explorer view better than the default window view, you can change the default so that Windows Explorer will be the default even when using My Computer, here's how. Open Windows Explorer, select View from the menu bar, Options, then the File Types tab. Find Folder in the Registered file types list, then double-click it. Select explorer from the Actions list, click Set Default, then close the remaining dialog boxes.

HOt Tip **Make a Selected Folder the Root of Your View:** To make the selected folder the root of your view add a new option to the Shortcut menu called "Explore from here." To create this option open Windows Explorer, select View from the menu bar, Options, then the File Types tab. Find Folder in the Registered file types list, then double-click it. Click New, type **Explore from here** in the Action text box, then press Tab. Type **c:\win-**

dows\explorer.exe /e,/root,%1 in the Application used to perform action text box, click OK, then close the remaining dialog boxes. Now if you right-click a folder the new option will appear.

HOt Tip **Change Registry to make Windows Explorer Always Open to a Specific Folder**: No matter which folder it is, you will need to make a change in the registry.

CAUTION: *The following instructions involve changing settings in the Registry. If the changes are not made properly, serious problems may result. Be sure to backup your Registry before continuing. See "Registry" for more information about backing up and editing the Registry.*

Using Regedit, open the Registry and move to: HKEY_CLASSES_ROOT\ Folder\shell\explore\ddeexec. In the right window pane, right-click on (Default), then select Modify. Change both instances of %1 to the path of the folder in which you want Windows Explorer to open. For example, [ExploreFolder("c:\My Documents", c:\My Documents, %S)]. Click OK to save your changes.

HOt Tip **Go to MS_DOS from Explorer:** Here's a way to set up a shortcut menu option to go directly to an MS-DOS prompt from Windows Explorer. In Windows Explorer click <u>V</u>iew on the menu bar, (Folder) Options, then the File Types tab. Next, scroll through the Registered file types list box and select Folder, then click the Edit button. Click the New button, type **Open an MS-DOS Window** in the Action text box, then press Tab. In the Application used to perform action text box type **c:\command.com /k cd %1**, then click OK. Now, whenever you want to go directly to MS-DOS, right-click the folder you want to be in, then click **Open an MS-DOS Window**. To return to Windows, type **exit**, then press *Enter*.

Go

The options on the *Go* menu provide functions to move backwards, forwards, and up one level in the hierarchy as well as direct access to various other destinations within Windows. Selecting an option from the menu will move you to the target destination without further interaction.

Favorites

The options on the *Favorites* menu are similar to the options on the Go menu in that they provide a method to move directly to a destination. Favorites, however, takes the concept a big step forward by providing a method to add and organize your own destinations, whether they be on your local drives, network drives, or on the Internet.

For more information see "Favorites," p. 203

Tools

There are several tools that are available for use in Windows Explorer. Some of these tools can also be used elsewhere in Windows. You can find tools on the *Tools* menu.

Find

The Find tool is described specifically under its own headings. For more information see "Find – Computers," p. 226; "Find – Files and Folders," p. 229; "Find – On the Internet," p. 236, or "Find – People." p. 237

Map Network Drive

Map Network Drive associates a drive letter to a specific path. For more information see "Map Network Drive" (p. 269).

Disconnect Network Drive

Disconnect Network Drive removes a drive letter mapping to a specific path. For more information see "Disconnect Network Drive."

95

Go To

The *Go To* command provides a way to quickly move to a specific folder within your file system. This command only works in Windows Explorer. There are two ways to execute the command:

Click <u>T</u>ools on the menu bar, then Go to.

or

Press *Ctrl+G*

In either case, the Go To dialog box is displayed.

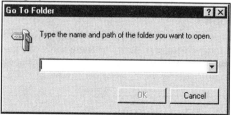

To find a folder type the exact path in the text box, for example: **\windows\system** then click OK. Go To will move you to the specified folder and then open the folder so that you can view the contents. The Go To Folder dialog box retains a history of the last 25 commands you have used, so you can use the drop-down list box to quickly return to a commonly used folder.

CAUTION: *The Go To Folder dialog box shares the history list with the Run dialog box. If you select a command that was used in the Run dialog box you may get an error message.*

 Find a Folder Quickly: To quickly move through a list of folders and files by name, click in the window pane you want to work in (if it's the right pane also click the column header for Name, to put the objects in alphabetical order), then press the first letter of the folder or file name you are looking for. The focus will move to the first folder or file that starts with the letter you typed. If you type the same letter again the focus will move to the next one that starts with the letter you typed.

Command

Explorer [/n] [/e][,/root,*object***][[,/select],***subobject***]**

Parameters:

/N................................Opens a new window regardless of whether a window is already opened for the same folder.

/E	Opens the Windows Explorer window with two panes rather than one.
/Root,*object*	Specifies the folder that Windows Explorer will use as the root when first displayed and restricts the user to that folder and the subfolders below it.
subobject	Selects a specified folder, highlights it and uses the parent object as the root unless **/select** is used.
/Select	Specifies that a parent folder is opened and the specified *subobject* is selected.

Notes:

1. Commas are required between the parameters.

2. If no parameters are used, C:\ is the root.

3. If /root is not used, but a folder is specified then that folder is used as the highest level displayed; however, you are not restricted to that folder and can move up the folder tree.

 Use MS-DOS to Create List of Folders or Files: If you need to print or capture a list of the folders and/or files see "Dir (MS-DOS)." Windows does not provide a direct method for accomplishing this task within the Windows environment.

Default Location: \Windows\Explorer.exe

See Also: Clipboard; Copying Files & Folders; Deleting Files & Folders; Dir (MS-DOS); Favorites; Section 4—File Types; Find–Files or Folders; Moving Files & Folders; My Computer; Quick View; Selecting Files & Folders; Shortcut Menu; Undo; View

---

98   Windows Update

Windows Update allows you to update your system files directly from Microsoft's web site. In the past you were faced with ordering update disks or CDs, but not anymore. As long as you are able to connect to the Internet you can have your files up-to-date in a matter of minutes.

Quick Access

Click **Start**, Windows Update

or

Click **Start**, Settings, Windows Update

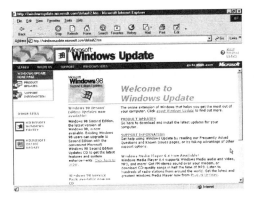

Update Wizard

Once you've connected to Microsoft's web site, start the Update Wizard. The Update Wizard checks your system and builds a database of your system files recording the date and size of each file. This database is then compared to Microsoft's, which produces a list of recommended updates that should be made. Select the updates you want installed, start the update process and watch Microsoft take care of the rest.

Note: Some updates can only be installed by themselves. Microsoft will notify you if this is the case. Just install those particular updates, independently of any other updates you need.

Default Location:
http://windowsupdate.microsoft.com

See Also: Version–Windows

Winipcfg

Winipcfg is a troubleshooting utility used for IP Configuration. If your computer is running Microsoft TCP/IP, it will display all current TCP/IP network configuration values. These include the network Adapter Type, Adapter Address, IP Address, Subnet Mask and Default Gateway.

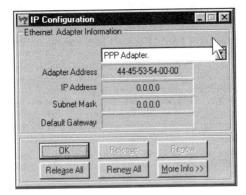

Quick Access

Click **Start**, Run, type **Winipcfg**, then click OK

Additional information is available by clicking the More Info button. This information is particularly useful on networks using DHCP. Using this information you can determine which TCP/IP configuration values have been configured by DHCP.

The Release All command will release all current IP connections. The Renew All command updates all IP connections.

Note: This utility does not dynamically refresh the information it displays. If you make changes you'll have to close the utility, then restart it to see the changes.

Xcopy & Xcopy32 (MS-DOS)

Xcopy and *Xcopy32* are MS-DOS commands that are very useful for copying large groups of files, especially when you want to retain a complex directory structure. They both are used the same way and use the same set of switches (see below). There is one major difference, however, between the two: Xcopy32 is a 32-bit version that can accommodate long file names while Xcopy is a 16-bit version and will not preserve the long file names.

> **Hot Tip** **Delete or Rename Xcopy:** To make sure you don't use the 16-bit version, Xcopy, you may want to rename it or delete it. You can then rename Xcopy32.exe to Xcopy.exe and feel right at home.

> **Hot Tip** **Xcopy vs. Diskcopy:** As opposed to the Diskcopy command, Xcopy can copy the contents of a disk to a disk of a different format.

Command

Xcopy or **Xcopy32** *source* [*drive:*] [/W] [/P] [/C] [/V] [/Q] [/F] [/L] [/D[:date]] [/U] [/I] [/S] [/E] [/T] [/K] [/R] [/H] [/A|/M] [/N] [/exclude:*filename*]

Options:

Source= ....The location of the files you want to copy. This must include a drive or path.

Destination= ....Destination of the files you are copying. This can include the drive, directory and file name. If *destination* is omitted, all files are copied to the current directory.

/A	Copies only files whose archive file attribute has been set. It does modify the archive attribute.
/C	Ignores all errors.
/D	Copies only the files changed on or after the specified date. If no date is specified, only the files whose date is later than the existing *destination* files will be copied. It's best to use four digit years to assure accuracy in the 21st century.
/E	Copies all subdirectories, even if they are empty. It's used with the /s and /t switches.
/Exclude:*filename*	Excludes all files listed in the specified text file. Each file name must be listed on a separate line in the file and no wildcards can be used.
/F	Displays *source* and *destination* files during the copy process.
/H	Copies files with the hidden and system file attributes. By default these files are not copied.
/I	Assumes *destination* specifies a directory if *source* is a directory or contains wildcards and *destination* does not exist. By default you are prompted to specify whether the *destination* is a directory or file.
/K	Copies and retains the read-only file attribute on the *destination* files, if present on

the *source* files. The read-only file attribute is removed by default.

/L .... Displays *source* and *destination* files but does not perform a copy.

/M .... Copies only files whose archive file attribute has been set and turns off the archive file attribute in the files specified in the *source*.

/N .... Copies files using the short file or directory names. If copying from a VFAT volume to a FAT volume or if the 8.3 file name convention is required on the *destination* volume this switch is required.

/P .... Confirms the creation of each *destination* file.

/Q .... Does not display the Xcopy messages.

/R .... Copies over read-only files at the destination.

/S .... Copies all directories and subdirectories unless they are empty. If not used, only a single directory is copied.

/T .... Copies only the subdirectory structure, not files. Use the /e switch to copy empty directories.

/U .... Copies only the files from the *source* that exist at the *destination*.

/V	Verifies each file as it is written to the destination. Not necessary for Windows 9x since the operating system performs this action. Only used for compatibility with previous versions of MS-DOS.
/W	Displays a message prompting you to press a key to begin the copy process. Waits at this prompt until a key is pressed.
/Y	Replaces existing destination files without a confirmation prompt.
/-Y	Replaces existing destination files after prompting for confirmation. This is the default.

Notes:

1. Both Xcopy and Xcopy32 use the same set of switches.

2. System and/or hidden files are not copied.

3. Xcopy generates exit codes that can be used in batch file programming to determine if an action should be taken based upon the code. Following are the exit codes:

Exit Code	Description
0	Files were copied without error.
1	No files were found to copy.
2	User pressed *Ctrl+C* to terminate Xcopy.
4	Initialization error occurred. Not enough memory or disk space, or you entered an invalid drive name or invalid syntax on the command line.
5	Disk write error occurred.

Here's an example of how the exit code can be captured in a batch file:

start /w xcopy c:\docs d: /s

if errorlevel *exitcode* goto *command*

The start /w command used in this example allows the batch file to stop and wait for Xcopy to finish running; otherwise, the batch file would try and continue as soon as Xcopy was launched.

Default Locations:
\Windows\Command\Xcopy.exe and
\Windows\Command\Xcopy32.exe

See Also: Copying Files & Folders; Copying Disk

File Types

Many different types of files are used for Windows 9x and the applications that run on these operating systems. Following is a list of the most common file name extensions and the file types they normally represent. An extension may be listed multiple times if the extension is used for more than one file type.

Windows 9x uses Quick View to view many different file types. Quick View, which is supplied with Windows 9x, is designed for specific file formats and can be used to read or display the file quickly, without having to load the application that created it.

Note: Quick View Plus 4.5 is a software product, published by Inso Corporation, that extends the viewing capabilities of Windows 9x to over 200 file formats.
A fully-functional trial version containing 30 file formats is available on their web site (http://www.inso.com). You can also contact them at:

Inso Corporation
401 N. Walbash, Suite 600
Chicago, IL 60611
800-333-1395
312-329-0700

Ext	File Type
.2gr	Video Grabber Library file, Microsoft Windows
.386	Virtual Device Driver
.3gr	Video Grabber Library file, Microsoft Windows
.abk	Backup (automatic) file, CorelDRAW
.ac1	ACL file; Action diagram file, FoxPro 2.0
.acm	Dynamic Link Library file, Microsoft Windows
.act	Action diagram file, FoxPro 2.0
.ai	Graphics file, Adobe Illustrator, Postscript
.aif	Setup file, Microsoft Windows
.aif,.aifc, .aiff	Audio file, AIFF
.all	Printer Information file, WordPerfect 6.0
.ani	Cursor file, Animated Cursors
.ann	Annotation Notes file, Microsoft Windows
.apd	Printing file; Microsoft Windows
.app	Application file, FoxPro 2.0
.asc	Text file, ASCII
.asm	Source Program file, Intel Assembly Language
.au	Audio file
.avi	Video file, MS Windows Digital-video

Ext	File Type
.awd	Fax file
.awp	Fax file, Microsoft At-Work Fax Key file
.aws	Fax file, Microsoft At-Work Fax Signature file
.bak	Backup file, FoxPro 2.
.bak	Backup file, Microsoft DOS
.bas	Basic Program file, Microsoft Basic
.bas	Basic Program file, Qbasic
.bas	Basic Program file, Visual Basic
.bat	Batch file, Microsoft DOS
.bcpio	Binary file, CPIO
.bin	Binary file,
.bk!	Backup file, WordPerfect 6.0
.bmk	Bookmark file, Microsoft Windows
.bmp	Graphics file, bitmap format, Microsoft Windows
.c	Source Program file, C
.c	Text file, ASCII text format
.c00	Print files, Ventura Publisher
.cab	Cabinet file, Microsoft Windows 9x
.cap	Captions file, Ventura Publisher
.cc	Text file, ASCII text format
.ccad	Drawing file, ClarisCAD
.cda	CD Audio file,
.cdf	Unidata net CDF
.cdr	Drawing file, CorelDRAW
.cdt	Template file, CorelDRAW

Ext	File Type
.cdx	Compound index file, FoxPro 2.0
.cgm	Graphics file, Computer Graphics Metafile, vector format
.cgm	Graphics file, Computer Graphics Metafile
.ch3	Chart file, Harvard Graphics
.chk	CheckDisk Command file, Microsoft DOS
.chp	Chapter file, Ventura Publisher
.cht	Chart file, Harvard Graphics
.cif	Chapter Information file, Ventura Publisher
.clp	Clipboard file, Microsoft Windows
.cmp	Compensation Map file, Zsoft's Publisher's Paintbrush
.cmx	Graphics file, Corel Presentation Exchange binary format
.cnf	Printer Information file, Ventura Publisher
.cnf	Scanner Configuration file, Zsoft's Publisher's Paintbrush
.cob	Source Program file, COBOL
.com	Command file, Microsoft DOS and OS/2
.cpe	Fax Cover Page Editor file, Microsoft Windows
.cpi	Code-page Information file, Microsoft Windows, OS/2 and DOS
.cpi	Graphics file, ColorLab

Ext	File Type
.cpi	Definition file, fonts and graphics, Microsoft DOS
.cpio	POSIX CPIO
.cpl	Control Panel file, Microsoft Windows 9x
.cpl	Palette file, CorelDRAW 5.0
.csh	Script file, C-shell
.csp	Graphics file, PC Emcee Screen Images
.ct	Graphics file, Scitex Continuous Tone
.cur	Cursor file, Microsoft Windows
.dat	Data file, Generic extension for files that contain data
.db	Database file, Paradox
.db2	Database file, dBase II
.dbf	Database file, dBase III, III+, and IV
.dbo	Command file, FoxPro 2.0
.dbt	Memo text file, FoxPro 2.0 and dBase
.dca	Text file, IBM
.dcr	Macromedia Director
.dcs	Graphics file, Desktop Color Separation protocol
.dcx	Fax file, Microsoft At-Work Fax View file
.def	Linker Definition file, Microsoft Windows
.dia	Graphics file, Diagraph

Ext	File Type
.dic	Dictionary file, Microsoft Word
.dic	Hyphenation dictionaries file, Ventura Publisher
.dif	Data Interchange Format file; Spreadsheet file, Visicalc
.dip	Graphics file,
.dir	Macromedia Director
.dlg	Dialog file, Microsoft Windows
.dll	Dynamic Link Library file, Microsoft Windows
.doc	Document file, FoxPro 2.0
.doc	Word processor (document) file, Multimate, Microsoft Word; Microsoft WordPad
.dos	Configuration files, Microsoft DOS, dual boot installation
.dot	Dot; Line Type file, CorelDRAW 5.0
.dot	Template file, Microsoft Word for Windows
.dpi	Graphics file, bitmap format, PointLine
.drv	Device Driver file, Microsoft DOS, Windows
.drw	Graphics file, Micrografx Designer 3.1; DRAW, vector format
.drw	MATRA Prelude drafting
.dvi	TeX DVI
.dwg	Graphics file, AutoCAD format
.dxf	Graphics file, AutoCAD 2-D, vector format

Ext	File Type
.dxr	Macromedia Director
.eps	Graphics file, Encapsulated PostScript format, with or with out .tif image file
.err	Error Log file, FoxPro 2.0
.esl	Extended Support Library file, FoxPro2.0
.etx	Text file, Struct-enhanced
.exe	Executable file
.f90	Text file, ASCII text format
.fax	FAX file, CCITT Group III Fax, Frecom Fax Board, IMAVOX Turbo Fax
.ffa	Index file, MS Office Find Fast Utility
.ffl	Index file, MS Office Find Fast Utility
.ffx	Index file, MS Office Find Fast Utility
.fky	Macro file, FoxPro 2.0
.flt	Dynamic Link Library, Microsoft
.flt	Filter file, Zsoft's Publisher's Paintbrush
.fmt	Format file, FoxPro 2.0
.fmt	Paper Description file, Microsoft Scheduler+ 7.0
.fnt	Font file, binary format, single font,
.fon	Font file, font directory
.fot	TTF File Locator
.fpt	Memo Text file, FoxPro 2.0

Ext	File Type
.frt	Report Form Memo Text file, FoxPro2.0
.frx	Report Form Database file, FoxPro 2.0
.fw2	Framework II file,
.fwd	Keyboard or Printer Support file, FoxPro 2.0
.fxp	Compiled Object-code file, FoxPro 2.0
.g	Text file, ASCII text format
.ged	Graphics file, Arts & Letters
.gem	Graphics file, vector format, GEM line art
.gen	Generated text, Ventura Publisher
.gif	Graphics file, Graphics Interchange format, CompuServe Inc.
.grf	Graphics file, Micrografx Charisma, vector format
.grp	Group file, Microsoft Windows
.gry	Gray Scale file, CorelDRAW 5.0
.gtar	GNU tar
.gx2	Graphics file, bitmap format, ShowPartner
.gz,.gzip	Compressed file, GNU ZIP achive
.h	Header file, C
.H, .hh	Text file, ASCII text format
.hdf	Data file, NCSA HDF
.hlp	Help file, Microsoft Windows, WordPerfect 6.0, FoxPro 2.0

Ext	File Type
.hpg	Graphics file, Hewlett-Packard, vector format
.hpl	Graphics file, Hewlett-Packard Graphics Language, vector format
.hqx	Macintosh BinHex format
.ht	HyperTerminal File
.htm,.html	Text file, Hypertext Markup Language
.hy1	Hyphenation algorithms file, Ventura Publisher
.icb	Graphics file,
.icc	Icon file, PubTech
.ico	Icon file, Microsoft Windows
.idx	Index file, WordPerfect 6.0, FoxPro 2.0
.ief	Graphics file, Image Exchange Format
.Iges, .igs	Graphics file, IGES graphics format
.il	Icon Library file, hDC
.im	Printer Calibration file, CorelDRAW 5.0
.img	Graphics file, GEM bitmap format
.inc	Include file, Microsoft Windows
.inc	Incremental Index file, WordPerfect 6.0
.inf	Setup file, Microsoft Windows
.ini	Initialization file, Microsoft Windows
.jas	Graphics file

Ext	File Type
.jff	Graphics file
.jpe,.jpeg, .jpg	Graphics file, compressed, Joint Photographic Experts Group format
.jt	FAX file, JT Fax
.jtf	Graphics file
.kbd	Keyboard Layout Definitions, Microsoft Windows 9x
.lab	Label Definition file, WordPerfect 6.0
.latex	Source file, LaTeX
.lbl	Label Definition file, LabelWorks for Windows
.lbt	Label Form Memo Text file, FoxPro 2.0
.lbx	Label Form Database file, FoxPro 2.0
.lex	Lexicon (dictionary) file, WordPerfect 6.0
.lib	Library file, Microsoft Windows
.ln	Graphics file, Scitex Line Work
.lnk	Shortcut File, Microsoft Windows 9x
.log	Error Message file, WordPerfect 6.0
.lrs	Language Resource file, WordPerfect6.0
.m	Text file, ASCII text format
.mac	Graphics file, MacPaint
.man	Troff with MAN macros
.mdx	Database Index file, dBASE IV format
.me	Troff with ME macros

Ext	File Type
.mem	Memory Variable file, FoxPro 2.0
.met	Graphics file, Microsoft OS/2 PM Metafile
.mid	Musical Instrument Digital
.mif	FrameMaker MIF format
.mmf	Mail file, Microsoft Mail
.mnt	Menu Memo Text file, FoxPro 2.0
.mnx	Menu Database file, FoxPro 2.0
.mod	Spreadsheet file, Multiplan
.mov	Video file, QuickTime video
.movie	Video file, SGI MoviePlayer format
.mpe, .mpg, .mpeg,	Video file, MPEG video
.mpr	Generated Menu Program file, FoxPro 2.0
.mpx	Compiled Menu Program file, FoxPro 2.0
.ms	Troff with MS macros
.msg	Message file, FoxPro 2.0
.msp	Graphics file, picture file format, Microsoft Paint
.nc	Unidata net CDF
.ndx	Database Index file, dBASE format
.oaz	FAX file, OAZ Fax Board
.obj	Object Module file, C
.otl	Outline Font file, Zsoft's Publisher's Paintbrush
.ovl	Overlay file, Microsoft DOS and OS/2

Ext	File Type
.p*	Graphics file, Mentor Graphics
.pal	Palette Definition file, Microsoft Windows and CorelDRAW 4.0
.part	PTC Pro/ENGINEER
.pas	Header file, Pascal
.pbm	Graphics file, PBM Bitmap format
.pcc	Graphics file, cutouts, Zsoft's Publisher's Paintbrush
.pcd	Graphics file, Kodak Photo CD format
.pct	Graphics file, Macintosh Picture
.pcx	FAX file, Intel Connection Co-processor
.pcx	Graphics file, bitmap format, Zsoft's Publisher's Paintbrush
.pdf	Document file, Adobe Acrobat
.pfb	Adobe Type I Font file
.pgm	Graphics file, PBM Graymap format
.pic	Graphics file, Lotus 1-2-3 Picture and Micrografx Draw, vector format
.pif	Graphics file, IBM Picture Interchange, vector format
.pif	Program Information File, Microsoft Windows
.pjt	Project Memo Text file, FoxPro 2.0
.pjx	Project Database file, FoxPro 2.0
.plb	Library file, FoxPro 2.0
.plt	Graphics file, AutoCAD Plotter file

Ext	File Type
.pnm	Graphics file, PBM Anymap format
.pnt	Graphics file, Macintosh Paint
.pol	Policy File
.ppm	Graphics file, PBM Pixmap format
.ppt	Presentation file, Microsoft PowerPoint
.prd	Printer Driver file, Microsoft Word
.pre	Graphics file, Freelance Graphics for Windows
.prg	Source Program file, dBASE, FoxPro 2.0
.prn	Print file, CorelDRAW 5.0
.prn	Printer Driver file, XyQuest's XyWrite
.prs	Printer Driver file, WordPerfect 6.0
.prt	PTC Pro/ENGINEER
.prx	Compiled Format file, FoxPro 2.0
.ps	Graphics file, PostScript
.psd	Graphics file, Adobe Photoshop for Windows
.pst	Macro (pre-sets) file, CorelDRAW 5.0
.pub	Publication file, Ventura Publisher
.pvd	Printer Driver file, PC Paintbrush
.qpr	Generated Query Program file, FoxPro 2.0
.qpx	Compiled Query Program file, FoxPro 2.0
.qt	Video file, QuickTime video

Ext	File Type
.r2d	Database file, Reflex, Version 2
.ra, .ram	Audio file, RealAudio
.ras	Graphics file, bitmap format, Sun Raster
.raw	Graphics file, Zsoft's Publisher's Paintbrush
.rc	Resource Compiler file, Microsoft Windows
.rec	Recorder file, Microsoft Windows
.reg	Registration Information file, Microsoft Windows
.res	Resource file, Microsoft Windows
.rft	DCA
.rgb	Graphics file, RGB
.rhn	Printer Characterization file, CorelDRAW 5.0
.ric	FAX file, Ricoh FAXNET
.rif	Graphics file, Raster Image File format, Fractal Design's Painter 2.0
.rle	Graphics file, Run Length Encoded format, Microsoft Windows
.rlz	Windows Application Program file, Realizer
.rmi	MIDI Sequence
.rpd	RapidFile Database file, FoxPro 2.0
.rpm	Audio file, RealAudio (plug-in)
.rtf	Text file, Rich Text Format
.rtx	Text file, MIME Rich Text Format
.rxd	Database file, Reflex, Version 1

Ext	File Type
.sam	Ami, Ami Pro
.scd	Graphics file, SCODL format
.scn	Scanner Calibration file, CorelDRAW5.0
.scp	MS Script File
.scr	Screen Saver File
.sct	Graphics file, Scitex format; Screen Form Memo Text file, FoxPro 2.0
.scx	Screen Form Database file, FoxPro 2.0
.sep	Graphics file, TIF 6.0 four-color bitmap
.set	Drawing file, SET (French CAD standard)
.sh	Script file, Bourne shell
.sh3	Slide Show file, Harvard Graphics
.shar	Archive file, Shell
.shw	Slide Show file, Harvard Graphics
.sit	Archive file, StuffIt
.sld	Graphics file, AutoCAD slide format
.slk	Spreadsheet file, Multiplan, Versions 1 or 2
.snd	Audio file
.sol	MATRA Prelude Solids
.spr	Generated Screen Program file, FoxPro 2.0
.spx	Compiled Screen Program file, FoxPro 2.0

Ext	File Type
.src	Source file, WAIS
.step	Data file, ISO-10303 STEP
.stl	Sterolithography
.stp	Data file, ISO-10303 STEP
.sty	Style Sheet file, Ventura Publisher
.sup	Supplementary Dictionary file, WordPerfect 6.0
.sv4cpio	SVR4 CPIO
.sv4crc	SVR4 CPIO with CRC
.sys	System file, Microsoft DOS and OS/2
.t	Troff
.tar	4.3BSD tar format
.tbx	Backup Memo Text file, FoxPro 2.0
.tcl	Script file, TCL
.tex	Source file, TeX
.texi, .texinfo	Texinfo (Emacs)
.tga	Graphics file, Truevision Targa bitmap format
.ths	Thesaurus file, WordPerfect 6.0
.tif	FAX file, Gammalink
.tif, .tiff	Graphics file, vector format, Tag Image File format, Aldus and Microsoft
.tmp	Temporary file, Microsoft Windows, FoxPro 2.0
.tpl	Word processor file (template), ACT!

Ext	File Type
.trf	Troff
.tsv	Text file, tab-separated values
.ttf	True Type Font file, Microsoft Windows 9x
.tut	Tutorial file
.txt	Text file, ASCII text format
.unv	SDRC I-DEAS file
.ustar	POSIX tar format
.vda	Data file, VDA-FS Surface data
.vda	Graphics file
.vew	Groupwise for Windows
.vgr	Graphics file, Ventura Publisher
.vrf	Script file, Oracle
.vsc	Configuration file, Virus Scan
.vsd	Drawing file, Visio 4
.vsh	Configuration file, VirsuShield
.vsl	Image file, Visio 4
.vss	Drawing file, Visio 4
.vst	Drawing file, Visio 4
.vsw	Drawing file, Visio 4
.vue	View file, dBASE III+, FoxPro 2.0
.vxd	Virtual Device Driver file
.w6w	Word processor (document) file, Microsoft Word
.wav	Digitized Sound file, Microsoft Windows Wave
.wb1	Spreadsheet file, Quattro Pro for Windows

Ext	File Type
.wb2	Spreadsheet file, Quattro Pro for Windows
.wdb	MS Works Database
.wid	Width Table file, Ventura Publisher
.win	Window file, FoxPro 2.0
.wk!	Spreadsheet file (compressed), Lotus 1-2-3, Version 2
.wk$	Spreadsheet file (compressed), Lotus 1-2-3, Version 1a
.wk1	Spreadsheet file, Lotus 1-2-3 VersionS 1 and 2
.wk3	Spreadsheet file, Lotus 1-2-3, Version 3
.wk4	Spreadsheet file, Lotus 1-2-3 Version 4
.wke	Spreadsheet file, Lotus 1-2-3, Educational Version
.wkp	Spreadsheet file, Surpass
.wkq	Spreadsheet file, Quattro
.wks	Spreadsheet file, Lotus 1-2-3, Version 1a or Microsoft Works Version 3
.wkz	Spreadsheet file (compressed), Quattro
.wmf	Graphics file, Microsoft Windows Metafile, vector format
.word	Word processor (document) file, Microsoft Word
.wp	Word processor (document) file, WordPerfect 4.2 and 5.0
.wp5	Word processor (document) file, WordPerfect 5

Ext	File Type
.wp6	Word processor (document) file, WordPerfect 6
.wpd	Word processor (document) file, WordPerfect 6.0 Demo
.wpf	Word processor file (document) Enable
.wpg	Graphics file, WordPerfect, bitmap format
.wps	Word processor (document) file, MS Works
.wq!	Spreadsheet file (compressed), Quattro Pro
.wq1	Spreadsheet file, Quattro Pro for MS-DOS
.wq2	Spreadsheet file, Quattro Pro for MS-DOS Version 5
.wr!	Spreadsheet file (compressed), Symphony, Version 2.0
.wr$	Spreadsheet file (compressed), Symphony, Version 1.2
wr1	Spreadsheet file, Symphony, Version 1.1; VRML Worlds
.wri	Word processor (document) file, Microsoft Write
.wrk	Spreadsheet file, Symphony, Version 1.0
.ws	Word processor (document) file, WordStar
.xbm	Graphics file, X Bitmap
.xfr	Font file, Bitmap format, Zsoft's Publisher's Paintbrush

.Ext	File Type
.xfx	FAX file, JETFAX
.xl	Spreadsheet file, Microsoft Excel
.xlc	Chart file, Microsoft Excel
.xlm	Macro file, Microsoft Excel
.xls	Spreadsheet file, Microsoft Excel, Version 2.0
.xlw	Workspace file, Microsoft Excel
.xpm	Graphics file, X Pixmap
.xwd	Graphics file, X Window dump format
.xwp	Word processor (document) file, Xerox Writer
.zip	Compressed file, PKZIP by PKW

See Also: Quick View, Explorer|Options|File Types

Technical Support Sources

Microsoft Corporation

1 Microsoft Way
Redmond, WA 98052-6399
Main:(425) 882-8080   Toll Free:(800) 426-9400
Fax:(206) 936-7329   Tech:(800) 322-1233
Web Page: http://www.microsoft.com
Internet:gopher.microsoft.com
BBS: (206) 936-6735

Access   (425) 635-7050
   Canada: (905) 568-2294
Authorized Support Centers   (800) 936-3500
Authorized Training Center   (800) 636-7544
   Referral
   Canada: (800) 563-9048
Automap   (425) 635-7146
   Canada: (905) 568-3503
Basic PDS   (425) 635-7053
Bob   (425) 635-7044
   Canada: (905) 568-3503
Bulletin Board System   (206) 936-6735
   BBS: (206) 936-6735
C/C++   (425) 635-7007
Canadian Support   (905) 568-3503
CD-ROM Installation   (206) 635-7033
Certified Professionals   (800) 636-7544
   Canada: (905) 712-0333
Consulting Line   (800) 936-5200
Consulting Services   (800) 426-9400
   Canada: (905) 712-0333
Delta   (425) 635-7019
Developer Network   (800) 759-5474
   Canada: (800) 759-5474
Download Service-USA   (206) 936-6735
Web Page: http://www.microsoft.com/
downloads/default.asp?

Excel for the Macintosh	(425) 635-7080
Canada: (905) 568-2294	
Excel for Windows and OS/2	(425) 635-7070
Canada: (905) 568-2294	
Excel SDK	(425) 635-7048
Fast Tips, Advanced Systems	(800) 936-4400
(NT, MS Mail)	
Canada: (800) 936-4400	
Fast Tips, Desktop Applications	(800) 936-4100
Canada: (800) 936-4100	
Fast Tips, Development Tools	(800) 936-4300
Canada: (800) 936-4300	
Fast Tips, Home Products	(800) 936-4100
Canada: (800) 936-4100	
Fast Tips, Personal Op Systems	(800) 936-4200
FORTRAN	(425) 635-7015
Forum on CompuServe	(800) 848-8199
Fox prods, MS-DOS, Windows & UNIX	
	(425) 635-7191
Fox products, Macintosh	(425) 635-7192
Front Page	(425) 635-7088
Canada: (905) 568-3503	
FTP Site - http://ftp.microsoft.com	
Web Page: http://ftp.microsoft.com	
Hardware-	**(425) 635-7040**
Mouse, BallPoint, etc.	
Internet Explorer	(425) 635-7123
Canada: (905) 568-4494	
Macro Assembler (MASM)	(425) 646-5109
Magic School Bus and	(425) 635-7140
Kids Products	
Canada: (905) 568-3503	
Microsoft Press	**(800) 677-7377**
Microsoft Wish Line	(425) 936-9474
Money	(425) 635-7131

Canada:	(905) 568-3503	
MS Plus		(425) 635-7122
MS-DOS 6.0/		(425) 646-5104
MS-DOS 6.2 Upgrades		
MSDL (Supported Products)		(425) 936-6735
Canada:	(905) 507-3022	
Multimedia Products		(425) 635-7172
Canada:	(905) 568-3503	
Office - Switcher Line		(425) 635-7041
Canada:	(905) 568-2294	
Office for the Macintosh		(425) 635-7055
Canada:	(905) 568-2294	
Office for Windows		(425) 635-7056
Canada:	(905) 568-2294	
Outlook		(425) 635-7031
Canada:	(905) 568-3503	
PowerPoint		(425) 635-7145
Canada:	(905) 568-3503	
Premier Support/Sales & Info		(800) 936-3500
Priority Comprehensive		
Priority Comprehensive-CC		(800) 936-5900
Priority Desktop App-CC		(800) 668-7975
Priority Desktop Applications		(900) 555-2000
Priority Desktop Apps. -CC		(800) 936-5700
Priority Develop. w/Desktop-CC		(800) 936-5800
Priority Development w/Desktop		(900) 555-2300
Priority Home Products		(900) 555-2400
Priority Home Products-CC		(800) 936-560
Canada credit card:	(800) 668-7975	
Priority Personal Op Sys-CC		(800) 936-5700
Priority Personal Operating Sys		(900) 555-2000
Profiler		(425) 635-7015
Profit		(800) 723-3333
Project		(425) 635-7155
Canada:	(905) 568-3503	

Publisher		(425) 635-7140
Canada:	(905) 568-3503	
QuickBasic		(425) 646-5101
QuickC		(425) 635-7010
Scenes and Games		(425) 637-9308
Canada:	(905) 568-3503	
Schedule		(425) 635-7049
Canada:	(905) 568-2294	
Solution Provider Line		(800) 765-7768
Solution Provider Sales & Info		(800) 765-7768
Canada:	(800) 563-9048	
Source Safe		(425) 635-7014
Support Consulting Line		(800) 936-1565
Support Network Sales & Info		(800) 936-3500
TechNet		(800) 344-2121
Canada:	(800) 344-2121	
Test for Windows		(425) 635-7052
Toronto, Canada BBS		(905) 507-3022
TT/TDD (Text Telephone)		(425) 635-4948
Canada:	(905) 568-9641	
Video for Windows		(425) 635-7172
Canada:	(905) 568-4494	
Visual Basic		(425) 646-5105
Visual Basic Professional Toolkit		(425) 646-5105
Visual C/C++		(425) 635-7007
Visual InterDev		(425) 635-7016
Visual J++		(425) 635-7011
Windows 95		(425) 635-7000
Windows Developer Stds Support		(206) 635-3329
Windows Entertainment Products		(425) 637-9308
Canada:	(905) 568-3503	
Windows NT (Installation Support)		(206) 635-7018

Windows/Windows for Workgroups	(425) 637-7098
Word for MS-DOS	(425) 635-7210
Canada: (905) 568-2294	
Word for the Macintosh	(425) 635-7200
Canada: (905) 568-2294	
Word for Windows	(425) 462-9673
Canada: (905) 568-2294	
Works for MS-DOS	(425) 635-7150
Canada: (905) 568-3503	
Works for the Macintosh	(425) 635-7160
Canada: (905) 568-3503	
Works for Windows	(425) 635-7130
Canada: (905) 568-3503	

World Wide Web

Main Support Site - http://support.microsoft.com/
DLL Help Database: - http://support.microsoft.com/
servicedesks/fileversion/dllinfo.asp

Non-Microsoft:

Windows Magazine: http://www.winmag.com/
ZD Journals: http://www.zdjournals.com/w95 or
http://www.zdjournals.com/w98

Glossary

This glossary includes listings for terms that are not defined explicitly within the topics themselves. It is not intended to be comprehensive, but seeks only to explain potentially unknown terms relating to Windows 98, Windows 95 and other directly related topics.

16-bit – A computer, program or application that uses data in groups of 16 bits at a time. IBM PC/AT class computers are 16-bit. Windows 3.x is a 16-bit operating environment.

32-bit – A computer, program or application that uses data in groups of 32 bits at a time. Computers using Intel 80386 microprocessors are 32-bit. Windows 9x and Windows NT are 32-bit operating systems.

64-bit – A computer, program or application that uses data in groups of 64 bits at a time.

active partition – The partition of a hard drive that contains the operating system that the computer boots from, usually the first partition. See also partition.

active window – The window that has focus. The active window's title bar will be colored while the others will appear dimmed. *See also* window.

American National Standards Institute (ANSI) – A nonprofit organization, supported by industry, that creates, coordinates and publishes standards which are used voluntarily throughout the United States.

American Standard Code for Information Interchange (ASCII) – A code, transmitted in seven-bit groups, almost always using an eighth-bit as a Parity Bit, for a total of eight bits per character. The code was developed by the American National Standards Institute to bring compatibility to text/data processing, and communication between computers and peripherals. *See also* bit.

analog – A system where an unlimited number of variables are used to represent the transmission of data. A value can be anywhere on a scale, in contrast with digital where each value conforms to limited predetermined number. Most commonly associated with radio waves. *See also* digital.

anonymous FTP (File Transfer Protocol) – A service that allows users to download files using FTP from Internet sites using a standard e-mail address and user name. No special password or security is required. *See also* File Transfer Protocol (FTP).

ANSI – *See* American National Standards Institute.

API – *See* Application Programming Interface.

application – A software program that performs a specific function that runs on an operating system, for example, a word processor, database or spreadsheet program.

Application Programming Interface (API) – A program designed to facilitate and execute the communication between an application and the operating system.

ASCII – *See* American Standard Code for Information Interchange.

asynchronous transmission – Communication between devices where the transmission of data can take place at anytime, by either device. The devices do not have to wait for a specific time to transmit as they would in a synchronous transmission. Asynchronous transmissions occur between computers and printers and/or modems. *See also* synchronous transmission.

attribute – A particular characteristic that describes data, fields, objects, etc. For example, bold would be an attribute of text as numeric would be an attribute of a field.

back up – To create a copy of original data files on disks, tapes, CDs or other media. *See also*- backup.

backup – The actual copy of original data files, created on disks, tapes, CDs or other media, using a back up procedure. If original data is lost, the data can be restored from the backups. *See also* back up.

bandwidth – The transmission capacity, usually measured in bits per second (bps), of a communication connection across a network or between computers.

Basic Input/Output System (BIOS) – A program, stored in Read-Only Memory (ROM), that controls start up and basic functions of a computer, such as operation of the keyboard, display, and drives. *See also* Read-Only Memory.

BIOS – *See* Basic Input/Output System.

bit – Short for Binary Digit, it's the smallest unit used for computer storage. Its value can only be 0 or 1. Seven or eight bits compose a byte. *See also* byte.

bits per second (bps) – In data transmission, the number of bits transmitted in one second. *See also* bit.

boot – The process of starting up a computer, the execution of the programs stored in the Basic Input/Output System (BIOS).

bps – *See* bits per second.

bug – An anomaly in software or hardware that causes a malfunction or undesired result.

bus – The connection to which all devices attach or interface within a computer. The capacity of the bus is measured by the number of bits that can be transmitted at one time, for example, 16-bit or 32-bit. The more bits transmitted the faster the communication within the computer.

byte – The standard unit for computer data storage. A byte usually contains seven or eight bits, depending on whether error correction is used. One byte can store the equivalent of one letter of the alphabet such as the letter B or the numeral 3. *See also* bit.

cache – 1) A portion of reserved memory used to store programs or data that is frequently accessed, thereby providing improved performance.
2) The process of placing programs or data in the location.

cascade – 1) A Windows term for the arrangement of windows or menus in an overlapping pattern where each window or menu is partially visible. 2) A series of connected hardware devices.

central processing unit (CPU) – The primary microprocessor chip that controls a computer.

client – 1) A computer that accesses or retrieves programs or data, from another computer called a server. 2) A software program that calls upon another program for data or a service.

cluster – 1) A number of disk sectors treated as one unit by the operating system and used for storage. 2) A group of computer terminals attached to a single controller or computer.

cold boot – *See* boot.

collapse – To change a hierarchical view so that only the root folder is showing. Used in Microsoft Explorer.

command – An instruction to a computer to have a function performed.

command button – A button generally on a toolbar or in a dialog box that when used executes a command.

communications protocol – A set of rules and standards that are used to exchange information between two computers. It serves to reduce errors, ensuring that what is received is the same as what was sent.

compression – The process of converting data from its original form to a condensed form that takes up less storage space on disk.

CPU – *See* central processing unit.

crash – When a computer stops processing instructions due to a serious hardware or software malfunction and cannot be restarted except by powering down and restarting.

cross-linked files – A condition when two or more files have stored data in the same cluster. This creates an unstable data storage condition, which can usually be corrected with ScanDisk.

data – Information that has been converted into a form that can be stored, transferred and processed electronically by a computer.

DDE – *See* Dynamic Data Exchange.

DDL – *See* Dynamic Data Link.

default – A setting, predetermined by the computer or program, that is used unless another setting is specified.

default printer – A printer that has been selected as a primary printer. When a print job is sent, if no other printer has been selected, the job will go to the default printer.

defragment – The process of reorganizing the files on a hard disk so that they are in contiguous order. This improves the time it takes to read files, thereby improving system performance. There are software utilities that perform this function such as Microsoft's DEFRAG. *See also* file fragmentation.

device – Any piece of equipment that can be installed in, or attached to, a computer. For example, drives, modems, scanners, etc.

device drivers - A software program that provides communication between the computer and a device. Device drivers can be generic or specific to a device. *See also* device.

DHCP – *See* Dynamic Host Configuration Protocol.

digital – A system where each value conforms to limited predetermined number which is used to represent the transmission of data. In contrast with analog where an unlimited number of variables are used to represent the transmission of data and a value can be anywhere on a scale. Most commonly associated with computers, where 0 and 1 represent all data. *See also* analog.

directory – An area of a storage device, uniquely identified, that contains files or other directories called subdirectories, arranged in hierarchical order. Synonymous with folders. *See also* folders; hierarchy.

disk compression – *See* compression.

disk partition – *See* partition.

Disk Operating System (DOS) – Software, retrieved from a disk, that is designed to start up and run a computer. Generally, associated with personal computers. Microsoft calls theirs MS-DOS, while IBM calls theirs PC-DOS.

DLL – *See* Dynamic Link Library.

DNS – *See* Domain Name Server.

domain – 1) A group of connected computers on a network. 2) A group of servers and clients secured by a common database.

domain name – A name which identifies a group of computers which includes the top domain and all its subdomains, for example, msn.com (Microsoft), ucla.edu (University of California – Los Angeles) or tnc.org (The Nature Conservancy).

Domain Name Server (DNS) – A computer on the Internet to which other computers of a domain or subdomain are eventually connected. This server translates domain names to Internet Protocol (IP) addresses and IP addresses to domain names. *See also* domain, domain name, and IP address.

DOS – *See* Disk Operating System.

download – To transmit a file from one computer to another. Download is synonymous with *receiving* a file, while upload is synonymous with *sending*. *See also* upload.

Dynamic Data Exchange (DDE) – A programming tool used to pass data and commands between two separate programs. DDE is older technology, which is being replaced by Object Linking and Embedding (OLE). *See also* Object Linking and Embedding (OLE).

Dynamic Data Link (DDL) – A Windows function that links data from one file to another. It could be used to link spreadsheet information to a word processing document. When information in the spreadsheet changed it would automatically update the word processing document with the same information.

Dynamic Host Configuration Protocol (DHCP) – A configuration protocol for TCP/IP commonly used for Internet connections.

Dynamic Link Library (DLL) – A program that is used as a subroutine by other programs. As a separate file, it is only called when needed, which saves valuable memory and operates more efficiently.

enumerating – The process of identifying which Plug and Play devices are in the computer and then assigning the appropriate hardware resources to the devices.

export – To transfer data from one file format to another. Used to convert files so that another program can read and use the same data. *See also* import.

FAT – *See* File Allocation Table.

File Allocation Table (FAT) – A method used by a disk operating system (DOS) to keep track of the location of files on a disk. The table stores a numeric value that corresponds to the cluster addresses where the file is located. When a request is made to find a file, DOS searches the FAT for the file location then goes to the specified location on the disk.

file server – A computer on a network that shares files.

File Transfer Protocol (FTP) – A standard protocol, which includes error checking, used to list and copy files over the Internet.

file type – The specific format in which an application saves its files. Usually a file type has a specific file name extension associated with it such as, .doc (Microsoft Word), .xls (Microsoft Excel) or .txt (ASCII text). *See also* the File Types section of this book where many file types are identified.

file fragmentation – A situation in which files are saved randomly in many different sectors of a disk. Reading and writing of such files is significantly slower than when files are not fragmented. *See also* defragment.

folder – An area of a storage device, uniquely identified, that contains files or other folders, arranged in hierarchical order. Synonymous with directories and subdirectories. *See also* directory; hierarchy.

FTP – *See* File Transfer Protocol.

Gb – *See* gigabit.

GB – *See* gigabyte.

gigabit (Gb) – A unit of measure used for data transfer—1,073,741,824 bits

gigabyte (GB) – A unit of measure used for data storage—1,073,741,824 bytes or 1,024 megabytes.

Graphical User Interface (GUI) – A user interface that uses symbols (icons), menus and dialog boxes to guide the user through a program

GUI – *See* Graphical User Interface.

hierarchy – A system of organizing folders, files and objects, ranked one above the other on a disk. Those items that have something in common are grouped together as people would be in a family tree. A hierarchical structure is often referred to as a tree.

high-level format – After a disk is low-level formatted a high-level format is executed which installs the programs necessary to boot the computer (boot track) and creates the file allocation table. *See also* low-level format; File Allocation Table (FAT).

home page – The main page on a Web site that the user generally goes to first. This page may have hyperlinks to other pages that are related to the home page.

host computer – A computer on a network that allows other computers to run their programs on it.

HTML – *See* Hypertext Markup Language.

HTTP – *See* Hypertext Transfer Protocol.

hyperlink – A word, icon, symbol, picture or graphic that when clicked with the mouse, opens another document (page). Hyperlinks allow the user to move directly to information they wish to view without having to page through large documents to get there. *See also* hypertext, Hypertext Markup Language (HTML); Web page.

hypertext – A word or words (text) that, when clicked with the mouse, opens another document (page). Hyperlinks allow the user to move directly to information they wish to view without having to page through large documents to get there. *See also* hyperlink; Hypertext Markup Language (HTML); Web page.

Hypertext Markup Language (HTML) – A programming language used to create documents on the World Wide Web which are displayed using a browser. The documents usually contain hyperlinks, which allow users to move from one page to another. HTML documents usually use either the .htm or .html file name extension. *See also* hyperlink; hypertext.

Hypertext Transfer Protocol (HTTP) – A set of standards that is used on the World Wide Web to exchange information contained in Web pages. Web browsers are used to read documents that comply with HTTP. *See also* Web browser; Web page; World Wide Web.

Glossary

icon – A graphical image representing a program or function. Usually icons are used on buttons, toolbars, as well as on the Windows desktop.

import – To transfer data from one file format into another. Used to convert files so that another program can read and use data created using a different application. *See also* export.

Internet – A large network composed of many interconnected smaller networks which allow the user to seamlessly access any part of the network. Today the Internet spans the world and provides services to millions of users.

Internet Protocol (IP) address – The address used on for a computer on a Transmission Control Protocol/Internet Protocol (TCP/IP) network. The addresses are formatted in four groups of up to three digits separated by periods, for example: 120.175.111.14. *See also* Internet; Transmission Control Protocol/Internet Protocol (TCP/IP).

Internet Service Provider (ISP) – A company or organization that provides access to the Internet. In most cases the ISP provides a local phone number that the user dials in to, to make a connection. Other ISPs provide a connection via a cable modem and do not require a phone number. Commercial operations charge a fee for this service; however, other organizations, such as colleges and universities may provide the service at no charge. *See also* Internet.

Intranet – An internal network, protected by a firewall server, that enables the sharing of information within a company. An Intranet is usually accessed using the same browser that one would use for the Internet. *See also* Internet; Web browser.

IP address – *See* Internet Protocol address.

ISP – *See* Internet Service Provider.

K – *See* kilobyte.

Kb – *See* kilobit.

KB – *See* kilobyte.

kilobit (Kb)-- A unit of measure used for data transfer—1,024 bits.

kilobyte (K or KB) -- A unit of measure used for data storage—1,024 bytes.

legacy system – A computer system, generally a mainframe or minicomputer, that has been in existence for a long period of time.

LAN – *See* Local Area Network.

Local Area Network (LAN) – A group of computers and/or peripherals, that are connected with cables and/or wireless connections, which communicate with each other through a network operating system. A LAN is usually contained within a small geographic area, for example, one building. *See also* WAN.

lock up - This occurs when the computer stops processing instructions due to erroneous software logic or malfunctioning hardware. *See also* bug.

lost file fragments - Pieces of data that are no longer associated with their original files.

low-level format – The format that takes place first, identifying the tracks and sectors, and preparing the disk for a high-level format. This process is usually performed by the manufacturer. *See also* high-level format.

Mb – *See* megabit.

MB – *See* megabyte.

megabit (Mb) – A unit of measure used for data transfer—1,048,576 bits.

megabyte (MB) – A unit of measure used for data storage—1,048,576 bytes or 1,024 kilobytes.

Microsoft License Pak (MLP) - This is a license agreement that permits you to install Windows on more than one computer from the same set of disks.

MLP – *See* Microsoft License Pak.

multi-tasking – The act of switching from one active program to another without closing down or losing your place in the programs you came from. Programs that are not in the active window continue to operate, performing their tasks in the background. *See also* active window; task switching.

network – A group of computers connected with each other either directly by cable or indirectly using telephone lines, radio waves or satellites for the purpose of sharing data, programs, or peripheral devices.

network drive – A disk drive in a server that is shared across a network by other computers. *See* network.

Network Operating System (NOS) – A software program that provides communication and security between computers and peripherals across cables and/or wireless connections.

NOS – *See* Network Operating System.

object – Any item that can be modified, manipulated or controlled by a user. Some examples of objects are files, folders, drives, buttons, screens, graphics, pictures and photographs.

Object Linking and Embedding (OLE) – A method used in Windows to share objects between applications. OLE offers two methods of using objects. Linking provides a link to an original object. Any changes made either to the link or the original will change the other. Embedding provides a copy of the original. When changes need to be made, both the original and the embedded copy need to be changed independently.

offline – The condition when a computer is not connected to a network, another computer, peripheral or service. A state of being disconnected. *See also* online.

OLE – *See* Object Linking and Embedding

online – The condition when a computer is connected to a network, another computer, peripheral or service. A state of being connected. *See also* offline.

Operating System (OS) – Software that starts and runs a computer facilitating communication between the computer, its devices, peripherals and application software.

OS – *See* Operating System.

partition – 1) A section of a hard drive used for the organization of files created during low-level formatting. 2) To create a partition. *See also* low-level format.

pathname – A combination of directories and subdirectories, or folders, that describe where a file is in a hierarchical file system. For example, c:\windows\system\sysedit.exe is the patinate for the sysedit.exe file.

PC card – An electronic device about the size of a credit card that slides into a slot on a portable computer and provides additional functionality, such as communication via a modem and/or network adapter. Originally the PC card was referred to as a PCMCIA card.

peer-to-peer network – A network of computers where workstations, nondedicated servers as well as, dedicated servers all work together sharing data, programs and peripherals. A nondedicated server is server that is also used simultaneously as a workstation. *See also* Local Area Network (LAN); network.

peripheral – A device connected to a computer that performs one or many functions for example, printers, scanners, monitors, keyboards, etc.

Point of Presence (POP) – The location where a long distance carrier connects to the line of the local phone company or user.

Point-to-Point Protocol (PPP) – A protocol used for communication on the Internet. It allows a user to connect directly to the Internet through their Internet Service Provider (ISP) using standard phone lines. It is becoming the de facto standard, replacing Serial Line Internet Protocol (SLIP), offering enhanced error checking and correction capabilities.

POP – *See* Point of Presence.

PPP – *See* Point-to-Point Protocol.

program – A set of instructions that tells a computer or electronic device what to do.

program file – The file that initiates or starts a program's operation, usually an executable (.exe) file.

property – A parameter that controls or describes how an object functions or looks.

RAM – *See* Random Access Memory

Random Access Memory (RAM) – The main memory used for processing instructions in a computer. It is used and reused randomly as a workspace and retains nothing once the computer is turned off. *See also* Read-Only-Memory.

Read-Only Memory (ROM) – A type of memory in a computer that retains the information stored in it, even when the computer is turned off, but cannot be changed. *See also* Random Access Memory (RAM).

reboot – The process of restarting a computer after it has been started previously. *See also* boot.

ROM – *See* Read-Only Memory

root – The highest level of a hierarchy, most often the first directory or folder on a disk. *See also* hierarchy.

run – 1) To start a software program. 2) A program in Windows that permits the user to start a software program using a command line approach.

server – A computer on a network that shares any of the following: processor, hard disk, CD-ROM, programs, files, printers, scanners, etc.

Serial Line Internet Protocol (SLIP) – A protocol used for communication on the Internet. It allows a user to connect directly to Internet through their Internet Service Provider (ISP) using standard phone lines. It is quickly being replaced by Point-to-Point Protocol, which offers enhanced error checking and correction capabilities. *See also* Point-to-Point Protocol.

Simple Mail Transfer Protocol (SMTP) – A communications protocol used for e-mail exchange on TCP/IP networks.

SLIP – *See* Serial Line Internet Protocol.

SMTP – *See* Simple Mail Transfer Protocol.

startup – The process of initializing a computer. *See also* boot.

status bar – A section of the screen, usually at the bottom, that provides information about the application being run.

subdirectory – A directory contained in or below a directory. *See also* directory; folder.

Super Video Graphics Array (SVGA) – A standard for video display, which supports 1,280 x 1,024 pixel resolution in 16 million colors. SVGA is the standard for most computers today. *See also* Video Graphics Array (VGA).

synchronous transmission – Communication between devices where the transmission of data can only take place at a specific point in time. The devices cannot transmit data, whenever they want to, as they can with asynchronous transmission. Synchronous transmissions occur within a computer and are controlled by the microprocessor. *See also* asynchronous transmission.

task switching – The act of switching from one active program to another without closing down or losing your place in the programs you came from. Programs that are not currently active do not continue to operate. *See also* multi-tasking.

TCP/IP – *See* Transmission Control Protocol/Internet Protocol

TELNET – A terminal emulation program that allows users to connect directly to a server on the Internet using a command-line interface.

tiling – An arrangement of open windows on the desktop that allows all windows to be visible, with no overlapping.

title bar – A section at the very top of a screen that displays the name of the window and may provide information about the application being run.

toolbar – A row or array of buttons, each of which perform specific functions within a software application. Toolbars are usually at the top of the screen just under the menu bar; however, they can also be undocked and reside as free-floating objects.

Transmission Control Protocol/Internet Protocol (TCP/IP) – A set of layered protocols originally developed by the U.S. Department of Defense to allow PCs, workstations and servers to communicate over the Internet. *See also* communications protocol.

UART – See universal asynchronous receiver-transmitter.

Uninterruptible Power Supply (UPS) – A battery that provides power to a computer or peripheral when a loss, degradation, or surge of power occurs. It has a limited delivery period and provides only a temporary solution to a power problem.

Universal Asynchronous Receiver-Transmitter (UART) – A circuit used to manage serial ports and modem connections. It converts data to be transferred as well as received. *See also* asynchronous transmission.

Universal Resource Locator (URL) – A standardized method of naming locations on the Internet. It allows a user to find Intranet sites, navigating through many interconnected servers and networks. An example of a URL is:
 http://www.microsoft.com.

Unix – A multi-user operating system, originally developed by AT&T Bell Laboratories, used primarily in universities and mid-sized businesses.

upload – To transmit a file from one computer to another. Upload is synonymous with *sending* a file, while *download* is synonymous with **receiving**. *See also* download.

UPS – *See* Uninterruptible Power Supply.

URL – *See* Universal Resource Locator.

VGA – *See* Video Graphics Array.

Video Graphics Array (VGA) – A standard for video display which supports 640 x 480 pixel resolution in 16 colors. Most computers today use a higher standard, Super Video Graphics Array (SVGA). *See also* Super Video Graphics Array (SVGA).

virtual device driver (VxD) – Software that allows different applications to address the same hardware devices without conflicting with each other.

volume – A named section of storage media whether it be a single diskette or a hard drive. A volume could refer to the whole diskette or drive or there could be many volumes on a diskette or drive.

VxD – *See* virtual device driver.

WAN – *See* Wide Area Network.

warm boot – The process of restarting a computer without turning the power off. *See also* boot.

Web browser – A software tool used to navigate to, access, and view Web sites and pages on the World Wide Web. It uses a Graphical User Interface (GUI) that can read HTML documents and display them in an easy-to-read format. The two most popular Web browsers are Microsoft Internet Explorer and Netscape Navigator. *See also* Graphical User Interface (GUI); Web pages; Web sites; World Wide Web.

Web page – A document contained in a Web site, written in Hypertext Markup Language (HTML), that contains information. It has it's own Universal Resource Locator (URL), but can also be reached using hyperlinks from other Web pages. *See also* hyperlinks; Hypertext Markup Language (HTML); Universal Resource Locator (URL); Web site.

Web site – A site established by a company, organization, or individual on the World Wide Web that offers information such as text, graphics, pictures, photographs, video and audio clips. The information is formatted primarily using the Hypertext Markup Language (HTML). Web sites may have hyperlinks to other sites that contain related information. *See also* hyperlinks; Hypertext Markup Language (HTML); World Wide Web.

Wide Area Network (WAN) – A group of computers and/or peripherals, that are connected with cables, wireless connections, and telephone lines which communicate with each other through a network operating system. A WAN is usually spread across a large geographic area, for example, from one city to another city. *See also* LAN.

window – An area on the screen, with a distinct border, that contains information, documents, or applications. A window can be resized in several ways and can be moved around the screen for the most effective use. *See also* active window.

Windows NT – A Microsoft network operating system that uses a graphical user interface very similar to Windows 9x.

workgroup – A group of computers usually in a small geographic location, such as a department, in which the users have a common focus and similar work strategy. The computers usually share peripherals, such as printers, in the immediate area but in most cases also share data and peripherals across a much larger network. *See also* network; peer-to-peer network.

workstation – A computer and associated peripherals, usually more powerful than a personal computer (PC), used by an individual to perform tasks.

World Wide Web (WWW) – A graphical user interface used to access information on Internet servers that provide information in the standard Hypertext Markup Language (HTML) format. *See also* Hypertext Markup Language.

WWW – *See* World Wide Web.

Appendix

Certificates of Authenticity

How to Recognize a Genuine Certificate of Authenticity

There are four versions of the Certificate of Authenticity, the OEM (Original Equipment Manufacturer) version and the Retail Version for each operating system, Windows 95 and Windows 98.

OEM Certificates

Windows 95

You can test for authenticity by checking the following things:

1. Raised print (also called Intaglio print) that feels like currency in the printed text, border, and the Microsoft Logo.

2. A strip of metallic holographic thread imbedded into the paper that appears to be a broken line. When held up to light, can be seen to be continuous.

3. Hold the certificate at an angle with the bottom edge at eye level and the top edge pointed toward an overhead light source. You should see two things as changes in texture on the certificate's surface:

   - The letters OK on top of the Microsoft Logo

   - The image of a woman's head on the left side of the certificate, slightly below the center.

The certificate should be 4.75 in. x 4.75 in.

See scan of Certificate on following page.

Certificate of Authenticity

This Certificate is your assurance that the software you obtained with your computer system is legally licensed from Microsoft Corporation. If you have concerns about the legitimacy of this Certificate or the software, call the Microsoft Piracy Hotline 800-RULEGIT (in the U.S. or Canada), or contact your local Microsoft sales office. For product support, contact the manufacturer of your computer system.

FOR DISTRIBUTION ONLY WITH NEW PC HARDWARE.

The continuous and interwoven metallic thread above indicates that this product is genuine Microsoft software.

Microsoft

Product ID: 28696-OEM-0015834-09363

Microsoft and the Microsoft logo are registered trademarks of the Microsoft Corporation. Reproduction of this Certificate of Authenticity is illegal and strictly prohibited by law.

A Windows 95 OEM certificate of authenticity

— Intaglio Print

— Holographic thread

— Latent image of word OK

— Latent image of woman

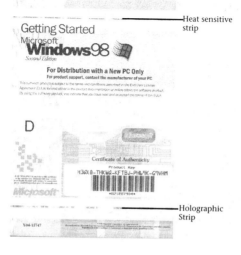

Heat sensitive strip

Holographic Strip

The Certificate of Authenticity for Windows 98 SE is on the cover of the manual. This is the OEM version.

Windows 98

Two security strips are woven into the cover of the Windows 98SE manual. The strip about 1 inch from the top of the booklet is heat sensitive. Rubbing the strip with your fingertip should reveal the word "GENUINE."

About 1 inch from the bottom of the book is a holographic thread. If you tilt manual in the light, you should be able to read the words "Microsoft" and "Genuine."

If you believe your copies are not authentic, contact Microsoft at piracy@Microsoft.com.

Retail Certificates

Retail Certificates of Authenticity are smaller, rectangular stickers on the side of the software box. They have three characteristics that identify them as authentic:

1. Heat sensitive ink that changes from blue to white when rubbed.
2. Perforations in the label that tear when the label is removed.
3. A latent image hidden in the Microsoft logo. It can be seen by holding the label at eyelevel under an overhead light source and then tilting it so that the top edge points toward the light.

The Windows 95 upgrade/Windows 97 product certificate is green on a white background with a red oval.

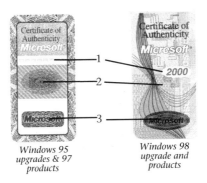

Windows 95 upgrades & 97 products

Windows 98 upgrade and products

The newer certificate is multicolored. The words "Certficate of Authenticity" are blue; the word Microsoft is white outlined in blue; the oval at the bottom is red and yellow with the word Microsoft in solid red.

Previous Certficates of Authenticity

Certificates of authenticity prior to about 1997 included an oval hologram, not possible to reproduce in print. The ovals were about 1 inch wide by $1\frac{1}{4}$ inches.

The pictures within the holograms were some variant of a baby or toddler sitting at a computer. The Word Microsoft or the Windows logo becomes visible on the computer screen when viewed from the left side.

Index